Praise for previous editions of

Colorado
Off the Beaten Path ®

"The narrative style is pleasant reading, with historic facts and fun people-stories enlivening each geographic area's 'uniqueness.' . . . Throughout the . . . pages of lively text and photos . . . the author's 'love and constant state of amazement' are contagious to the reader."

—*Nederland* (Colo.) *Mountain-Ear*

"*Colorado: Off the Beaten Path* may well be the perfect guide for newcomers to our slice of the continent. . . . Offers a refreshing change of pace and a delightful new vision of our state."

—KCFR Radio, Denver

"This book even holds surprises for natives or longtime inhabitants and will delight the mountain climber, the wildflower enthusiast . . . and the history buff."

—*Colorado Outdoors*

"A fascinating guide that enables the reader to explore . . . little-known areas of the state. Using the book as an aid, you will discover your own Colorado."

—*The News Tribune,* Fort Pierce/Port St. Lucie, Fla.

"A great guide, solidly packed with information and fun."

—*Travelwriter Marketletter,* New York, N.Y.

Help Us Keep This Guide Up-to-Date

Every effort has been made by the author and editors to make this guide as accurate and useful as possible. However, many things can change after a guide is published—establishments close, phone numbers change, and facilities come under new management.

We would love to hear from you concerning your experiences with this guide and how you feel it could be improved and be kept up-to-date. While we may not be able to respond to all comments and suggestions, we'll take them to heart and we'll also make certain to share them with the author. Please send your comments and suggestions to the following address:

The Globe Pequot Press
Reader Response/Editorial Department
P.O. Box 480
Guilford, CT 06437-0480

Or you may e-mail us at:
editorial@globe-pequot.com

Thanks for your input, and happy travels!

OFF THE BEATEN PATH® SERIES

Colorado

SIXTH EDITION

Curtis Casewit

Revised and updated by
Alli Rainey

The
Globe
Pequot
Press

Guilford, Connecticut

Copyright © 1987, 1991, 1994, 1997, 1999 by Curtis Casewit
Revised text copyright © 2001 by The Globe Pequot Press

Off the Beaten Path is a registered trademark of The Globe Pequot Press.

Cover and text design by Laura Augustine
Cover photo by Index Stock
Maps created by Equator Graphics © The Globe Pequot Press

Art Credits: page 4, rendered courtesty of Denver Metro Convention & Visitors Bureau; page 92, based on a photograph by Carl Scofield.

Library of Congress Cataloging-in-Publication Data is available.

ISBN 0-7627-0920-0

Manufactured in the United States of America
Sixth Edition/First Printing

Acknowledgments

This book was written with the help of many people. The author would like to thank Richard Grant, Denver Metro Convention and Visitors Bureau; Deborah Powell, C.E.C.S. Wordprocessing; Bill Saul, National Western Stock Show; Leo Goto, Wellshire Inn; Lillian Wyles, Denver researcher; JoAnn Sims, Central City Opera House Association; Elena Valdez, Aspen Ritz Carlton Hotel; J. S. Munn, Vista Verde; Christy Metz, National Park Service; Kristine Meyer, Beaver Village, Winter Park; Robert Levine, Antlers Lionshead Vail; Barbara Jennings, Colorado Ski Country USA; Paula Sheridan, Winter Park Resort; Kristine L. Bittner, researcher, and Sarah Lawlor, assistant editor; and finally, Helen Evans, my special travel companion.

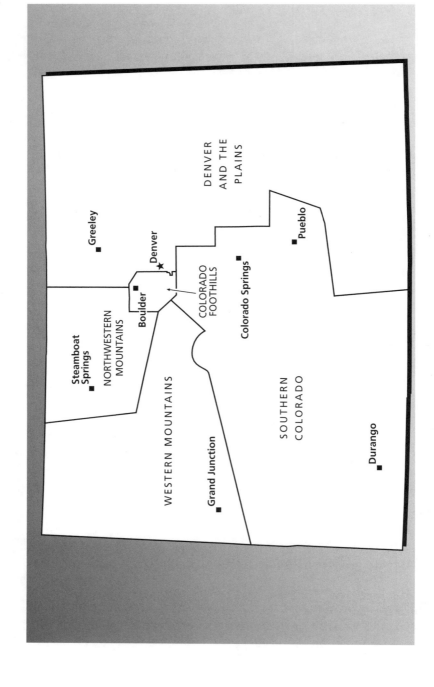

DENVER AND THE PLAINS

Greeley

Denver

COLORADO FOOTHILLS

Pueblo

Colorado Springs

Boulder

NORTHWESTERN MOUNTAINS

Steamboat Springs

SOUTHERN COLORADO

WESTERN MOUNTAINS

Grand Junction

Durango

Contents

Introduction

I first saw Colorado in 1948.

It was love at first sight. I have never been able to tear myself away, despite opportunities elsewhere. The state's beauty kept me here; indeed, there followed almost forty years of exploration. By automobile, train, plane. On foot and on horseback. On skis and on snowshoes.

From the tourist's viewpoint, Colorado has everything one could desire; travelers spend more than $7.1 billion here each year. The state even holds surprises for natives or longtime inhabitants. Indeed, after all those years of roaming through Colorado, I still wrote this book in a constant state of amazement.

Denver itself is packed with the unexpected. And remarkably enough, you can drive a mere thirty minutes from the state capital to reach the swish and rush of mountain streams, view dramatic rocks, or wander among thick forests. Higher and higher mountains beckon to the west; to the east the placid plains offer new sights as well.

Colorado: Off the Beaten Path® has assembled some of the state's most unique locales—some of which are rarely found in travel books. The selections cover a wide area but are purely personal choices. Some of

Author's Note

I lived in the Austrian Alps before I settled in the United States, or more precisely, in the Colorado Rockies, first in Aspen and then in Denver. High mountains have attracted me most of my adult life. The beauty of Southern Colorado—"The Switzerland of America"—always leaves me spellbound. In my younger years, I skied almost every weekend. In summer, I rock-climbed or followed one of the myriad hiking trails to higher elevations (Colorado has 1,500 peaks more than 10,000 feet above sea level and 53 giants over 14,000 feet). Flowers were everywhere. I breathed deeply and decided that I was very lucky.

The mountains gave health and contributed to inner peace.

As I grew older, I shortened distances and switched from high-powered downhill skis to old-fashioned cross-country skis. I learned to pace myself and to put in rest stops. One afternoon not long ago, on the return from a summer hike, I paused at one of those Forest Service information posts with maps and the usual mountain do's and don'ts. Another Colorado outdoor worshiper, perhaps aging, too, and equally fatigued, had affixed one more message onto the post. "GO UP INTO THE MOUNTAINS," it read. "YOUR BODY NEEDS IT."

the attractions may be readily recognized but were visited and reviewed by this writer with a fresh slant. Many of the descriptions will interest new settlers as well as those who have lived here for many decades. Naturally, suggestions for future editions are welcome. You may contact Curtis Casewit c/o The Globe Pequot Press.

About the Book's Organization

Few people hereabouts know the names of counties. So each chapter deals with a region. In chapter 1, for instance, you visit the foothills and front range. In chapter 2 you explore the interesting sights of Colorado's northwestern mountains via the important US 40 and the unusual Trail Ridge Road through the magnificent Rocky Mountain National Park. Chapter 3 takes you along one of Colorado's main arteries— I–70—to famous western mountains, all the way from historic Georgetown to Glenwood Springs and beyond, with one or two side trips into nearby valleys. Chapter 4 deals with the state's southern region, including Colorado Springs. Lastly, Denver and the plains are the subjects of chapter 5. In every instance the focus was on the uniqueness of a destination.

Finally, a word about prices. Globe Pequot Press books aim to be practical, so the reader of *Colorado: Off the Beaten Path*® deserves to know what to expect. The rates for hotels are as follows: inexpensive (less than $75 a night), moderate ($75 to $100 a night), expensive $100 to $150 a night). A few establishments get a "deluxe" label (more than $151 a night). The rates for restaurants are as follows: inexpensive (entrees less than $10), moderate (entrees $10 to $15), expensive (entrees $15 to $20), and deluxe (entrees more than $20). Most of the state's hoteliers and restaurateurs believe in good values, though.

Happy traveling!

Fast Facts About Colorado

Colorado Tourism Office
1625 Broadway, Suite 1700,
Denver, CO 80202;
(303) 892–3840; fax 892–3725
Internet: www.colorado.com
E-mail: gayle.brody@state.co.us

Colorado's Major Newspapers
The Denver Post *(daily)*
The Rocky Mountain News *(daily)*
Westword Newspaper *(weekly)*

Transportation: Regional Transportation District (RTD)
Buses connect with downtown Denver, Lakewood, Villa Italia, and Cherry Creek
Shopping Center. RTD offices are at 1600 Blake Street, Denver, CO 80202. More
information: (303) 299–6000 or (800) 366–7433.
Internet: www.rtd-denver.com

Climate Overview
Semiarid
Short springs
Dry summers
Mild winters, except in mountains

Average highs and lows in Denver (temperatures Fahrenheit)

Jan 43/16	Apr 62/35	July 88/59	Oct 66/36
Feb 47/20	May 71/44	Aug 86/57	Nov 53/25
Mar 52/26	June 81/52	Sept 77/48	Dec 45/17

Famous Coloradans
Clive Cussler (world-famous author)
Major Stephen Long (explorer)
Lieutenant Zebulon Pike (expedition leader)
Kit Carson (trapper)
H. A. W. Tabor (miner)
Marshall Sprague (historian)

Brief Fun Facts about Colorado
The weather—if you don't like it, wait an hour—is known to go from clear skies to thun-
derstorms, tornadoes, and flash floods and back before you've had time to complain about
any of it. It also can drop 30 degrees overnight, and just when you thought it was Indian
summer in October, a blizzard can dump 3 feet of snow in two days' time.

Colorado Foothills

Front Range

When you come upon the seventy-million-year-old ***Red Rocks Park and Amphitheatre,*** west of Denver, for the first time, the primeval scene takes your breath away: Huge reddish sandstone formations jut upward and outward. Each is higher than Niagara Falls. The view conjures up dinosaurs, sea serpents, and flying reptiles; indeed, tracks of those long-extinct creatures have been found here, along with valuable fossil fragments. The colors are those of the Grand Canyon; one can easily believe the geologists who speak of earth-shattering, monolith-building cataclysms, of retreating ancestral oceans, iron oxide color, water erosion. Geographers once considered this site one of the Seven Wonders of the World.

The U.S. Geographical Survey showed up eager for surveys in 1868. By 1906 financier John Brisben Walker had acquired the land; the acoustics of these rocks would be perfect for an amphitheater. A visiting opera singer, Dame Nellie Melba, was quick to agree; it would make one of the world's greatest open-air stages. John Brisben Walker eventually donated the land to the community, and in 1927 it was incorporated into the Denver Mountain Parks System.

Construction started a few years later; dedication of the tiered outdoor area followed in 1941. The local symphony soon brought its famed orchestra to the site. The latter not only produced perfect sound and aesthetic inspiration but also allowed a magnificent look at Denver far below.

During many years the outdoor theater experienced triumphant ballet performances, and audiences heard celebrated orchestras and even portions of Wagner operas. Singers like Lily Pons, Jennie Tourel, Jessye Norman, and Helen Traubel all raved about Red Rocks. Even the difficult-to-please Leopold Stokowski was impressed by a setting that included a "Creation Rock."

Colorado Foothills

Boulder
36
119
72
7
287
119
Nederland
ROCK CANYONS
AND
BOULDERS
Lafayette
7
7
93
36
287
72
Broomfield
287
36
"RICHEST
SQUARE MILE
ON EARTH"
119
72
121
Central City
93
70
40
Golden
76
70
Idaho
Springs
6
6
6
40
70
40
6
Lakewood
95
FRONT
RANGE
74
74
Morrison
8
Evergreen
8
285
N
285
470
121

0   10 mi
0   10 km

COLORADO FOOTHILLS

In 1959, in the interests of still further improvements, Denver's manager of parks flew to Germany at his own expense. He persuaded Wolfgang Wagner, grandson of the composer, to inspect Red Rocks. Wagner eventually remodeled the orchestra pit and made other design changes.

The cost of bringing large groups of classical musicians and opera companies proved to be financially difficult, however. What's more, performers sometimes fought with winds that would tear away the orchestra's notes or with sudden five-minute rains that would drench the singers to the depth of their costumes.

Since 1961 Red Rocks rarely heard any more classical music; instead, by the mid-1960s the Beatles made a full-throttle appearance here. Through the seventies and eighties and into the nineties, there followed assorted high-decibel rock, pop, blues, jazz, and country western stars—often with sell-outs of the 9,000 seats. Tickets are expensive. However, the public gets free admission to Red Rocks facilities at all other times. Traditionally, too, a free Easter Sunrise Service has taken place here for several decades. (The stage has meanwhile been covered.)

Red Rocks, located at 12700 West Alameda Parkway in Morrison, is easy to reach via numerous routes. From Denver you can take West Alameda Avenue west, drive US 285 west to C470 to Morrison Road, or follow I–70 west and watch for the marked exit. The total distance varies between 14 and 17 miles, depending on your route. Hours are 5:00 A.M. to 11:00 P.M. daily; admission is free. Call (303) 640–2637 or fax (303) 572–4792 for more information. Web site: www.redrocksonline.com.

You can see the stunning Red Rocks Amphitheatre from the hiking trails of Mount Falcon

---

AUTHOR'S FAVORITE ATTRACTIONS IN THE COLORADO FOOTHILLS

Red Rocks Park and Amphitheatre, (303) 640–2637, www.redrocksonline.com

Buffalo Bill Museum and Grave, (303) 526–0747, www.buffalobill.org

Lookout Mountain, (303) 526–0594, www.co.jefferson.co.us/dpt/openspac/natstart.htm

Beaver Brook Trail, (303) 271–5925, www.co.jefferson.co.us/dpt/openspac/

Flagstaff Mountain, (303) 441–3408, www.ci.boulder.co.us/bmp/

Central City Opera House, (800) 851–8175, www.centralcityopera.org

Eldorado Canyon, (303) 494–3943, parks.state.co.us/eldorado/

Cold Stone Creamery, (303) 541–0668, www.coldstonecreamery.com

Tiny Town, (303) 697–6829, www.designcircuit.com/eic/tiny.html

Matthews/Winters Park, (303) 271–5925, www.co.jefferson.co.us/dpt/openspac/maw.htm

---

Trivia

Long ago, a vast inland sea covered the Colorado area, which contained sediments that gradually built up on its floor. After the sea receded, the sediments hardened and the forces of geology and erosion went to work over the next few million years to sculpt the formations you see at Red Rocks today.

Red Rocks Park and Amphitheatre

Park, for which we can thank the same John Brisben Walker, financier, entrepreneur, visionary. Walker wanted to build a Summer White House in the park, and a marble plaque still indicates the spot. He had an eye for the best views: The Mount Falcon area is surrounded by blue mountains, and at a distance you can recognize Mt. Evans (elevation 14,264 feet) and the Continental Divide. Other vistas of the 1,415-acre Mount Falcon Park include the Colorado plains and, with a little imagination, Nebraska.

The park seems surprisingly serene; it is so vast that the walkers and the occasional horseback rider and mountain bikers can spread over many a flowered hill and dale. No motorcycles are permitted, and cars are restricted to a few parking lots—the latter concealed by trees. The exceptionally well-marked foot trails are often shaded by conifer forests.

Picnic tables invite families, and there are meadows for kiters and butterfly fans. Lovers find privacy among the daisies, the scrub oak, and the spruce. Here, at 7,750 feet above sea level, a light breeze blows often. Summers are cooler here than in Denver, in the smog far below. For once, you hear only the light Colorado wind. The traffic has been silenced.

COLORADO FOOTHILLS

AUTHOR'S FAVORITE EVENTS IN THE COLORADO FOOTHILLS

Bolder Boulder 10K race;
Boulder; May;
(303) 444–7223;
www.bolderboulder.com

Colorado Music Festival;
Boulder Chautauqua Park;
June through August;
(303) 449–2413;
www.coloradomusicfest.com

Colorado Shakespeare Festival; CU-Boulder;
June through August;
(303) 492–0554;
www.coloradoshakes.org

Boulder Climbing Series;
Boulder Rock Club;
October through March;
(303) 447–2804;
www.boulderrock.com

Morrison Cowboy Celebration; Morrison;
September; (303) 697–1747;
town.morrison.co.us/
cowboys/index.shtml

Walker's fortunes ultimately waned: The Summer White House was never built, and the financier's own castlelike home was struck by lightning and burned in 1918. The stone walls and chimneys, and even the fireplaces, are still there—an interesting destination for hikers. A few minutes away, the stables do a good summer business. Cross-country skiers enjoy the park in winter. No charge.

Mount Falcon Park is accessible via Highway 8 to Morrison or via US 285 and the Parmalee exit. Be prepared for dusty roads to the park entrance. For more information contact Jefferson County Open Space, (303) 271–5925. Fax (303) 271–5955. E-mail: outreach@co.jefferson.co.us. Web site: www.co.jefferson.co.us/dpt/openspac/falcon.htm.

Surprise! Morrison, Mount Falcon Park, and Red Rocks are just twenty minutes west of Denver. As **Morrison Road** shoots through the foothills toward higher altitudes, many travelers will be preoccupied with reaching their goal: "the mountains or bust." Nonetheless, along the way there are jewels to be found.

One such jewel is the town of **Morrison.** On any given weekday small groups of congenial neighbors meet on the street

Tracks in Time

A visit to the Morrison area would not be complete without a stop at the outdoor museum known as Dinosaur Ridge. View more than 300 dinosaur footprints, all preserved in the sandstone of the Dakota Formation on the east side of the hogback. This National Natural Landmark is open for free viewing year-round, with seventeen interpretive signs providing information about the tracks and other fossils found in the area.

Visitors can also arrange for a guided tour with the Visitor Center or call ahead to find out about the next Dinosaur Discovery Day, a day when free tours are offered to the general public. For more information, call (303) 697-3466 or write Friends of Dinosaur Ridge, 16831 West Alameda Parkway, Morrison 80465. E-mail: director@dinoridge.org. Web site: www.dinoridge.org.

corners to exchange pleasantries. A man with his dog drives a golf cart down the main thoroughfare toward the edge of town. Children maneuver mountain bikes onto paths that run along a rippling stream opposite the rushing Bear Creek. Indeed at times, Morrison is very Norman Rockwellesque.

But more than a pleasant atmosphere, this community offers a treasure trove of antiques that will please collectors and browsers alike. A 1910 phonograph. A wooden wagonwheel, circa 1895. You might like to try *Lacey Gate Antiques,* 116 Stone Street, Morrison 80465, (303) 697–4407; *Little Bits of Yesterday & Today,* 309 Bear Creek Avenue, Morrison 80465, (303) 697–8661; or *El Mercado,* 120 Bear Creek Avenue, Morrison 80465, (303) 697–8361.

Whatever your pleasure, buying, selling, or window shopping, Morrison is a pleasant place to while away an hour or two. For more information call (303) 697–8749, fax (303) 697–8752, or write 321 Highway 8, Morrison 80465. E-mail: office@town.morrison.co.us. Web site: town. morrison.co.us.

A five-minute uphill drive from Morrison will take you to the much photographed locale of *The Fort,* which is a replica of Bent's Fort, an 1834 early Colorado fur-trading post. The thick, picturesque adobe building contains a small shop that sells authentic Indian jewelry, tomahawks, feathers, and other items. But The Fort is best known as a restaurant. The walls are covered with western oil paintings and original etchings celebrating the West. The cuisine is southwestern, with appetizers like rattlesnake cake, delicate buffalo tongues, and Rocky Mountain "oysters." Among other entrees, you can order elk medallions, grilled quail, surprisingly tender buffalo filets, buffalo T-bones, game hens, and fresh mountain trout, all washed down with first-class, high-priced wines and followed by original desserts. The Fort is at US 285 and Colorado 8. The restaurant is open for dinner Monday through Friday from 5:30 to 9:30 P.M. and Saturday and Sunday from 5:00 to 9:30 P.M. E-mail: fortdenver@mindspring.com. Web site: www.thefort.com. For reservations call (303) 697–4771 or fax (303) 697–4786.

To the west of Morrison, as the crow flies, a mere 16 miles west of Denver on US 285, you suddenly see the sign for *Meyer Ranch Park.* Here are 397 quiet acres replete with nearly 4 miles of well-maintained hiking trails. You climb gently through young aspen groves and pine forests. Your eyes are soothed by meadows filled with Colorado's state flower, the columbine, that give way to grasslands. Depending on the season, you spot shooting stars, lady slippers, and the purple Indian paintbrush. What remarkable serenity so close to the big city of Denver! The trail names fit perfectly: Owl's Perch, Lodge Pole, Sunny Aspen.

Motorized vehicles are not permitted here, and dogs belong on a leash. The Meyer Ranch Park area has a history of homesteading, haying, and grazing. According to local legend, during the late 1880s the animals of the P. T. Barnum circus wintered here. The Victorian-style Meyer Ranch—still occupied by the Meyers—stands proudly and handsomely across the highway. For more information about the park, call Jefferson County Open Space at (303) 271–5925. Web site: www.co. jefferson.co.us/dept/openspac/meyer.htm.

The same US 285 will take you to a truly offbeat family destination. Denverites, twenty minutes down the valley, know about *Tiny Town;* out-of-town visitors probably haven't heard about this Lilliputian village and its miniature railway.

Tiny Town appeals to children. Imagine about one hundred toy-size, handcrafted buildings! To peek into, sometimes to crawl into as well! Old miniature log cabins, fire station, post office, water tower, flourmill, bank, stables, schoolhouse, roominghouse, farms, ranches, barns and windmills, mines and miners' shacks, and many, many more. There's even a miniature train ride around the entire Tiny Town village loop.

Trivia
Colorado's Front Range has an average of 300 days of sunshine per year—second only to Miami, Florida.

The attraction is run on a nonprofit basis by a foundation. The distance from Denver is about 12 miles via US 285, turning south at South Turkey Creek Road. Bring a picnic and be prepared to pay $3.00 for adults, $2.00 for children ages three to twelve, younger than three free, and $1.00 per person train fare.

Open every day from Memorial Day weekend through September 1, 10:00 A.M. to 5:00 P.M. Open weekends in May, September, and October, 10:00 A.M. to 5:00 P.M. For more information: Tiny Town, 6249 South Turkey Creek Road, Tiny Town 80465; (303) 697–6829. Web site: www.designcircuit.com/eic/tiny.html.

US 285 is sometimes narrow and curvy, so it's easy to miss an entrance to an offbeat retreat for vacationers. One example? The modest little wooden sign that reads *Glen-Isle Resort.* These humble log cabins and a well-worn lodge are hidden by a tiny bridge and assorted bushes and trees off the highway between Grant and Bailey. This unpretentious holiday settlement dates back to 1900 and works out fine for families, couples, and singles who want to cook (wood furnished) and who appreciate the silence of a 160-acre forest. The latter is honeycombed with footpaths for hikers; horse trails are nearby, too. Glen-Isle is nicely old-fashioned; the last time I visited, there was not even a television set. For folks who don't want to cook, a dining room offers homey food. The tab for everything seems reasonable enough. Expect basic (not luxurious) accommodations. For more information: Glen-Isle Resort, 573 Old Stagecoach Road, Bailey 80421; (303) 838–5461. Web site: www.caccl.com/glenisleresort.

Matthews/Winters Park derives its importance from its location: The park lies astride the entrance to Mt. Vernon Canyon, which is one of the early routes to the gold fields of Central City (then known as the Gregory Diggings) and South Park. Other canyons were also used, and at each portal a town was founded to try to get a share of the quick fortune the Fifty-niners were scrambling to uncover.

The big year here was 1859. The stagecoaches and wagons rolled through, and the new town of Mt. Vernon had a 150-horse corral. A local paper declared that "timber, stone, lime, and coal are abundant in the vicinity." For a while Mt. Vernon became a stage stop. An inn, a saloon, and a schoolhouse were built, used, and abandoned. Once "boasting forty-four registered voters," the town of Mt. Vernon lost its place in history after the railroads arrived.

And now? Sunflowers, chokecherries, and willows lean over the gravestones and crosses of long-gone pioneers: I.I. DEAN, DIED AUGUST 12, 1860, AGED 31 YEARS, I AM AT REST. And the marker of a younger man: JAMES JUDY, DIED SEPTEMBER 8, 1867, AGED 21 YEARS. Just a few square gravestones, some crosses, and wild vegetation. Not far away, next to Mt. Vernon Creek, picnic tables sit under leafy trees.

The rest of the park consists of undulating grasslands, trails, and fields of sedges—bleached in summer—silver-green sage, purple thistles, wild roses, and wild plums. Trails run through rabbit brush and tall dill, and there's nary a sound, despite the nearby highways.

In recent years the park has become a popular after-work and weekend destination, not only for hikers but also for mountain bikers. A fun, $4^1/_{10}$-mile out-and-back ride on the Village Walk Trail and the Red Rocks Trail is suitable for intermediate riders, with only a few moderately difficult technical sections. Serious mountain bikers can make the ride into a loop by crossing the street and testing their skills on the $2^4/_{10}$-mile Dakota Ridge Trail, a technically challenging ride across the hogback.

For more information contact Jefferson County Open Space at (303) 271–5925. Fax: (303) 271–5955. Mailing address: 700 Jefferson County Parkway, Suite 100, Golden 80401. E-mail: outreach@co.jefferson.co.us. Web site: www.co.jefferson. co.us/dpt/openspac/maw.htm.

The public parking area is located off SR 26, just south of I–70, and lies within the Mt. Vernon town site. The park is open from 5:00 A.M. to 11:00 P.M.

The front-range mountain settings come with precious few dinner retreats—particularly not historic ones like the **Manor House Restaurant.** From afar the white Georgian mansion makes its appearance on top of a green hill, amid footpaths and an equestrian center. White columns give the building a fairy-tale quality.

The Manor House was built on a vast ranch in 1914 by John C. Shaffer, industrialist, owner of the *Rocky Mountain News,* importer of Hereford cattle from distant points, and collector of antiques. Shaffer's wife, Virginia, hosted President Theodore Roosevelt and other notable figures, who raved about the magnificent fireplaces, statuary, elegant carpets, and valuable nineteenth-century paintings. Various ranchers raised cattle nearby, with a view to faraway Denver. Virginia Shaffer wrote a poem about the landscape: "Where the sunsets are entrancing / where one sees a sight sublime / Come again! Come again!"

Now the elegant ranch house serves distinctive food in sumptuous surroundings. The restaurant is a little hard to get to. Look for US 285 and exit at Highway C 470, then to Ken-Caryl Avenue, to Mountain Laurel, and finally onto Manor House Road. It's a complicated trip, at least the first time. The thirty-minute drive from Denver is worthwhile, however. The Manor House has an imaginative chef who starts you off with wild-mushroom strudel or smoked salmon (smoked right on the premises), roast rack of lamb, veal medallions, and many more fine dishes, graced by elegant glassware and shining silver. Good service plus mountain views. Dinner is served Tuesday through Sunday, lunch on Friday, and brunch on Sunday. Contact Manor House Restaurant, 1 Manor House Road, Littleton 80127; (303) 973–8064.

If you travel west on US 40 out of Denver, you abruptly leave behind the plains of Denver and eastern Colorado and enter a long valley with the jagged foothills of the Rockies rising on both sides. As you proceed, you may see some horses grazing on the slopes.

If you're hungry, make a stop at 14195 West Colfax Avenue, at **Healthy Habits Restaurant** (303–277–9293). It may be one of the secrets kept

Mother Cabrini Shrine

*O*n a 900-acre hilltop on Lookout Mountain sits the Mother Cabrini Shrine. There is no charge to enter the famous little chapel, which was built in 1954 and devoted to Saint Frances Xavier Cabrini. The setting includes lovely fields, surrounding forests, and quite a few steps that will make hikers happy. For more information call (303) 526–0758. E-mail: info@den-cabrini-shrine. Web site: www.den-cabrini-shrine.org.

by diet-minded Denverites; here you get some sixty salads plus four fiber-rich soups, all buffet-style; an assortment of muffins; spinach and other pastas; and fresh fruit and other vegetarian goodies. But beware the dessert table! Healthy Habits is a delightful place, especially in summer, when you can sit outdoors, "al fresco," and view the flower-dotted foothills from your table. It's a great break on your trip west to **Golden.**

Soon you reach the heart of Golden with its eight churches, all of them small and varied in architecture. The churches give the impression that even institutionalized religion can still be personal.

Across the wide main street, just before you come to the bridge over Clear Creek, an arch shouts, HOWDY FOLKS, WELCOME TO GOLDEN, WHERE THE WEST LIVES.

Consider a trip to **Heritage Square,** in the Golden area. The rustic artisan and entertainment village was built on the 1860 townsite of Apex, another mining boomtown. It has metalsmiths, jewelers, candy makers, and more, including horseback rides, a narrow-gauge train trip, a large melodrama theater, tree-lined, lamplighted streets and plenty of free parking. Exit 259 off I–70 and go north 1 mile. For more information call (303) 279–2789.

To the west there rise range after range of mountains, each higher than the last. These mountains, besides having whatever aesthetic or spiritual value you may find in them, serve the practical purpose of limiting the size to which Golden can grow—it currently has about 16,000 inhabitants. But the Rockies have protected the city from becoming part of a growing urban sprawl.

The Golden story began back in 1859, when a man named Tom Golden set up a hunting camp with a couple of other men. Soon some representatives of the Boston Company passed by on a wagon train, looking for a suitable place to establish a trading and supply base for the prospectors who were flooding the mining areas to the west. They liked the site and stayed.

Golden grew rapidly. Within a year it had a population of 700. By 1862 it became the territorial capital but lost this honor five years later to Denver. There was sporadic gold excitement in the immediate area—people still occasionally pan Clear Creek, west of town—but there were no big gold findings. (The primary reward for panning here is the sight of gold in your pan. You can work all day for a dollar.) Its early economy was built on trading. It was the major supply center for the mining operations at Black Hawk, Central City, Idaho Springs, and other communities.

With the decline of mining, new economic bases emerged. Golden's present economy is based primarily on two institutions, both of which have brought it international recognition: the Colorado School of Mines, for a century the leading school in the world devoted to mining and minerals, and a brewery, one of the largest in the country.

Trivia

Golden once rivaled Denver; it was the capital of the Colorado Territory from 1862 to 1867.

The Colorado School of Mines, while not open to the public for tours, does have a museum that fits the theme of the school. The **Geology Museum,** on the corner of Sixteenth and Maple on campus, is almost an art gallery. Murals by Irwin Hoffman depict many periods in the development and history of mining. See Egyptian slaves working a human-powered mill. Learn how Greeks and Romans mined by burning bushes over the area they wanted to excavate, then throwing cold water on the hot rocks, causing them to break apart. The museum is at Sixteenth and Maple Streets in Golden. Regular hours are 9:00 A.M. to 4:00 P.M. Monday through Saturday and 1:00 to 4:00 P.M. Sunday; closed all CSM holidays and Sunday during summer. Admission is free. Contact Colorado School of Mines Department of Geology and Geological

Golden Adventures

*S*eekers of unusual family fun will want to check out Heritage Square's **Alpine Action.** After riding a chairlift nearly 500 feet up the mountainside, visitors can cruise downhill for half a mile aboard a toboggan that fits on the tracks of the alpine slide. Those who can't get enough of heights can leap from a 70-foot tower—attached to a bungee cord, of course! Or they can slip and slide down a 330-foot water slide into a heated pool. Contact Alpine Action, Heritage Square, Golden 80401, (303) 279-1661. Web site: www.alpineslide-bungee.com.

Engineering, Golden 80401; (303) 273–3823. Fax (303) 273–3859. E-mail: vamast@mines.edu.Web site: www.mines.edu/Academic/geology/museum.

What does it mean, that slogan "Where the West Lives," so proudly proclaimed on the banner? *West* is the most basic word in American folklore. Its connotations extend well into the realms of history, morality, and philosophy. To the tourist, out to see the country, it's obviously a matter of history. Golden, with its ten museums—a record for a town of its size—does not disappoint in the "History of the American West" department.

Start out at the ***Colorado Railroad Museum,*** which displays many ancient, narrow-gauge locomotives and even a small depot. The narrow-gauge railroads of Colorado made it possible for miners and other fortune seekers to access the mineral riches of the Rocky Mountains. These tracks also allowed the wealth to be carried out and spread. The history of railroads in Colorado is preserved in the twelve-acre Colorado Railroad Museum.

Here you will see the original rolling stock, including locomotives. A rail spur allows the facility to "steam up" different engines through the year.

The building itself, a masonry replica of an 1880 depot, houses some 50,000 photographs and artifacts. The basement contains one of the state's largest model railroad exhibits. It re-creates some of Colorado's old rail lines, such as the one in Cripple Creek. Famous relics of the museum include the Rio Grande Southern 1931 Galloping Goose No. 2 and the steel observation car used on the Santa Fe Super Chief, the Navajo. A bookstore sells about 1,000 specialized titles and magazines, tapes, gifts, and mementos.

Open every day except Christmas and Thanksgiving. Hours are 9:00 A.M. to 5:00 P.M., September–May; 9:00 A.M. to 6:00 P.M., June–August. Small charge for admission. Colorado Railroad Museum, 17155 West Forty-fourth Avenue, Golden 80402; (800) 365–6263 or (303) 279–4591. Fax (303) 279–4229. E-mail: corrmus@aol.com. Web site: www.crrm.org.

If the West remains here in Golden in any living sense, it can only be in the character of the people.

What kind of people were they? As with all pioneers, they had to be extremely self-reliant. They were dissatisfied with what they had left behind and were willing to take all necessary risks to try to find something better. They were doers rather than theoreticians.

COLORADO FOOTHILLS

Trivia

Golden's Armory Building, built in 1913, is the largest cobblestone building in the country. Workers hauled 3,300 wagonloads of stream-worn boulders from nearby Clear Creek and quartz from Golden Gate Canyon to construct the building, which is located at Thirteenth and Arapahoe in Golden.

The current Golden folks love the outdoors. Everywhere there are campers, tents, jeeps. Backpackers can be seen heading out of town toward the mountains. The cultural life seems aimed at "doing" rather than the less demanding "appreciating." For example, the Foothills Art Center devotes its major effort to workshops and lessons along with the display of art.

For all this, and much more, Golden is certainly worth a visit. Additional information: Greater Golden Chamber of Commerce, 1010 Washington Avenue, P.O. Box 1035, Golden 80402; (303) 279–3113 or (800) 590–3113. Fax (303) 279–0332. E-mail: info@ goldencochamber.org. Web site: www.goldencochamber.org.

Before you're done with Golden, ask yourself what could possibly epitomize "the West" more than the place where Buffalo Bill asked to be buried? Buffalo Bill was a unique character of the frontier. And the museum that bears his name, 12 miles west of central Denver, on Golden's Lookout Mountain, has a uniquely western character. Here are the mementos that bring a fascinating man to life: the paintings and posters that show him in full regalia on his white horse, white of beard, cowboy hat jaunty on his head. You can see his clothes, saddles, old weapons, even a mounted buffalo, and lots of artifacts. (In 1989, Buffalo Bill's museum and grave attracted 53,000 visitors.)

The ***Buffalo Bill Memorial Museum and Grave*** is crammed with photographs that retrace his careers as a buffalo hunter, Indian fighter, and army scout (for U.S. Army General Sheridan, among others).

Born as William F. Cody, Buffalo Bill led an extraordinary life. As a long-time Pony Express rider, he was pursued by Indians, escaping (as he wrote), "by laying flat on the back of my fast steed. I made a 24-mile straight run on one horse." On another occasion he rode 320 miles in some twenty-one hours to deliver the mail. (En route he exhausted twenty horses for the journey.) He had few rivals as a hunter and was said to have shot 4,280 bison in a $1^1/_2$-year period. His slogan: "Never missed and never will / always aims and shoots to kill."

The buffalo shooting had a purpose, of course; the meat was needed to feed some 1,200 men who were laying track for the railroad. And though William Cody had his battles with the Indians, he later learned the Sioux language and befriended the Cheyennes, among other tribes.

William Cody may have had his best times as a circus rider, actor, and showman, gaining fame all over the world. The first "Buffalo Bill's Wild West" show opened in 1883. The extravaganza toured for nearly three decades, spreading the myths and legends of the American West around the globe. Almost a hundred mounted Sioux Indians chased wagon trains and a stagecoach; Annie Oakley and Johnny Baker amazed audiences with their marksmanship; eighty-three cowboys rode bucking broncos, thereby formalizing a cowboy sport into rodeo; and the entire Battle of Little Big Horn was re-created. Spectators could see live elk and deer from Colorado. There were horse races and even a bison hunt complete with a charging herd. At its height Buffalo Bill's show employed more than 600 performers. And in one year he traveled 10,000 miles, performing in 132 cities in 190 days. (He was particularily popular in Europe.)

Cody's flowing white hair, short white beard, and rifle-holding figure symbolized the Wild West in many European capitals. Buffalo Bill gave a command performance for Queen Victoria at Windsor Castle and amused Kaiser Wilhelm II in Berlin.

No fewer than 557 dime novels were written about Cody during his lifetime. His face beamed out from hundreds of thousands of posters. Even today the distinctive goatee and silver hair continue to make him as recognizable as the kings, generals, and presidents who may have honored him.

Cody made one of the first movie Westerns ever produced. Although near the end of his career, he also lived to see the start of the tourist industry as he opened the first hotel near Yellowstone National Park.

Toward the end of his life, he turned into an entrepreneur and author. He gave most of his life's savings away to various good causes. His money ran out; his fame did not.

When Buffalo Bill died, President Woodrow Wilson wired his condolences. Former president Teddy Roosevelt called Cody "an American of Americans." The Colorado legislature passed a special resolution ordering that his body lie in state under the gold-plated rotunda of the State Capitol in Denver. Nearly 25,000 people turned out to pay their last respects and march in his funeral on Memorial Day, June 3, 1917.

Buffalo Bill's grave is a few steps from the museum atop Lookout Mountain, with a good view of Denver and the plains. Anyone can come and see the burial place. It is marked by white pebbles. The simple legend reads: WILLIAM F. CODY 1846–1917.

The museum stands in a quiet conifer forest. First opened in 1919, it has been restored and improved over the years. A gift shop sells arrowheads, carpets, and other fitting items.

The hours are 9:00 A.M. to 4:00 P.M. daily in winter, except Monday and Christmas; 9:00 A.M. to 5:00 P.M. daily in summer. Call (303) 526–0747 or write to 987½ Lookout Mountain Road, Golden 80401. Web site: www.buffalobill.org. Small fee. For the most scenic drive, take US 6 west of Denver to Golden, turn left on Nineteenth Street, and proceed uphill via *Lookout Mountain Road,* also called Lariat Trail because it twists and turns all the way up Lookout Mountain.

As you continue south on Lookout Mountain Road after leaving Buffalo Bill's grave, a sign on Colorow Road will direct you to turn right toward the *Lookout Mountain Nature Center.* Situated on 110 acres of a fenced nature preserve, the center has a museum, plant and animal displays, and a self-guiding nature trail. All are handicapped-accessible, and admission is free. Hours are 10:00 A.M. to 4:00 P.M. Tuesday through Sunday; the facility is closed Monday and holidays. Also offered are nature classes that range from "Messages from the Wild" to wildflower and bird walks to night tours to discover constellations and nocturnal animal activity. All sessions require preregistration. Contact the nature center at 910 Colorow Road, Golden 80401; (303) 526–0594. Web site: www.co.jefferson.co.us/dpt/openspac/natstart.htm.

Step aside, you hardy mountaineers! Make room for some hiking tourists—the sort who can spare only a couple of hours for a gentle excursion into the Colorado front range. Easy, mountain flower-bordered trails abound in the foothills near the state capital.

One of the least-known paths curves around *Lookout Mountain,* which was first used by the Cheyenne and Arapaho Indians as a lookout. Now

Home on the Range

*T*he city of Denver has continuously maintained a herd of bison since 1914 at Genesee Park, just down the hill from the Buffalo Bill Memorial Museum and Grave. The buffalo roam free in their natural habitat and are best seen in fall, winter, and early spring when park officials feed them daily. Take I-70 west to exit 254 (Genessee Park). The twenty-four adult cows and two bulls can be seen on either side of the highway—a tunnel under the road allows the animals safe passage.

Flying Over Golden and Lookout Mountain

A bright weekend in the foothills. The air above Lookout Mountain sparkles. You get here via Highway 6; after the traffic light changes, you turn left on SR 68 and let your car curve uphill.

Suddenly, something catches your eye at the top of your windshield. A hang glider circles above calmly, quietly, like a bird of prey. He soars above the highway that brought you here. As you climb higher on Lookout Mountain, you spot two more human flyers just taking off. You stop the car and learn that this 7,000-foot mountain is the gateway for these daredevils. Do they belong to a club or organization? Apparently not. They're simply individuals who enjoy hang gliding.

known as the **Beaver Brook Trail**, it is one of the state's most interesting paths, yielding views of the gorges below, dipping and climbing with a varied landscape of leaf trees and dramatic Douglas fir. Although you're close to Denver, you're quickly led away from civilization.

Instead of highways there are fields of asters, yucca, and wild roses under you. In the forests the path is moss bordered, and spring beauties show their heads in season.

The Beaver Brook Trail makes some demands on your balance because you need to maneuver across several small boulder fields. Due to the rock scrambling required, the hike is inappropriate for small children and mountain bikes. The trail is a little more than 14 miles out and back, Beaver Brook remains blissfully quiet during the week. On Sundays, however, you sometimes see church groups and lines of scouts and other hikers coming up from the city. If you hike up here in July and August, you'll be surrounded by lots of color. On the trail you may also spot the state flower, the blue Rocky Mountain columbine.

It's true that wildflowers bloom later at the higher elevations. By the time plants have already wilted above Golden (elevation 7,600 feet), other flowers on the Beaver Brook Trail just begin to unfold. The higher you climb, the later the growth, the smaller the flower, and the colder the air.

Small Colorado plants appear and disappear with the seasons, go underground, or take many years to mature. Certain wildflowers can sleep peacefully under the thickest snow cover, biding their time until spring. In summer, the large fields of mountain flowers on the Beaver Brook Trail meadows give pleasure to your eyes.

The Beaver Brook Trail is within easy reach from Denver by car. Just take

US 6, turn left at the first traffic light (Nineteenth Street) in Golden, then drive up the curvy Lookout Road for 3 miles. Before you get to Buffalo Bill's grave, you spot a sign on your right: BEAVER BROOK TRAIL: WINDY SADDLE ENTRANCE. Free, the trail is open one hour before sunrise, until one hour after sunset year-round. For more information contact Jefferson County Open Space, 700 Jefferson County Parkway, Suite 100, Golden 80401; (303) 271–5925. Fax: (303) 271–5955. E-mail: outreach@co. jefferson.co.us. Web site: www.co.jefferson.co.us/dpt/openspac.

Finally, see Colorado's remnant of the Ice Age, called a glacier but actually an icefield, covering a steep year-round snowbowl of about ten acres. In summer, when Denver swelters in a 95°F heat wave, it's about 45°F on the glacier, and young people come to ski here in July and August. Other visitors to the famous snowfield bring platters or auto tubes or even race downhill on shovels. Hikers, campers, and backpackers can be spotted at the 11,000-foot level as they scramble uphill past the last scrub pines. A few tourists come to sit on rocks and soak up the Colorado sun.

All that eternal snow and ice make **St. Mary's Glacier** unusual, of course. The trip is a pleasant one, attracting Sunday drivers from the big city. Once you exit I–70, you follow a creek flanked by stands of conifers and aspen trees. After about 8 miles the road steepens and leads into a series of driver-challenging curves and serpentines. Then the valley widens and the forest thickens. You see several rushing waterfalls. At an elevation of 10,400 feet you notice a free parking lot; leave your car and hike up the rocky jeep trail or follow the uphill footpaths through kinnikinnik (evergreen groundcover), past the many fallen trees that age gracefully in gray. On weekends you meet lots of families on your way up to the glacier. People are friendly and talkative. "Been to the top yet? How was it? Do we have far to go?"

After half an hour you see a cold lake, topped by the glacier. It's less harmless than most folks think. Mountain dwellers know the glacier's record: Almost every year someone who skis too fast or careens downhill on a shovel somehow gets bruised, bloodied, or even killed. On rare occasions cross-country skiers are buried by an avalanche up here. In winter, the ill-prepared, ill-clothed can get frostbitten on top of the glacier at the 11,400-foot level. The prudent know that mountains are unforgiving; these visitors come to St. Mary's only when it smiles.

From I–70 just past Idaho Springs, take exit 238, known as the Fall River Road. A 12-mile drive brings you to the parking lot and the start of your St. Mary's Glacier adventure.

Richest Square Mile on Earth

At one point in history, **Central City** vied with Leadville for the bonanzas. They called Central City the Richest Square Mile on Earth. In all, some $75 million in gold was found there. Tourists can still do a bit of gold panning in nearby creeks. And through Labor Day you can ride a re-created narrow-gauge railway along the bleached mountainsides, past the old abandoned mounds of earth, mines of yesteryear.

Sloping, winding **Eureka Street** has been kept up. The redbrick buildings look as well preserved as those of Denver's restored Larimer Square. Central City's pharmacy and several other stores put their oldest relics into the windows. The **Teller House Hotel**—a rediscovery of Victorian times—is still worth seeing today.

The Teller House and the well-appointed Central City Opera House contrast with the miners' dwellings. The latter are small, modest cubes scattered across the pale gold or ochre and russet slopes.

The first frame houses sprang up during the 1860s, along with the mine dumps. Gold! Not just in a river but in the mountain, too. A man named John Gregory had plodded to 8,500-foot-high Central City from Denver, a trip of some 35 miles with an elevation gain of more than 3,000 feet.

That was in 1859. Gregory soon dug up a fortune. The word raced as fast as the spring waters of Clear Creek. Horace Greeley, the New York editor, heard about Gregory Gulch and traveled west to take a personal look. Greeley reported: "As yet the entire population of the valley, which cannot number less than four thousand, sleep in tents or under pine boughs, cooking and eating in the open air."

A mass of prospectors swarmed into the hillsides. Some people had a grand time. A theater was built. Sarah Bernhardt and Edwin Booth came to perform. The Teller House Hotel rose in 1872, attracting the finest artisans. Large, carved bedsteads, marble-topped commodes, and tall rosewood and walnut highboys were ferried across the prairies and up the rough roads by teams of oxen and mules and on woodburning trains. Central City's hotel hosted famous people. President Ulysses S. Grant, Walt Whitman, Oscar Wilde, Baron de Rothschild, and assorted European noblemen and their wives all slept in Central City.

In 1874 most of the community burned down, but gold rebuilt it. Fewer than four years later there was a new opera house, which still stands. Built in 1878 by Welsh and Cornish miners, the **Central City Opera House,** located on Eureka Street, is home to the fifth-oldest opera

Central City Opera House

company in the nation. This restored Victorian opera house holds an annual summer festival that draws patrons from nearly every state. Performances range from its popular one-act opera "The Face on the Barroom Floor," which recounts the local lore behind the painting on the Teller House Bar floor, to classic operas like Giuseppe Verdi's *La Traviata*. Central City Opera House invites opera buffs to sink into one of the 550 new theater seats installed in 1999 while they take in performances by both known stars and future divas.

For show dates (performances are in summer), prices, and times, write to Central City Opera at 621 Seventeenth Street, #1601, Denver 80293 or call (303) 292–6700 or (800) 851–8175. Fax: (303) 292–2221. E-mail: info@centralcityopera.org. Web site: www.centralcityopera.org.

Opening night remains Colorado's great social event. Cars and busloads of operagoers from nearby cities climb the road along Clear Creek Canyon, the same route taken by John Gregory more than one hundred years ago.

Now masses of gamblers also swarm into the area, since gaming was approved some years ago for Central City and Black Hawk. New casinos have replaced many historic buildings and shops. Where parking was once hard to find, it is now almost impossible, but shuttle services run from Golden and other areas in Denver on a regular basis.

Trivia

Sherill Milne and Beverly Sills both got their operatic starts in Central City.

If you want to try your luck, stop at these Central City establishments: Central Palace, Tollgate Casino, Famous Bonanza, and Harvey's Wagon Wheel. Down the road in Black Hawk, try Bullwackers and Colorado Central Station.

Central City is about an hour's drive from Denver via US 6 and Colorado 119. For more information, call (800) 542–2999. City offices are located at 141 Nevada Street, Central City 80427. Web site: www.centralcitycolorado.org.

Rock Canyons and Boulders

As you descend into **Boulder,** Colorado, the towering Flatirons, huge slabs of metamorphic sandstone lifted up by the same geologic forces that account for the birth of the Rocky Mountains, will command your view to the west. Now the city's trademark, the Flatirons—some of which reach heights of more than 1,000 feet—offer ample opportunities for rock climbers of all abilities. These monoliths also beckon to hikers and trail runners due to the abundance of trails interwoven among the tree-lined hills that surround them. Forming the abrupt border between the plains and the Rocky Mountains, this stunning assortment of rock formations in all shapes and sizes is a true paradise for the outdoor enthusiast. Located 22 miles northwest of Denver, Boulder is easily reached in about half an hour via the Boulder Turnpike, US 36.

Trivia

Boulder is the only U.S. community that uses its own city-owned glacier, Arapahoe Glacier, for its water supply.

Arguably in possession of the highest population of rock climbers per capita of any city or town in the United States, Boulder enjoys its status as one of the centers of U.S. rock climbing. This reputation becomes even clearer when you drive up Boulder Canyon or consider the proximity of Eldorado Canyon—a mere ten-minute jaunt from South Boulder. A vast amount of world-class climbing areas within several hours' drive only beefs up the city's appeal, not to mention one of the best indoor climbing facilities in the country. Added to this, rock climbing's popularity has witnessed a tremendous explosion since the early 1990s. Those seeking more rock to climb tend to flock to areas rife with quality cliffs—like Boulder—while those living in such places find the transition from nonclimber to climber relatively painless.

Eldorado Canyon is counted among the birthplaces of rock climbing

COLORADO FOOTHILLS

Trivia

in the United States. Gorgeous sandstone cliffs soar above the canyon floor in shades of red speckled with greenish and golden-hued lichen that appears to take on its own luminescence when viewed in the right light. Formed of the same type of hardened sandstone that makes up the Flatirons—known as the Fountain Formation—the world-class walls of Eldorado Canyon enjoy international prestige within the rock-climbing community.

Hundreds of established routes await rock climbers of all abilities on the canyon walls, but none should be taken lightly. "Eldo," as climbers affectionately refer to the place, is known for its stiff grades, polished rock (especially on popular climbs), and sometimes scanty protection. All of these factors mean that climbers should take caution when they first start out climbing in the canyon, perhaps choosing an easier route to allow themselves time to grow accustomed to the area.

Once a bastion for some of the state's hardest routes, Eldorado Canyon's heyday as far as pure difficulty for climbing moves has passed, but that doesn't relegate its challenges to second-tier status by any means. Exposure—that sensation you get when you can truly feel just how high above the canyon floor you are—is the name of the game on classic routes like the Naked Edge, the Yellow Spur, and even Bastille Crack. Easily identified as the crack that divides the Bastille formation (the crag that sits on the left of the auto road as soon as you start to drive up the canyon), it is an ever-popular classic; more likely than not you will see someone climbing it any given day, at any given time.

Seeing the climbers in Eldorado Canyon, you might wonder what—if anything—the kind of climbing they're doing has in common with reaching the summit of Mount Everest. The answer, simply put, is, "not much!" These days, the term climbing encompasses a variety of subdisciplines. Among these disciplines is rock climbing, which itself can be broken down into even more categories, from bouldering to big wall climbing to free climbing. Free climbing, by the way, is not soloing—the term free climbing means that the climber uses his or her own physical

The first train from Denver to Black Hawk rolled through on December 15, 1872. It took another six years for the line to extend to Central City. Regardless of the railroad's success, writer-explorer Isabella Bird once complained that she had never seen such "churlishness and incivility as in the officials of that railroad." She wrote of her disapproval in her 1875 book, A Lady's Life in the Rocky Mountains.

Back then, the train traveled a 200-foot-per-mile grade through Clear Creek Canyon. Black rock walls rose more than a thousand feet on either side. You can still look at the ominous walls if you travel Highway 6 through the area; it follows the same route as the railroad did.

Trivia

ability to climb the rock, with the safety gear and rope serving only as a backup should he or she slip and fall (this does happen more often than you might think and usually has no serious consequences). Climbing without ropes or gear is called free soloing.

Modern rock climbers revel in an abundance of varied challenges, from less-than-vertical slabs of rock (like the Third Flatiron) that require precision footwork and perfect balance to overhanging ceilings that demand explosive power and the ability to literally leap dynamically from hold to hold. Even more amazing (to nonclimbers) is that a climb of 15 feet or less in length can pose a far greater challenge, in terms of pure difficulty level, than a climb of 100 or even 1,000 feet! Rock climbs in this country are rated for difficulty on the Yosemite decimal scale, which assigns a rating of 5 to any rock climb that requires ropes for safety, and then a number following the decimal point telling how hard the route is. Starting at 5.10, climbs are further broken down into ascending degrees of difficulty with the letters a through d placed after the decimal (so a climb rated 5.10a will be significantly easier than a climb rated 5.10d). On this open-ended scale, climbs currently range from 5.0 to 5.15a. Bastille Creek is rated 5.7, Yellow Spur 5.10a, and Naked Edge 5.11a.

The type of rock climbing that you will most likely observe in Eldorado Canyon will be free climbing of the "traditional" sort. The climbing here generally requires forearm and calf endurance, poise under stress, the ability to place gear quickly and effectively, a strong sense of balance and technique, and, of course, experience. Climbers utilize modern, specialized equipment, from virtually unbreakable nylon ropes to soft, formfit-

Traditional vs. Sport Climbing

*M*ost of the rock climbing done in Eldorado Canyon falls under the definition of traditional climbing, meaning that climbers place and remove virtually all the pieces of protection that they utilize on any given climb. More recently, "sport climbing" has taken off in a variety of locations, including Boulder Canyon. In sport climbing, climbers hook devices called quickdraws into pre-placed expansion bolts that are relatively permanent fixtures to the rock face, meaning that the bolts remain in the rock for the use of future parties.

Eldorado Enchantment

*W*hile the parking lot in Eldorado Canyon bustles with activity on the weekends, on weekdays the canyon tends to see far less traffic. For rock climbers, this is the preferred way to enjoy the fabulous Eldorado classics. One magical weekday morning, I set out with a partner in the brilliant Colorado sunshine. We hiked the steep hill up to the base of Red Garden Wall, the largest crag in the entire Boulder area. As we rapidly danced our way up one of the area's classic routes, I reveled in the vastness and beauty of the canyon as it swept away beneath me. Sitting on the top of the buttress, I watched my partner surmount the final arête, dazzlingly outlined by the morning sun just as it started to envelop the cliffs—caught up for a moment in the magic of Eldo.

ting shoes soled with "sticky rubber" that gives them greater purchase on tiny dime-edge footholds. Strong, lightweight, removable pieces of protection—including passive metal wedges called stoppers or nuts and active mechanical gear known as camming devices—are placed in cracks and other aberrations in the rock as a climber (the leader) works his or her way up the rock. The climber then attaches his or her rope to these pieces, thus ensuring that any fall will be relatively short and safe, so long as the piece is properly placed to arrest the fall. The following climber (the second) then removes the pieces as he or she climbs the route, as the rope is now attached to a safety anchor above.

If scaling the walls isn't your idea of fun, Eldorado Canyon has plenty to offer in the way of alternative recreation. Tourists flock to the canyon in at least as many numbers as rock climbers, often clogging the narrow road up the canyon as they stop to gawk at their vertically inclined brethren. At the end of the canyon's road lies a lovely streamside picnic area with tables,

Trivia

President Dwight Eisenhower and his wife, Mamie, spent their honeymoon in Eldorado Canyon.

barbecue grills, and individual sites, perfect for a family outing. Numerous hiking trails allow those who prefer to keep their feet on the ground a chance to explore the canyon's deeper realms. Kayakers and anglers delight in South Boulder Creek, which burbles its way down the canyon for most of the year, freezing over during winter months.

Mountain bikers, too, are not left out—they can be seen slogging their way up the unrelenting **Rattlesnake Gulch Trail,** a strenuous but short trail that challenges the rider with 1,200 feet of elevation gain in 2 miles, not to mention some tight, technical single track. To find the trail, turn left on the Fowler Trail after passing through the first parking area in Eldorado Canyon State Park.

To reach Eldorado Canyon State Park, 25 miles northwest of Denver, take the Boulder Turnpike to the Superior exit; Highway 170 will take you to Eldorado Springs. From Boulder, head south on SR 93 and then take a right (west) on SR 170 (Eldorado Springs Drive). Eldorado Canyon State Park is open from dawn to dusk year-round. A $4.00-per-vehicle charge is required for entry. For more information, write 9 Kneal Road, P.O. Box B, Eldorado Springs 80025, or call (303) 494–3943. E-mail: eldorado@csn.net. Web site: parks.state.co.us/eldorado.

Make sure you don't miss out on **Eldorado Springs** as you leave the canyon. This tiny, eclectic town not only serves as a gateway to the park but also is home to the Eldorado Springs Pool at the historic **Eldorado Springs Resort,** which makes for a great place to cool off during hot summer months. Once a major tourist destination known as the "Coney Island of the West," more than 60,000 guests flocked to the Eldorado Springs Resort every summer during the early 1900s. The pool, built in 1906 and then advertised as the largest pool in the country, is filled to the brim with artesian water from the springs. Open from 10:00 A.M. to 6:00 P.M. daily from the Saturday before Memorial Day through Labor Day. Admission is $5.00 for adults, $3.00 for children three to twelve, under five free. Phone: (303) 499–1316. Fax: (303) 499–1339. Email: info@eldoradosprings.com. Web site: www.eldoradosprings.com/about/resort.html.

To find out more about the history of rock climbing, as well as moun-

Boulder Hiking

*T*he **Mesa Trail,** one of Colorado's most scenic introductions to year-round hiking and trail running, can be accessed easily. From Denver, drive the Boulder Turnpike (US 36) until you get to the "Superior" exit; Highway 170 will take you toward Eldorado Springs. Slow down until you notice the picnic tables and a small parking area on the right. The Mesa Trail is well marked. You cross a little bridge and soon zigzag through a landscape enhanced by sumac bushes, ferns, and sedges. The uphills are gentle enough, leading you before long into impressive pine forests, with glades to view the Flatiron citadels. (You see climbers here all summer.) The Mesa Trail winds up in Boulder's Chautauqua Park, from where some people actually embark on the same journey in the other direction and head back down. (An added note: In winter, the terrain is delightful for cross-country skiers.)

COLORADO FOOTHILLS

Trivia

The pure, 76° water of Eldorado Springs flows at a constant rate of 200 gallons per minute. Bottled at the source, Eldorado Springs drinking water is available for purchase at local grocery stores.

taineering and skiing, stop by **Neptune Mountaineering** on your way into Boulder. There you can explore owner Gary Neptune's impressive collection of climbing and skiing artifacts while you stock up on hydration packs, hiking boots, and energy bars. Make sure you grab an event schedule—Neptune Mountaineering hosts weekly slide shows, bringing some of the most famous names in the climbing community to Boulder. Usually held on Thursday nights, the slide shows are generally low in cost and high in fun.

Neptune Mountaineering can be reached at (303) 499–8866. The store (633 South Broadway) is located on the upper level of the Table Mesa Shopping Center at the corner of Broadway and Table Mesa in Boulder. From Eldorado Springs, take SR 93 north (it turns into Broadway). Open Monday through Friday, 10:00 A.M. to 8:00 P.M.; and Saturday and Sunday, 8:00 A.M. to 6:00 P.M. Web site: www.neptunemountaineering.com.

Trivia

Boulder has no shortage of trails to explore: Boulder Mountain Parks is home to approximately 50 miles of trails, and the City of Boulder Open Space has 80 miles of trails.

After stopping at Neptune's, continue along Broadway to Baseline Road, turning west to head up **Flagstaff Mountain,** the perfect place to mingle with some rock climbers while taking in some beautiful scenery. Bouldering—a type of rock climbing that involves short, intense movements up the sides of the rocks, with the climber normally staying low to the ground—is a popular pastime on Flagstaff, and for good reason. As plentiful as the spots on a Dalmatian's back, high-quality boulders dapple the flanks of Flagstaff, serving up myriad boulder problems that both delight and frustrate the numerous rock climbers who flock to test their skills on the sharp, rough sandstone. Pull out at any of a number of locations along the road and follow the paths back to the boulders where you'll likely find some climbers who have come to test their skills for an afternoon. You can either continue strolling along one of the mountain's marked trails, or just grab a seat on one of the surrounding smaller boulders and relax in the shade of ponderosa pines while you watch the boulderers. The jagged ridge of the First Flatiron pokes out above the trees to the south, and obstructed views of the city of Boulder can be seen to the east.

For more information on Flagstaff Mountain, contact Boulder Mountain Parks, Parks and Recreation Deptartment, P.O. Box 791, Boulder

80306; (303) 441–3408. Fax: (303) 441–4408. E-mail: sutherlandD@ci.
boulder.co.us. Web site: www.ci.boulder.co.us/bmp/. Open year-round,
5:00 A.M. to 11:00 P.M. (midnight for Panorama Point parking lot). Daily
permits can be purchased for $3.00 from any of the six well-marked,
self-service stations located along Flagstaff Road.

For a big treat, make dinner reservations at the *Flagstaff House
Restaurant,* one of Boulder's finest dining establishments. Nestled on
the side of Flagstaff Mountain, this lovely restaurant is a sure bet to
delight even the most discriminating of palates. Expect to shell out a
bundle (think $60 to $70 per person) for gourmet New American cuisine complete with impeccable service, complimentary appetizers from
the chef, and a terrific wine list, not to mention the stupendous views of
Boulder. The Flagstaff House Restaurant (1138 Flagstaff Road, Boulder
80302; 303–442–4640) is on the right as you drive up the mountain.

After dinner walk off your meal with your date by taking a romantic
moonlight stroll at *Panorama Point* (1 mile up Flagstaff Road from the
base of the mountain) or one of the many other overlooks that line
Flagstaff Road. If you're still feeling guilty about your marvelous dinner
the next morning, you can always come back and bike up Flagstaff
Road; it's one of the most popular workouts for local bikers of both
breeds: mountain and road.

The tree-lined campus of the University of Colorado at Boulder (known
to locals as simply "CU") warrants a visit, particularly in the summer
when the university stages its annual *Colorado Shakespeare Festival.*
During the season, you'll notice banners proclaiming the performances—and telling you to keep quiet—along Broadway as you head
toward downtown Boulder. The festival performs several Shakespeare
plays in July and August. National auditions attract actors from all over.
Contact the festival at (303) 492–0554 or write Colorado Shakespeare
Festival, CB-277, Boulder, 80309. E-mail: shakes@colorado.edu. Web
site: www.coloradoshakes.org.

Macky Auditorium, also on the CU campus, hosts performances by the
Boulder Philharmonic, the College of Music, visiting musicians partici-
pating in the Artists Series, and concerts by nationally known groups.
For information, call (303) 492–8423. E-mail: macky@stripe.
colorado.edu. Web site: www.colorado.edu/Macky.

Boulder also hosts the *Colorado Music Festival* from June through
August. Visiting performers and composers lend their talents and
energy to the festival. Reservations are required. Call (303) 449–2413 or

Trivia

CU-Boulder's mascot is a live buffalo named "Ralphie." Four Ralphies—all females – have trotted around the football field since the original Ralphie made her debut in 1966.

write to the festival at 1525 Spruce Street, Suite 101, Boulder 80302 for details. E-mail: cmf@coloradomusicfest.com. Web site: www.coloradomusicfest.com.

Hopefully you haven't tired of rock formations yet—Boulder has still more to offer in this department. Turn your sights north and then west for a drive up **Boulder Canyon,** with a stop, of course, at beautiful **Boulder Falls.** Tall, granite outcroppings line Highway 119 as it wends its way up toward the rustic town of Nederland and the Peak-to-Peak Highway. Find the canyon via Broadway (SR 93) in Boulder. Head west on Canyon Boulevard (SR 119)—you can't miss it! Stop at the pullout 11 miles up the canyon on your left to park, and then cross the street for a short walk back to the falls. Free; open from dawn to dusk. Contact Boulder Mountain Parks, Parks and Recreation Department, P.O. Box 791, Boulder 80306. Phone: (303) 441–3408. Fax: (303) 441–4408. E-mail: sutherlandD@ci.boulder.co.us. Web site: www.ci.boulder. co.us.

You'll probably catch glimpses of rock climbers here and there on the formations as you drive up the canyon, weather permitting. Of course, come winter, you're more likely to see people with crampons (metal-toothed attachments) on their boots and ice axes in their hands hacking their way up frozen waterfalls and sheets of ice—Boulder Canyon attracts ice climbers, too. But with its classic rock climbs, both traditional and sport,

South Boulder Creek Trail

*R*ain or shine, summer and winter, at least once a week I venture out to run along my favorite stretch of trail in all of Boulder. Located east of the main part of town, South Boulder Creek Trail doesn't tackle any of Boulder's hilly terrain but rather offers a nice, flat, 3½-mile dirt trail alongside South Boulder Creek. This path winds through trees and grasslands, offering interpretive signs along the way as well as the opportunity to see wildlife, from coyotes to entire prairie dog towns. To me, this trail always seems to epitomize the season—in fall, the trees lining it burst into glorious shades of orange and yellow, while winter finds them stark and bare as my feet crunch the packed snow and ice on the trail. Spring brings with it budding greenery and the most fragrant smells of new growth, and summer bursts with bountiful life. From Broadway in Boulder, head east on Baseline, passing Foothills Parkway. The trailhead, with plenty of parking, is on the right side of the street. Located on City of Boulder Open Space.

The area around Boulder Falls is made up of five acres of mining claims donated to the City of Boulder in 1914 by Charles G. Buckingham, president and cofounder of Buckingham Brothers Bank (now Norwest Bank). Since 1881 Buckingham had held a patent on the American Mill site, which included Boulder Falls. He gave the land with the intent of preserving it for recreational use.

the canyon most likely sees far more traffic from those who like to feel the rock beneath their fingers and under their feet in warmer weather. After all, some claim that the canyon's famous Country Club Crack (5.11a) was the hardest rock climb in the country for a period of time!

Seeing all the rock climbing around Boulder might spark your interest in trying out rock climbing yourself—but don't head out there uninformed. Though rock climbing is a relatively safe sport—despite the media's perpetual desire to portray it as "extreme" or "death-defying"— you should receive proper instruction and learn the safety basics before trying it out on your own. Rock climbing also requires specialized equipment that can take a big bite out of your wallet. Though rock climbing these days is a relatively safe endeavor when properly undertaken with an understanding of ropes and gear, novices must take a lesson or find an experienced mentor to show them the ropes, so to speak. Of course Boulder has a number of local services that cater to the needs of newcomers to the sport.

One of the best places to learn rock climbing in Boulder is ***Boulder Rock School.*** Affiliated with ***Boulder Rock Club,*** the AMGA-accredited school offers a wide range of classes for all ages and ability levels. The school teaches a two-hour class called Introduction to Indoor Climbing for $45. After this lesson, the novice climber should be able to go to any gym around the country and pass the belay test, the rope safety skills test required by all climbing gyms.

Pretty much anybody can take a beginning climbing class—rippling abs or bulging biceps are not prerequisites. It's not unusual to see couples enroll for a climbing class together only to discover that the female partner can immediately climb harder routes than her brawny male counterpart, much to his surprise. This only goes to show that, especially at the more moderate levels of the sport, technique, balance, and flexibility count just as much as, if not more than sheer strength.

More adventurous novices can try an outdoor lesson. Generally, experienced rock climbers use the gym for training and workout purposes but find that the indoor environment does not compare to the outdoor experience of climbing on real rock. Most guiding services, Boulder Rock School included, offer beginning climbing courses, with the option for private instruction (more expensive). As with indoor classes, the service provides all the necessary climbing equipment, allowing the student to sample rock climbing without making any monetary investment beyond the price of the class. Boulder Rock School's Introduction to Outdoor Climbing class costs $119 for a six-hour class.

Contact the Boulder Rock Club/Boulder Rock School by calling (303) 447–2804 or (800) 836–4008. Fax: (303) 447-8356. E-mail: mattyoc@ aol.com. Web site: www.boulderrock.com. The facility is located at 2829 Mapleton Avenue in Boulder. Take US 36 into Boulder, and then head east on Mapleton. The club is on the north side of the street. You must call for class schedules and to reserve a space.

The mood of Boulder can perhaps be felt most at the *Pearl Street Mall,* easily found by taking Broadway north from Canyon; the mall intersects Broadway a few blocks up. Both locals and visitors mingle among boutiques and restaurants, many of which feature outdoor patios. Some people simply hang out on the mall's strip and watch the eclectic crowd. Besides the shoppers and the leisurely crowd of patrons, Pearl Street has musicians, jugglers, and many other types of street performers (some of whom may not necessarily intend to perform, but perform nonetheless). The mall's sidewalk is a street that has been closed to traffic since the seventies, and this street never fails to excite.

Don't miss out on a cool treat from *Cold Stone Creamery,* located just south of Pearl Street at 1964 Thirteenth Street, Boulder 80302; (303)

Boulder Creek Path

*F*rom Eben G. Fine Park at the base of Boulder Canyon to Fifty-fifth Street on the east side of town, the 7-mile-long wooded Boulder Creek Path winds its way through. You can run it, walk it, bike it, or blade it. You never have to stop for a second; underpasses protect you from car traffic at every intersection. And there's plenty to see along the way: Xeriscape gardens, a fish observatory, and a fishing pond for the kids. (The pond is actually designed for children.) A network of other paths connect with this main artery, allowing for easy access to virtually all areas of Boulder. West of town, the path follows Boulder Creek up Boulder Canyon for a ways, turning to dirt before it ends.

541–0668. E-mail: bconley@coldstonecreamery.com. Web site: www. coldstonecreamery.com. The ice cream (and frozen yogurt) is made fresh daily, and customers create their own flavors from a choice of more than forty mix-ins. Waffle cones are standard at this ice cream lover's paradise, where a small-size ice cream is bigger than a large at most other shops.

For a preview of what you can expect to see during a stroll down Pearl Street, check out the virtual tour available at www.virtualviews. com/views/pearl/index.html.

Where should you stay? Contrasting with the vivacious pace of Pearl Street is the stately *Boulder Victoria Historic Inn.* At this seven-room bed-and-breakfast, you're aware of understated Victorian hues, vast and sparkling bay windows, and a sea of well-tended delphiniums. Everything asks the traveler to slow down and drink in all the rich history that this Victorian architecture has to offer.

While the original 1876 structure was a modest frame house, major renovations in 1889 transformed it into a showpiece, complete with carved posts and arched balconies. Now, more than one hundred years later, new owners have added their own lavish accents to make this one of the more beautiful historical residences around.

Outside, unique sandstone furniture in a garden of pansies and roses invites you to take in the views. Inside, large guest rooms decorated with dark wood and richly patterned wall coverings, as well as period antiques and brass beds, make travelers feel as if they've just stepped into the pages of a Jane Austen novel. Indeed, the Boulder Victoria won't disappoint. It's a genuine glimpse of nineteenth-century elegance and propriety. For information write 1305 Pine, Boulder 80302; (303) 938–1300. Web site: www.bouldervictoria.com/victoria.html.

**PLACES TO STAY IN
THE COLORADO FOOTHILLS**

*(ALL AREA CODES 303 UNLESS
NOTED OTHERWISE)*

BLACK HAWK
Gold Dust Lodge (good access to all summer opera productions; moderate); 5312 Highway 119; 582–5415

BOULDER
Alps Boulder Canyon Inn, 38619 Boulder Canyon Drive (expensive to deluxe); 444–5445

Boulder Mountain Lodge (rooms and campsites, scenic; inexpensive to moderate); 91 Fourmile Canyon Drive; 444–0882

Boulder Victoria Historic Inn (relatively quiet B&B; recently restored; expensive to deluxe); 1305 Pine; 938–1300

Briar Rose Bed and Breakfast Inn (small, but prestigious and distinguished, moderate to expensive); 2151 Arapahoe Avenue; 442–3007

Broker Inn (moderate to expensive); 555 Thirtieth Street; 444–3330

Courtyard by Marriott (moderate to expensive); 4710 Pearl East Circle; 440–4700

Hotel Boulderado (well-established, centrally located hotel; deluxe); 2115 Thirteenth Street; 442–4344

Sandy Point Inn (some rooms with small kitchens; condominiums; nonsmoking; moderate to expensive); 6485 Twin Lakes Road; 530–2939 or (800) 322–2939

CENTRAL CITY
Harveys Wagon Wheel Hotel/Casino (moderate); 321 Gregory Street; (800) 924–6646

GOLDEN
Glen-Isle Resort (cool retreat on river, simple accomodations; inexpensive to moderate); Bailey 80421; 838–5461

La Quinta (clean; inexpensive to moderate); 3301 Youngfield Service Road; 279–5565

Table Mountain Inn (fine mountain views; moderate to deluxe); 1301 Washington Avenue; 277–9898

Colorado Foothills General Information Resources

BOULDER

Boulder Convention and Visitors Bureau, 2440 Pearl Street, 80302; (303) 442–2911 or (800) 444–0447; fax (303) 938–8837
E-mail: visitor@bouldercvb.com
Web site: www.bouldercoloradousa.com

CENTRAL CITY/BLACK HAWK

Gilpin County, 203 Eureka Street, P.O. Box 366, Central City 80427; (303) 582–5214; fax (303) 582–5440
E-mail: commpubcomment@gilpincounty.com
Web site: www.gilpincounty.com

Gilpin County Chamber of Commerce, P.O. Box 343, Black Hawk, 80422; (303) 582–5077 or (800) 331–5825

GOLDEN

Greater Golden Chamber of Commmerce, P.O. Box 1035, 80402; (303) 279–3113 or (800) 590–3113
E-mail: info@goldencochamber.org
Web site: www.goldencochamber.org

PLACES TO EAT IN THE COLORADO FOOTHILLS

(ALL AREA CODES 303)

BLACK HAWK/CENTRAL CITY
Tony Roma's (voted "best ribs in Colorado," located at Harvey's Wagon Wheel Casino; inexpensive); 321 Gregory Street, Central City; 582-0800

BOULDER
Café Gondolier (moderate to expensive except for the all-you-can-eat homemade spaghetti for $3.95 on Tuesday and Wednesday nights); 2845 Twenty-eighth Street; 443-5015

Dandelion (contemporary American; deluxe); 1011 Walnut Street; 443-6700

Flagstaff House (historic; innovative American menu; mountain cabin setting; deluxe); 1138 Flagstaff Road; 442-4640

Q's (Hotel Boulderado; deluxe); 2115 Thirteenth Street; 442-4880

Royal Peacock (East Indian; expensive); 5290 Arapahoe Avenue; 447-1409

Sunflower (innovative, gourmet vegetarian and organic cuisine, expensive to deluxe); 1701 Pearl Street; 440-0220

DENVER
Healthy Habits (vegetarian buffet-style, one-price salad bar; indoor, outdoor; inexpensive); 14195 West Colfax Avenue; 277-9293

GOLDEN
Chart House (steak, seafood; Sunday brunch; deluxe); 25908 Genessee Trail; 526-9813

Cody Inn (Continental; moderate to expensive); 866 Lookout Mountain Road; 526-0232

Hilltop Café (bistro; moderate to expensive); 1518 Washington Avenue; 279-8151

Table Mountain Inn (Southwestern; expensive to deluxe); 1310 Washington Avenue; 277-9898

LITTLETON
Manor House Restaurant (salmon, veal, lamb; deluxe); 1 Manor House Road; 973-8064

MORRISON
The Fort (beef, buffalo; deluxe); 19192 Highway 8; 697-4771

Other Attractions Worth Seeing in the Colorado Foothills

BOULDER
University of Colorado, (303) 492-1411
Boulder Museum of History, (303) 449-3464
Collage Children's Museum, (303) 440-9894

CENTRAL CITY
Gilpin Historical Society Museum, (303) 582-5283

GOLDEN
Golden Gate Canyon State Park, (303) 582-3707
Coors Brewing Company, (303) 277-2337

Northwestern Mountains

Rocky Mountain National Park Territory

I f you happen to come to **Estes Park** during the high summer season—and want to be above the melee—you might consider the short uphill drive to the **Stanley Hotel and Conference Center.** It stands above the busy town like a white castle. The one-hundred-room Stanley reminds you of those old Swiss Grand Hotels—aristocratic, flawlessly kept up, frequently restored, a monument to good taste and good manners.

The hotel is all stately white columns, Victorian furniture, fireplaces crackling in the lobby, rooms with impeccable white linen, polished cherrywood furniture, and antique dressers. The handwrought leaded-glass windows, the spotless white tablecloths in the (deluxe) dining room, and the comfortable bar add to a vacation feeling. Miles of walks surround the hostelry, which is at an elevation of 7,500 feet.

The historic hotel was built by the inventor of the Stanley Steamer automobile. Back in 1905, doctors gave F. O. Stanley, the inventor, only a few months to live. Stanley gathered his wife, her maid, and his controversial Steamer and headed for the Colorado Rockies. The undaunted old gentleman was determined to drive his vehicle to Estes Park, Colorado, regardless of roads declared impassable. He victoriously covered the 20-mile stretch in a record one hour and fifty minutes. The inventor suffered from tuberculosis, and his doctor had sent him to Estes Park with the hope of prolonging the patient's life "for a year or so." The sturdy old gentleman was to live for another thirty-seven years. (He reached the age of ninety-one.)

The ingenious, eccentric millionaire ran his lavish hotel facility with a style all his own. In order to bring chamber music to Estes Park for his

Northwestern Mountains

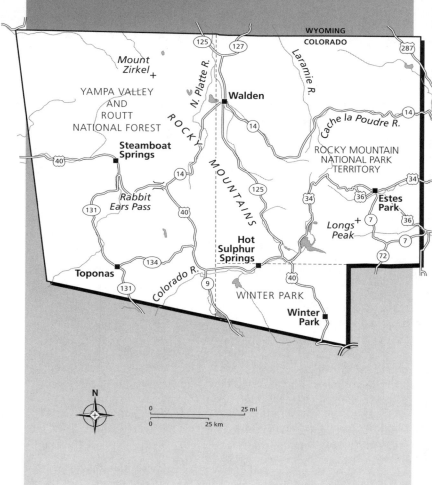

WYOMING
COLORADO

125   127   287

Mount
Zirkel +   N. Platte R.

YAMPA VALLEY   Walden   Laramie R.
AND   Cache la Poudre R.
ROUTT   14   14
NATIONAL FOREST
                          R   ROCKY MOUNTAIN
Steamboat   O   NATIONAL PARK
Springs   C   TERRITORY
40   K
                          Y   14   34

Rabbit   M
Ears Pass   O   125   34   36   Estes
131   40   U   Park
                              N   34
                              T   Longs +   7
                              A   Hot   Peak   36
                              I   Sulphur   7
Toponas   134   Colorado R. N   9 Springs
131   S   40   72
                                    WINTER PARK
                                          Winter
                                          Park

N

0   25 mi
0   25 km

AUTHOR'S FAVORITE ATTRACTIONS
IN THE NORTHWESTERN MOUNTAINS

Trail Ridge Road (Rocky Mountain National Park between Grand Lake and Estes Park), (970) 586–1206, *www.nps.gov/romo*

Stanley Hotel, (970) 586–3371 or (800) 976–1377, *www.stanleyhotel.com*

Rocky Mountain National Park, (970) 586–1206, *www.nps.gov/romo*

Grand Lake, (970) 627–3372 or (800) 531–1019, *www.grandlakechamber.com*

C Lazy U Ranch, (970) 887–3344, *www.clazyu.com*

Winter Park, (970) 726–5514 or (303) 892–0961, *www.skiwinterpark.com*

Beaver Village Condominiums, (970) 726–8813 or (800) 824–8438, *www.beavercondos.com*

Strawberry Park Hot Springs, (970) 879–0342, *www.strawberryhotsprings. com*

Vista Verde Ranch, (800) 526–7433, *www.vistaverde.com*

Ponderosa Lodge, (800) 628–0512, *www.estes-park.com/ ponderosa*

guests, he had a huge New York Steinway piano shipped to Colorado by oxcart. His resort, located on 160 acres of land, was part of the 6,000-acre Lord Dunraven hunting estate.

Most of the guests arrived by train, to be picked up in Stanley's steaming ten-horsepower automobile. The "all-electric" hotel charged $8.00 a day, gourmet meals included.

The Stanley Hotel opened in June 1909. It had cost $1 million to build and was described as "simply palatial." The materials had come by horse teams on roads that Stanley himself designed. A magnificent white edifice with dormers and flagpoles and elegant porches welcomed the hotel guests. Once inside the lobby, the arrivals were dazzled by the hand-carved wooden staircase, the ornate brass elevator, and the carpeted halls that led to rooms with lead-glass windows and four-poster beds.

Stanley, who'd made huge sums with the invention of his automobile and later with photo-dry plates, personally designed the hotel's electric kitchens. He ordered the decor of a music room, arranged for a gentlemen's smoking room (even if he never touched tobacco himself), and enjoyed showing up in the billiard room. The legendary Stanley Hotel eventually attracted celebrities such as Theodore Roosevelt, John Philip Sousa, and Molly Brown.

Remarkably enough, F. O. Stanley's creation still stands; indeed, it prospers. It can be found in the National Register of Historic Places. The music room is still there, as is a writing room. Picture windows and restaurant views give to the mountains, including Longs Peak. Sunning and swimming are available in summer. A professional theater flourishes; in fact, the hotel stays open through the winter as well. Rates are moderate when the snow falls; summer accommodations are more expensive, as they should be at this palace.

Trivia

The Stanley Hotel earned some of its more recent notoriety as the setting that inspired Stephen King's novel, The Shining. *King wrote roughly half of the manuscript for the novel while staying in room 217 at the hotel. He returned to the Stanley Hotel in 1997 to make the ABC miniseries version of* The Shining *(the motion picture was filmed elsewhere).*

A 1906 Stanley Steamer automobile stands in the lobby, as a reminder of how it all began. Contact Stanley Hotel and Conference Center, P.O. Box 1767, Estes Park 80517; (970) 586–3371 or (800) 976–1377. Fax (970) 586–4964. E-mail: stanley@estes-park.com. Web site: www.stanley hotel.com.

On a July day in 1982, a flood roared into one of Colorado's most visited tourist centers. The water raged through Elkhorn Avenue, Estes Park's main street, breaking shop windows and causing wholesale destruction. The Fall River rose, tearing into motels and mountain cabins. Three people drowned. The damage was estimated at $31 million. For the remainder of that season—and part of the next—the flood stopped tourism in its tracks.

Estes Park has long been rebuilt. The reborn main street offers prettily painted benches, trees and planters, new sidewalks, and souvenir stores. A church has become an array of shops. Someone coined the slogan "The Gutsiest Little Town in Colorado!" Some 250,000 to 300,000 tourists come to stay here each year. They enjoy themselves in myriad ways. Rock climbers flock to climb not only on aptly named **Lumpy Ridge,** which rises above the town to the northwest, but also to attempt some of the other, more remote cliff faces so abundant in Rocky Mountain National Park. You may see them in town picking up a coffee in the morning, or more likely after a climb, when, dirty and tired, they'll stop

Aspen Lodge at Estes Park

What a contrast! Estes Park, the stylish community that became famous with the Stanley Hotel, also gave us the Aspen Lodge at Estes Park, a rugged, typically western log-cabin lodge with sixty spacious rooms. The main year-round focus here is on the outdoors. In winter, you skate or play ice hockey or broomball, go sledding or tubing, enjoy a sleigh ride, rent snowshoes or cross-country skis. In summer, there are short or long hikes (this writer required three hours to reach the summit of the Twin Sisters peak), hot tubs, mountain bikes, and a weight room, all to stimulate your appetite; restaurant on the premises. The Aspen Lodge at Estes Park is at 6120 Highway 7, Estes Park 80517; (970) 586–8133 or (800) 332–6867, fax (970) 586–8133. Web site: www.ranchweb.com /aspenlodge.

in at a restaurant to fill their bellies. Other visitors carry fishing tackle; trout are plentiful (Colorado license required). Wildlife abounds, and the air is pure in the surrounding mountains.

Estes Park has two golf courses, including one that occupies land once owned by the famous Earl of Dunraven, an Irish nobleman who discovered the area in 1827 while on a hunting trip. The American homesteaders followed during the 1870s. Nowadays Estes Park has about 4,000 permanent inhabitants, plus 25,000 others who own mountain cabins, show up briefly in summer, and often keep to themselves.

To be sure, the town is ideal for vacationing families. Estes Park makes boredom impossible. In summer, the ***Estes Park Aerial Tramway*** ascends the flank of Prospect Mountain, located a few blocks from Elkhorn Avenue. ***Trout Haven,*** also close by, features several ponds stocked with rainbow, plus gear for rent. (See sidebars for contact information). On nearby ***Lake Estes*** lie boating possibilities and free access to terrific family hiking terrain. For more information, contact Estes Valley Recreation and Park District, 1770 Big Thompson Avenue, P.O. Box 1379, Estes Park 80517; (970) 586–2011. Fax (970) 586–8193. E-mail: EVRPD@aol.com. Web site: www.estesvalleyrecreation.com/marina.html.

The reborn Estes Park presents some contrasts: new and old, serene and loud, natural and artificial. The touristy aspects of the town will disturb the sensitive traveler. Mountains don't seem to suffice. Your children can race noisy little go-carts ("Grand Prix! Thrilling! A

Estes Park: The Best Views

The Estes Park Aerial Tramway, west on US 34 to Moraine Park Road, carries passengers to the 8,896-foot summit of Prospect Mountain for an unmatched look at the community and surrounding mountains. Sit on one of two suspended cabins and view the Continetal Divide, and then picnic at the summit. For more information: 420 Riverside Drive; (970) 586–3675.

Blast!"). On Elkhorn Avenue, a store prints handbills with headlines ("The Smiths having a Ball in Estes!" or "Patsy Saw Her First Snow!!") and sells T-shirts with silly messages ("Colorado is owned by Canadians").

For all visitors there are rodeos, parades, chamber music concerts, and Rocky Mountain National Park talks, walks, and campfire programs. Still other possibilities: You can shop for Native American crafts or jewelry, sporting goods, western wear, or mineral specimens.

When should you come to Estes Park? Avoid July and August. Elkhorn Avenue then turns into a tourism circus, with thousands of people descending upon the town. Early June and September are good months. A tranquil time begins after Labor Day.

Accommodations? The redecorated **Ponderosa Lodge** overlooks the now peaceful Fall River; some units were damaged by the flood but were rebuilt (1820 Fall River Road, Estes Park 80517; 800–628–0512. E-mail: ponderosa@estes-park.com. Web site: www.estes-park.com/ponderosa). The Ponderosa also added a large cedar log cabin for families or groups.

The YMCA in the Rockies rents housekeeping cabins. Estes Park has a Holiday Inn with a large indoor swimming pool. The Stanley Hotel is the most elegant and historic in town. Except for the moderately priced YMCA, the tariff for summer accommodations is high.

Estes Park is 65 miles northwest of Denver and easy to reach via the

Estes Park Speciality—Fly Fishing

*E*ven the most avid of anglers will want to cast their attention toward the Estes Park area.

For fly fishing, the **Colorado River**, west of Estes Park, cannot be faulted. Your frying pan will be kept busy, because the fish thrive in the chilly waters here. Indeed, the "Colorado," as it's called, has been named a Gold-Medal trout stream. The reason? The high number of trout over 14 inches long that have been pulled from its waters.

If you prefer to drop your line in a lake, you won't want to miss **Grand Lake,** south and west of Estes Park. This is the largest natural lake in Colorado and is home to Kokanee, brown, rainbow, and lake trout.

One more tip: **Trout Haven** (810 Moraine Avenue, Estes Park 80517; 970–586–5525; E-mail: fish4u@gte. net; Web site: www.trouthaven.com) may just be your ticket. This farm fishery allows you to fish without a license, and you pay only for what you catch. As an added bonus, the proprietors will clean and pack your catch on ice.

Break the Ice: Ice Climbing near Estes Park

*E*stes Park is home base for the **Colorado Mountain School** *(CMS), the sole concessionaire permitted to guide rock and ice climbs in nearby Rocky Mountain National Park. Wintertime is the perfect season to test yourself on the park's frozen waterfalls under the watchful eyes of one of CMS's expert guides. From introductory one-day courses to an intensive, multiday advanced course, CMS has classes appropriate for all skill levels. Contact CMS at 351 Moraine Avenue, P.O. Box 1846, Estes Park 80517; (970) 586-5758, fax (970) 586-5798. E-mail: cmschool@cmschool.com. Web site: www.cmschool.com.*

Boulder Turnpike and US 36 through Lyons. For more information, write Estes Park Chamber Resort Association, 500 Big Thompson Avenue, P.O. Box 3050, Estes Park 80517; (970) 586–4431 or (800) 443–7837. Fax (970) 586–0144. Web site: www.estesparkresort.com.

For those who prefer to do their nature exploration by automobile, a drive along the spectacular **Trail Ridge Road** (US 34) in Rocky Mountain National Park shouldn't be missed. Lying within the park, Trail Ridge Road winds along for 48 miles through the high country, connecting the towns of Estes Park and Grand Lake. Eleven miles of the road are above tree line, with the high point at 12,183 feet. Take some time to enjoy your passage along the highest continuously paved highway in the United States, but make sure you plan your trip with the weather in mind.

The season is short for a visit, though. Deep snows and snowdrifts cover Trail Ridge all winter and spring; indeed, the famous road is open only from Memorial Day until the first heavy snowfall, usually in mid-October. Then it closes down.

Starting from Estes Park, you climb for some 4,000 feet on a highway that has serpentines like those of Alpine passes. Reaching 12,183-foot (3,713-meter) level, you find that the air is thin and the ultraviolet rays are strong. Eventually you descend through the clouds to Grand Lake, which is 4,000 feet below. In between you spot some of Colorado's highest mountain ranges. When you park, you find yourself in view of rock piles, known as moraines, deposited here during the Ice Age. There's the Iceberg Lake View at 12,080 feet, and there's high meadowland known as tundra, which is reminiscent of Alaska.   •

Your family can learn much about forestry below timberline. The lovely aspen tree occurs in stands at elevations of about 9,000 to 10,000 feet.

Trail Ridge Road also provides a home for alder trees and Douglas fir. In the conifer family you find blue spruce, lodgepole pines, and the beautiful *Pinus ponderosa*. At some higher levels, 9,500 feet and up, grow the subalpine fir and the Engelmann spruce.

How do you distinguish between the many species of conifers? The differences are noticeable. Spruces, for example, can be identified by cones that stand up straight like candles, and spruce needles are attached singly to the twigs. By contrast, ponderosa pine needles come in clusters of two to three; the bark is a dark brown. Lodgepole pine needles are attached in pairs.

Like most important Colorado highways, Trail Ridge has a long history. First came the Utes and other Native American tribes, who actually followed the already marked trails of wild animals. Miners used it in the 1880s. In 1929, Congress appropriated almost $500,000—a large sum in those days—to build a highway over the Continental Divide. Engineers called it Tombstone Ridge, which became Trail Ridge Road. The paving was finally completed in 1935.

The government engineers, normally cool and scientific, became eloquent enough in their final analysis, which mentioned the "deep canyons, many lakes and perpetual snow." The route report concluded: "Below lie streams, valleys, forested slopes, and the realms of

Coping with the Altitude

*M*ost out-of-state visitors need a day or two to become accustomed to the altitude. Los Angeles, New York, and Dallas are at sea level. Colorado's resorts and the lifts are from 8,000 to 12,000 feet up. Some midwestern skiers may fly to Vail and immediately storm the slopes. The abrupt altitude change will affect flatlanders, of course. They'll probably ski their initial runs with knees made of Jell-O. And they'll tire more easily. A suddenly transplanted midwesterner or southerner may not sleep well the first night in the high mountains. And, if one were to ask the ski patrol

about the acclimatization of older visitors, the advice is always the same: Please don't overdo it on the first day! According to the patrol, people with chronic heart or lung problems should take it especially easy at the higher elevations.

Doctors claim that it takes one day to get used to each additional thousand feet. An exaggeration? The point seems valid enough, however. A New York skier needn't rush up to his final Colorado destination as though he were trying to catch a commuter train or subway at home.

NORTHWESTERN MOUNTAINS

civilization. All around are mountains and peaks, no longer towering above but close at hand or seen across some mighty valley."

Travel some 70 miles north and west from Denver (I–25 north to SR 66, west on 66 until it joins US 36) to Estes Park and Trail Ridge Road (US 34. See Rocky Mountain National Park entry for contact information).

One hundred and twenty years ago, an Englishwoman named Isabella Bird waxed enthusiastic about this Colorado landscape. She came upon the nearby Longs Peak region on horseback. What expressions of wonder! "Exquisite stretches of flowery pastures dotted with trees sloping down-like to bright streams full of red waistcoated trout or running up in soft glades into the dark forest, above which the snow peaks rise," wrote the lady, and the description still fits.

The peaks and lakes of ***Rocky Mountain National Park*** have present-day names that bear witness to it all: The tourist can view Deer Mountain, Isolation Peak, Snowdrift Peak. Those who come afoot—and more people do every year—may head for Dream Lake, Lone Pine Lake, Fern Lake, and up to Chasm Lake.

All belong to the impressive 415-square-mile span of Rocky Mountain National Park. Established by the federal government in 1915, the park now encompasses more than one hundred upthrusting peaks higher than 11,000 feet above sea level. Longs Peak is the highest mountain in the park at 14,255 feet.

> **Trivia**
>
> *The 1,000-foot east face of Longs Peak, a vertical granite cliff known as the Diamond, attracts rock climbers from all over the world.*

Bureau of Land Management and U.S. Forest Service

*T*he Bureau of Land Management (BLM) adminsters millions of acres of public lands around the country, including 8.3 million acres in Colorado, while the U.S. Forest Service (USFS) manages 14.3 million acres in the state. State offices for both organizations can direct you to specific regional and local offices, many of which are listed throughout this book as well. For more information, look on the USFS Web site— www.fs.fed.us/recreation/states/co.shtml—or contact the USFS Rocky Mountain regional office at (303) 275–5350. For information about BLM lands in Colorado, visit Web site www.co.blm.gov/index.htm or contact the BLM Colorado state office at (303) 239–3600.

There are lots of things to do here, yet the expanse also brings happiness to the inactive. Nearby resort hotels are inviting with clean rooms and deck chairs, and the area appeals to the most sedentary motorist.

Nature studies, lectures, and tours are conducted by park rangers. The many summer doings make this part of Colorado especially attractive to visitors. There are not only campfire programs, but also a number of short, self-guiding nature paths for the benefit of families. (You can bring small children, too.) A Colorado fishing license entitles you to angle for trout in the park's many lakes; some 350 well-marked trails invite the hiker. Wildflowers abound in late spring. Bring your camera.

Trivia

Rocky Mountain National Park's annual budget is about $850,000—which may seem like a lot, until you consider that the park has nearly 3.4 million visitors each year!

Walking is the best way to see this national park. One of the most scenic and easily accessed trails is the one to **Bear Lake.** Nine different hikes begin here. Difficulty ratings range from the half-mile "easy" stroll around the lake to the $8^8/_{10}$-mile round-trip to Flattop Mountain that is rated "strenuous." Rocky Mountain National Park is especially popular with backpackers, who need a permit, and with rock climbers.

The Park Service exacts a small fee ($10 per vehicle) to enter the mountainous domain; if you plan to visit other parks, it will be worth your while to buy a Golden Eagle Pass ($65). It's good for your car and its occupants during the entire year. Travelers age sixty-two and older may ask for the Golden Age Pass—a lifetime pass to all federal recreation areas for a onetime $10 charge. Hikers can reach the park gratis by setting out from the main parking lot of the Longs Peak Trail toward Chasm Lake, below the summit of the peak. The trails are marked and not too steep.

Please note that the Rocky Mountain National Park has become so popular that every year some three million people stream through four entrances, especially in summer. The major highway, Trail Ridge Road, closes from mid-October through Memorial Day.

Rocky Mountain has only six campgrounds, fewer than a third of Yosemite's or Yellowstone's. No hookups are available for trailers; the big ones, like Airstreams, are hard to navigate on the curvy park roads. Some tents go up early in the morning, and at the peak of the season—June through Labor Day—accommodations may be hard to come by, even in neighboring towns.

There are several ways to avoid the crowds and still enjoy the Rockies' pleasantly cool summers; the green of pine, spruce, and fir; the mosaic of wildflowers; and the water that cascades down those Rockies. For instance, you can arrive early in the season or after the children are back in school. You can relax by renting a mountain cabin.

Autumn is the best time of all, bringing with it a seemingly endless string of clear, warm days. The evenings turn crisp and the nights are chilly, so bring an overcoat. Mid-September seems the best period. Come after Labor Day and you'll find less competition for the area's good rooms, restaurant tables, and traffic lanes.

In winter, cross-country skiing is plentiful. In summer, the patient animal watcher can see deer, elk, sheep, beaver, pikas, and many birds as well.

The Englishwoman was right about the park and its "exquisite stretches."

From Denver you can arrive at this ultrascenic region via several routes. Some summer motorists head west from the Mile High City on I–70, cross Berthoud Pass via US 40, and then get to the Rocky Mountain National Park via Grand Lake (altitude 8,367 feet and icicle-cold). You can also come on the spectacular Peak-to-Peak Highway (SR 119, SR 72, and SR 7) from Black Hawk. The drive is especially enjoyable in late fall when the aspen trees burst into gold. Earmark at least half a day to get to the national park via this route. To save time, you can drive through Boulder and Lyons instead (use US 36); from Boulder it's about 34 miles to Estes Park and the Rocky Mountain National Park gates.

For more information: Rocky Mountain National Park, 1000 Highway 36, Estes Park 80517-8397; (970) 586–1206. Fax (970) 586–1256. E-mail: ROMO_Information@nps.gov. Web site: www.nps.gov/romo.

If you've decided to spend a day driving along Trail Ridge Road from Estes Park, the end of your journey will deposit you in the town of **Grand Lake,** which skirts the shores of Grand Lake itself. This unusually blue lake—the largest glacial lake in the state—will be dotted with sailboats in August, its marinas filled up with yachts. At an elevation of almost 8,400 feet above sea level, Grand Lake boasts the "World's Highest Yacht Club." The mountain giants of Rocky Mountain National Park cast a watchful presence over the stunning, Swisslike scene.

The slightly offbeat location doesn't prevent the international sailing elite from competing here for trophies. Regattas are frequent. During the summer marinas get busy with vacationers who rent rowboats, paddleboats, or motorboats.

You see sailboarders. The lake and the nearby streams are populated by anglers. Four river-rafting companies take you out on various excursions. You have limitless opportunities for hiking. Stables with horses beckon. The surrounding peaks are forested by healthy aspen trees, ponderosa pine, and Douglas fir. You will find waterfalls and mountain flowers.

In winter the handsome, wooden, lakeshore summer homes are abandoned by their rich midwestern and Texan owners; the souvenir shops along the boardwalk close down. Only a few saloons, a tiny grocery, and the pharmacy stay open. Trail Ridge Road is closed. At the same time, the cross-country ski possibilities are plentiful. The Rocky Mountain National Park entrance is only a mile away, and you see Nordic skiers even on the golf course. Noisy snowmobile enthusiasts show up with their machines. Most winter tourists stay in nearby Granby; the wealthy ones repair to the C Lazy U Ranch.

Trivia

Grand Lake is also known as the "Snowmobile Capital of Colorado," due to its more than 300 miles of trails.

For those who wish to enjoy the deep silence that winter in the Rockies can bring, the smell and roar of snowmobiles shatters any attempt to enjoy the deep quiet of winter. One escape from the snowmobiles: the ***Grand Lake Touring Center*** (Box 590, Grand Lake 80447; 970–627–8008. Web site: www.grandlakecolorado.com/touring center). Although few people know about it, the location is easy to find; just turn left on County Road 48 and proceed to the west entrance of Rocky Mountain National Park. The Ski Touring Center is more scenic than most, and the 30 kilometers of trails are immaculately kept up. Some of the runs are surprisingly steep—especially for a golf course!— but other trails are gentle enough for beginners. Among the many runs, experts will enjoy the Spirits Haunt; good skiers can be seen on Ptarmigan Tuck. Actually, you rarely see many people up here in this pristine territory; Grand Lake just doesn't get many visitors in winter. And, of course, snowmobiles are verboten in the Ski Touring Center. Full-moon ski adventures and spaghetti dinners take place throughout the season; call for details. The center is open daily from 9:00 A.M. to 4:00 P.M.

Grand Lake's history is also worth writing about. The Native Americans called it Spirit Lake. According to local historians, the first Indians arrived around A.D. 900 to 1300. They no doubt stayed during the summer and late fall. Game, fish, and other food were plentiful.

The earliest legend of the region tells of Ute, Arapaho, and Cheyenne squabbles. Apparently, the Utes living in this summer paradise were suddenly attacked by marauding Cheyennes. Fearing for their women and children, the Ute braves hastily loaded them on rafts and shoved the rafts onto the lake for safety. As the battle with the Cheyennes raged among the trees and along the lakeshore, a storm came up, blowing the rafts far out onto the 400-foot-deep lake. The Indians watched helplessly as the rafts were overturned and the women and children drowned. After this time the Utes regarded the lake as dangerous and stayed away, naming it Spirit Lake.

The first white visitors probably showed up in 1855 to hunt for furs and catch the plentiful trout. Although he is best known for his discovery of the Gore Range near Vail, Sir George Gore, the Irish nobleman, also explored the Grand Lake wilderness for a couple of years. He arrived with a party of fifty people and thirty supply wagons. He brought guides, secretaries, and hunt-and-fish-supply artisans. The country then abounded with game, including elk, bear, deer, and buffalo.

Other hunters and trappers of lesser stature came next, and some, attracted by the remote beauty of the area, remained to become the region's first settlers. Among these was Joseph L. Westcott, who became the first postmaster of Grand Lake in 1877. Westcott, later known as Judge Westcott, remained here most of his life.

In 1881, the little hamlet of Grand Lake got its first sizable general store, and the Grand Central Hotel was completed. It was a decade of summer residents building homes that looked out on the water. The first big regatta took place here in 1912, on the 12-mile-long lake. It is measured only a mile across, so you always see the other shore. The mountain backdrop is as stunning as any in Switzerland.

While a somewhat lengthy trek is required for a summer visit (via Trail Ridge Road), winter renders Grand Lake an even more out-of-the-way destination. A circuitous route can be followed from Denver, taking I–70 to SR 40 north, then breaking off after Granby onto SR 34 to head farther north. For more information: Grand Lake Area Chamber of Commerce, P.O. Box 57, Grand Lake 80447-0057; (970) 627–3402 or (800) 531–1019. Fax (970) 627–8007. E-mail: glinfo@grandlakechamber. com. Web site: www.grandlakechamber.com.

The *C Lazy U Ranch,* ensconced in its own Willow Creek Valley some 100 miles west of Denver, is no ordinary guest ranch.

At the stables, the wranglers assign you a personal horse for your stay, and you and your group set out into a quiet, slightly remote, truly relaxing 5,000 acres of mountains and hillsides, forests and rivers, ponds and lookout points.

In winter, the ranch turns into Grandma Moses scenery, all white, with brown barns and fences and the children—colored dots—playing ice hockey, skating, and tubing. At the Nordic shop, one hundred pairs of cross-country skis and boots and poles await the lucky guests. Some 30 miles of trails are packed and ready; you share these winter woods with elk and deer, which show up in the meadows, stealing the horses' hay. You ski in privacy, in a private preserve. When the snow falls, some summer wranglers turn into cross-country guides. No extra charge for lessons or rentals.

Rates are high and commensurate with the ranch's amenities and all-inclusive package. C Lazy U is closed in October and November and in April and May. Access: I–70 to exit 232, then along US 40 to SR 125. You'll see the sign. For more information: C Lazy U Ranch, 3640 Colorado Highway 125, Granby 80446; (970) 887–3344. E-mail: ranch@ clazyu.com, Web site: www.clazyu.com. Don't be surprised if the ranch is sold out in July and August.

Spend a day traveling a little farther west along US 40 to reach *Hot Sulphur Springs Resort,* located between Granby and Kremmling. This tiny resort has reinvented itself after having been practically forgotten for decades. Handsomely restored in 1996, the resort is now outfitted with a half-dozen tiny pools, a massage room, and a solarium. Anyone age sixteen or older can soak in the outdoor pools for $13.50 a day; the price is $11.50 for kids age six through fifteen and free for children age five or younger. Reservations are highly recommended for all services; call for details. For more information: Hot Sulpher Springs Resort, P.O. Box 275, Hot Sulphur Springs 80451; (970) 725–3306 or (800) 510–6235. Fax (970) 725–3206. E-mail: HotSprings@ RkyMtnHi.com. Web site: www.rkymtnhi.com/hotsprings.

South of Granby beckons the *Devil's Thumb Ranch Resort,* P.O. Box 750, Tabernash 80478; (970) 726–5632 or (800) 933–4339, fax (970) 726–9038. E-mail: devthumb@rkymtnhi.com. Web site: www.rkymtnhi. com/devthumb. The 400-acre Shangri-la is idyllic in summer, picturesque in fall, and one of Colorado's best places for horseback riding, trail hiking, and trout fishing. In winter, the ranch reinvents itself as a first-class cross-country center with rentals, instruction, and 105 kilometers of varied, lone trails. Most of the accommodations can be described as rustic, even primitive, without TV and the bathroom down the hall. The scenic beauty—pure Colorado!—makes up for the lack of hotel-style amenities or the feeling of loneliness. The price is right, though, and the Devil's Thumb Ranch Resort guarantees memories. You get here via US 40 past Fraser. About 2 miles after Fraser, turn right on CR 83. The road forks a short distance after this; turn onto the right-hand fork and follow it for 3 miles.

Winter Park

How does a large ski area come to be? Where did it all start? To understand *Winter Park* and its landscape better, some historical background may be in order.

A few hardy Denverites already skied in the region around 1920. Winter Park (then West Portal) consisted of sawmills and railroad shanties; a tunnel construction shack served as a warming house to skiers who sought their thrills in forest glades and down logging roads. They climbed the Winter Park hills under their own steam, all the while dreaming of real trails. The dream became a reality in the mid-1930s when several ski clubs laid out better runs.

Denver's manager of parks and improvements was among the first to see the potential. He appropriated the funds for a first ski tow, a "T-bar of sorts," built with staves from old whiskey barrels. In March 1937 the Denver official told an astonished Colorado audience, "We'll create a winter playground unequaled in the world!" He brought in Otto Schniebs, then one of America's most famous skiers. Schniebs, who spoke of the sport as "a way of life," was enthusiastic about the runs.

Winter Park's official dedication took place on January 28, 1940. A ski band played. Hans Hauser, a handsome ski school director, had been commandeered from Austria. Alf Engen, the jumper, came from Utah to show his stuff. A ticket for the 1/2-mile-long lift cost $1.00 (50 cents for students).

By 1947, Winter Park (which got its name from its designation as a winter park in Denver's park system) had three T-bar lifts and four rope tows. Owned by the city of Denver, the area made good progress during the early fifties; soon there were numerous chairlifts, which multiplied every season. (The area now has twenty lifts.)

The history of this ski mecca was crowned in 1975 when its capacity was almost doubled. To drum up $6 million for lift construction and base facilities seems an even greater feat when you consider the tight money situation of the early seventies.

Twin factors—fairly easy access and adequate accommodations—always helped Winter Park's cause.

To avoid the hassle of renting a car, many families take advantage of *Home James Transportation Services'* frequent shuttle vans that run from Denver International Airport (DIA) directly to lodging properties in Winter Park. Cost is $39 per person age twelve or older for one way in winter. The price is $34 for children two to eleven. Children younger than two ride free if sitting on an adult's lap. Advance reservations are required. Contact Home James Transportation Services, P.O. Box 279, Winter Park 80482; (970) 726–5060 or (800) 359–7536. Fax (970) 726–4730. E-mail: homejames@rkymtnhi.com. Web site: www.homejames-shuttle.com.

Trivia

Winter Park's Mary Jane area offers seventy trails on three mountains for more advanced skiers, including the mountain known as Mary Jane itself, which has been voted the best mogul mountain in North America.

To be sure, Winter Park always attracted customers of every age and ability. The slopes are well groomed. The lifts run without fail. A large ski school teaches beginners in record time; three days of lessons should get you up and down many slopes. The area boasts more than 120 ski runs that satisfy the most fanatic mogul skier as well as the rank novice.

Winter Park vies with Colorado's top resorts, yet it has none of the poshness, the celebrity parade, the hectic atmosphere of other international ski resorts, or the wild nightlife of the Beautiful People. The resort works out well for nonskiers also. Resort managers make it possible for anyone to reach the Winter Park summit (elevation 10,700 feet) in comfortable, heated vehicles called snow cats. For $10 to $25, a nonskiing vacationer can thus mingle with the fast downhill crowd, take pictures of the deep sun-flecked woods, and lunch al fresco. Several ski lodges offer heated swimming pools, and even older people like to spend a few unstrenuous hours on light cross-country skis or guided snowshoe tours.

Other resort activities include moonlight snowmobile dinner tours, nighttime gondola rides, and even rock climbing at the 30-foot *Base Camp 9000 Climbing Wall,* located in Winter Park's West Portal Station ($15 for three climbs, equipment available for rent). Call (970) 726–1616 or (303) 316–1616 for more information about or reservations for Winter Park's nonskiing activities.

Sleigh rides are available in the evenings. The families climb aboard, snuggle under warm blankets, breathe the forest air, and listen to the sleigh bells and the crunch of snow. Along the way, there will be hot chocolate for the kids, hot spiced wine for adults. Call (970) 726–1446 for reservations and information. In the same Colorado valley, at the same time, vacationers enjoy themselves on a lighted hill, slithering down the slopes on snow tubes.

The 67-mile drive from Denver across Berthoud Pass to Winter Park won't take much longer than two hours on I–70 and US 40. The roads are kept sanded. Winter Park Resort opens in early November and closes in late April. Resort hours are 9:00 A.M. to 4:00 P.M. Monday through Friday and 8:30 A.M. to 4:00 P.M. Saturday, Sunday, and holidays. For more information: Winter Park Resort, 150 Alpenglow Way, P.O. Box 36, Winter Park 80482; (970) 726–5514 or Denver direct (303) 892–0961. E-mail: wpinfo@mail.skiwinterpark.com. Web site: www.winterparkresort.com.

Reveille to a winter morning in the Colorado ski country. Outside your windows, the sun slants through the conifers; from the condo cross-country ski tracks take off for the snow-covered forest. You're on the quiet edge of Winter Park. You gratefully set out, skiing through light and shade, breathing deeply. Ah, to be alive! To be in motion!

Later you return to the comfortable condominium for lunch. Some people are unaware that they can rent these vacation apartments for a night or a weekend, solo, coupled, or as a family of six. Kristine Meyer, the manager at the *Beaver Village Condos,* puts it this way: "Your time with us will be special. You can cross-country ski outside your door or catch a free shuttle to Winter Park's downhill runs. Afterward, you can sit in our sauna, enjoy a whirlpool, or swim in the indoor pool. It's all included."

Beaver Village is typical for Colorado's condo pleasures: a well-equipped kitchen, matching dishes, pots and pans, ironed sheets, clean towels, shiny glassware, and cozy, generous furniture in mountains hues. The 120 units contain moss-covered fireplaces, plus free wood. And each *room* has its own thermostat. The management hands honeymooners a gratis bottle of vintage wine. For reservations: P.O. Box 349,

Grand Adventure Balloon Tours

*P*assing through Winter Park in the summer and looking for a fun adventure? Try out a hot air balloon flight. The tour takes you and your companions up, up, and away, soaring up above the treetops with astounding views of the surrounding mountainous terrain. For reservations and information about prices, contact Grand Adventure Balloon Tours, P.O. Box 3423, Winter Park 80482; (970) 887–1340 or (888) 887–1340. Web site: www.vacationsinc.com/general/balloon.html.

Winter Park 80482; (970) 726–8813 or (800) 824–8438. Fax (970) 726–5313. E-mail: bvcinfo@beavercondos.com. Web site: www.beaver-condos.com.

At the west end of town, the somewhat removed *Alpine Vacations* occupies a multiview hillside above the little hamlet of *Fraser,* which was President Eisenhower's favorite. Year-round lodging here exudes charm. Reservations: Box 3123, Winter Park 80482, or call (970) 726–8822 or (800) 551–9943. Fax (970) 726–5949. E-mail: alpinevacations@alpinepeaks.com. Web site: www.alpinevacations.com.

Size doesn't mean impersonality. In the *Hi Country Haus* unit 1510, for instance, the coffee mugs come with greetings:

> *My best to you*
> *Each Day*
> *My best for you*
> *Each Day*

For reservations: Vacations, Inc., Box 3095, Winter Park 80482; (888) 686–3325. Web site: www.reunionspecialists.com.

The little-known *Meadow Ridge Complex* sits astride a promontory. Meadow Ridge enjoys an outdoor swimming pool plus outdoor and indoor hot tubs. The condos are attractive and come with maid service and gratis ski area shuttles. It is very quiet on the promontory. Arrange a rental through Alpine Vacations (see previous entry for contact information.)

Several times each winter the slopes of this giant area are alive with

Winter Park: Rail Trips

*T*he U.S. west and Colorado always appreciate a ski train; for some sixty years, Denverites have supported the rail trip to Winter Park. It starts at Denver's Union Station and ends on the ski area's slopes. Tradition! The first such train ran in 1936. Nowadays, skiers welcome the reliable schedule, departing on weekends at from Denver at 7:15 A.M. and leaving Winter Park to return to Denver at 4:15 P.M. The two-hour adventure covers 56 miles, travels through 29 tunnels, and climbs almost 4,000 feet. For guests who arrive in Winter Park by train, Beaver Village Condos has arranged a complimentary pick-up and drop-off service. For more information: Ski Train, P.O. Box 481234, Denver 80248–1234; (303) 296–4754. E-mail: skitrain@skitrain.com. Web site: www.skitrain.com.

Playground for Cross-Country Skiers

A ten-minute drive north from Winter Park, near Tabernash, you come upon the year-round **Snow Mountain Ranch/YMCA** of the Rockies. Thanks to its 100km of cross-country skiing, the ranch is popular with large groups—especially religious and educational groups. True, you find yourself in a somewhat remote country: no shops or restaurants or movies in the vicinity, no television in the spartan rooms; for dinner you line up for the simple, wholesome meals. Who comes here? Lots of midwestern folk to whom spiritual values

and prayer are important. Recreation makes for a better Colorado vacation. Apart from cross-country skiing, you can try showshoeing, swimming in an indoor pool, or guided hiking in summer. The route to all these goodies is the $150 YMCA membership. Lodging is extra, of course.

More information: Snow Mountain Ranch/YMCA, P.O. Box 169, Winter Park 80482, (970) 887–2152 or (303) 443–4743. E-mail: info@ymcarockies. org. Web site: www.epcenter.org.

multicolored pairs of flags, and through these gates, at intervals, there descend a succession of skiers. In a downhill race they're clocked at 40 miles an hour.

Nothing unusual? Not for the ordinary ski racer. But these people are not ordinary. Many of the competitors have only one leg. Others have only one arm or no hands. The rest fly down the Colorado mountain despite paralyzed joints, missing kneecaps, absent toes, or stiffened backs.

The skiers are all disabled, the result of disease, accidents, or their conditions at birth. Yet these people show that you can conquer almost any barrier. Eyes shining, cheeks glowing, the racers speed through the finish line.

Colorado's Winter Park Ski Resort offers the **National Sports Center for the Disabled (NSCD),** the world's largest teaching program for physically challenged skiers. Some thousand volunteers and fifteen professional instructors participate in it. Each ski season, thousands of lessons are given here to people with cerebral palsy, spina bifida, polio, multiple sclerosis, and paraplegia. Some of the students are blind. All in all, forty-five different disabilities are handled in Winter Park.

Skiing requires perfect coordination and a good balance. To hurtle down a snowy slope, two-legged sighted skiers use all of their God-given limbs—their feet to direct the two skis, their hands and arms to hold the poles, which act as stabilizers.

The loss of an arm throws the body out of kilter. With only one ski pole, it's more difficult to make the turns or to walk up a hill. Yet, where there's a will, there's a way, and practice and determination will make a one-armed skier as good as a two-armed one.

The sudden loss of a leg is more serious, yet even that can be overcome. At first there will be pain, and when the stump has healed, the person will feel off-balance. Then come the weeks of learning the use of crutches. The amputee must strengthen the remaining leg—and how the muscles will ache for a while! There's also the self-consciousness. But only at first.

A positive mental attitude will put the disabled person onto the right track within a few weeks. The individual realizes that one can do many things with an incomplete body. Winter Park simply calls it "rehabilitation through recreation." The students themselves often see it as a lark. "Skiing on one leg is easier than on two," chuckles one participant. "The trouble with *two* skis is that they don't go in the same direction for the beginner!"

The NSCD started in 1970 and has become the largest of its kind in the world. The program began with twenty-three amputees from the Children's Hospital in Denver, and each year new disabilities were added. Most of the students are now adults. One of the highlights has been the introduction of mono skis and a sledlike device used by paraplegics or any individual confined to a wheelchair.

Skiers with one good leg and two usable arms are taught the three-tracking technique, which means skiing with small outriggers. The outriggers consist of a ski tip attached to the bottom of a modified crutch. In full gear, the three-tracker has contact with the snow on the bottom of the full-length ski and balances with both ski tips. In due time, amputee skiers become so proficient that they can enter races.

How is it possible to teach skiing to the sightless? In some countries instructors ring a little bell at every dip of a mountain. Winter Park has used bamboo poles that link instructor and pupil; the key teaching elements, however, are touch and verbal contact. The sightless individual has to begin from the beginning: He or she has to learn all about ski boots (and how to put them on) and then about the skis themselves. The feeling of standing on skis comes next, with the feet parallel to each other, then walking to the sound of the instructor's ski poles tapping.

Next, the pupil sidesteps up a gentle slope, constantly in communication with the instructor. Chairlift loading has to be taught, too. Again, with proper instruction and good communication, it proves to be no problem.

A Member of the National Sports Center for the Disabled (NSCD)

The sightless person eventually moves on to steered turns, parallel turns, and, finally, mogul skiing. Oftentimes a sightless skier will progress down the hill to the sound of the instructor calling, "Turn, turn, turn!" In due time, a close bond develops between student and instructor.

How is this large Colorado program financed? Funds come from general donations, program fees, grants from private corporations and foundations, and special events. A large Denver bank finances a major race. The participants also pay a small daily fee toward lessons and equipment rental.

The learning experience isn't too difficult for athletic individuals who already skied before injury or illness hit them. Thanks to the use of special gear, people can now take up skiing despite physical problems.

One good example is Larry Kunz, who was born with a spina bifida condition that gave him little muscle control from the knees down. Thanks to the Children's Hospital in Denver, Larry was introduced to Hal O'Leary, a Winter Park coach who specializes in teaching the physically impaired. "At first Larry couldn't even walk," O'Leary says. "But in a week, he was able to use his crutch skis and get around in heavy ski boots. Today, he soars down the slopes despite his spina bifida."

Some of the most exciting moments occur on the racecourse. At one competition a Winter Park official handed out trophies to the three fastest skiers. "You three won this slalom," he said. "But actually, all you people were winners. You won over your disability."

More information on the program can be obtained by writing or calling National Sports Center for the Disabled, P.O. Box 1290, Winter Park 80482; (970) 726–1540 or (303) 316–1540. Fax (970) 726–4112. E-mail: info@nscd.org. Web site: www.nscd.org.

Honestly now, did you ever dream of a family ski vacation, yet not dared to go because the resorts all seemed too big, too famous, too overrun, or too expensive?

Hesitate no longer. Small can be beautiful, too. And to the novice skier, less can indeed be more.

A case in point? *Ski Idlewild,* a miniresort 3 miles west of Winter Park, has excellent cross-country trails in Idlewild's conifer forests. The landscape here is kindly, too. And someone will often stop to point out the tracks of deer, ermine, or snowshoe rabbits. The trails reflect the character of this country. You tour along a Winterwoods trail and descend a

Serendipity path. A barn stands amid lovely white meadows flanked by frozen ponds and a little river. The scenery is relaxing. Someone actually suggested that Idlewild change its name to "Idyllwild." Perhaps so; you're off the highway, away from the thunder of trucks and the caravan of cars. You can park yours here and forget it.

There is no charge for using the cross-country trails. Ski Idlewild is 69 miles west of Denver via I–70 and US 40. The phone number is (970) 726–8352 or (800) 705–8352.

The various condos and lodges also offer a memorable family diversion—a nighttime sleigh ride. The sleighs are pulled by sturdy draft horses. You glide through spruce forests, bundled up in warm blankets. The destination, 2 to 3 miles yonder, may be an old homesteader's cabin or a bonfire, where a western steak dinner awaits. The various Winter Park–based sleigh teamsters have been at their trade for many years, including **Dashing Through the Snow** (970–726–5376 or 888–384–6773; www.toski.com/dtts/dashing.html), **Devil's Thumb Ranch Resort** (970–726–8231; www.rkymtnhi.com/devthumb/activities. html), and **Grand Adventures** (800–726–9247; www.grandadventures.com). Rates are reasonable for all.

High up, a ski jumper pushes off, sinks into a crouch, chest tight against his knees. He accelerates in the two steep snow grooves toward the platform. Suddenly, his body uncoils, straightens, dives upward. He is airborne. Seconds tick away. The spectators gasp. Still he soars through the Colorado sky, then a smooth landing. Judges note the distance. The audience roars.

Ski jumping is sensational to watch. Especially in this case. *The competitor was six years old!* And his leap was the result of a unique school for youngsters at Winter Park. For the past several decades, thousands of kids have been trained in human aviation here at the **Nordic Program at the Winter Park Competition Center,** where children begin training at the age of six. The upper limit for competitors is eighteen. Even middle-aged parents have turned up for lessons. And why not? The school is for first-timers. There is a small charge to enroll on a regular basis.

During the season's first get-together, anxious parents ask: Could a child come to harm here? Ski jumping is actually safer than downhill skiing. For one thing, the special hills are well prepared. For another, the youngsters jump in a straight line, and training is worked out with great care. No person, therefore, ever suffered a serious accident at this Colorado school.

Before being taken on, a youngster must know how to ski at least a little. The coach gives a brief test for this purpose. Then he groups his pupils by age. Class I is for sixteen- to eighteen-year-olds; Class II includes ages fourteen and fifteen; Class III, twelve and thirteen; Class IV, nine through eleven; and Class V, six through eight. All are taught separately. Fortunately, Winter Park's Nordic Program is lighthearted enough for an occasional snowball fight, and there are neither roll calls nor other regimentation.

How do you create a young ski jumper? The novices first learn the basic aerodynamic position for the inrun, meaning the short chute spurt before takeoff. They're taught the precise instant for leaping. They're shown how to stop safely and gracefully. When the youngsters are ready to make actual jumps, they always start with the smallest hills.

They only fly for a few feet at first, but they nonetheless get an idea of what it's like. A few novices may have their hearts in their throats. After a single leap, though, the kids like the flight so much that they come back for more. Most of the little jumpers feel like conquerors. "I'm a pilot!" they cry. "I'm a bird!" "Look at me! I'm a kite!"

A few jumps later they graduate to bigger hills, where they can zoom 30, 40, or more feet. In all, Winter Park has five jumping installations. The largest allows distances of 200 feet; here speeds of 55 miles per hour are normal. And from time to time, the winners battle it out at other Colorado ski areas as well. To be sent to Steamboat Springs or Summit County is a great honor, of course.

The jumping meets pack the greatest excitement, both for the young athletes and for the spectators. The eager, freckled faces, the colorful suits, the splashes of reds, greens, and blues of parkas and ski pants and caps are a delightful sight. Before each leap tension fills the thin, sweet mountain air. Up on top the eyes squint under big goggles. Competitors get last-minute advice from coaches. Six-year-olds wonder: Will they jump far enough? Will they look good enough in the air? Will they beat the competition?

These junior affairs are staged much like adult championships: The entrants wear bibs with starting numbers. The reporters are there; the ski patrol stands by in case of the rare sprain; the judges sit sternly in a tower, ready to compute results. The jumpers are judged not only by what distances they can reach but also by their style. They lose points, for instance, by standing straight after takeoff. (The jumper must be forward while in flight.) They lose points if their skis flutter in all directions. (The skis must be together.) They cannot win if their arms go like windmills. And they're evaluated for their landing—which should be steady—and for the ease of coming to a halt (no flailing hands).

This is the real thing, and even the tiniest of the fifty to seventy-five youngsters try to do their best. Afterward the kids get ribbons, and the year's final championship means a trophy for at least one jumper.

Some of the jumpers keep training until the sun goes down behind the darkened fir trees. The youngsters struggle upward to fling themselves into the sky, soaring and soaring. At a time when we're often told that the American youth is going soft, Winter Park must command attention. Soft? The fresh, scrubbed, entrancing faces may look it. But after one or two winters, these leaping children become as hard as the steel edges under their skis. Surely, some of them will do us proud in a future Olympics!

For more information contact Competition Center, Winter Park Recreational Association, P.O. Box 36, Winter Park 80482; (970) 726–1588. Fax (970) 726–1690. E-mail: bob_dart@mail.skiwinterpark.com. Web site: www.skiwinterpark.com/competition/nordic.html.

Yampa Valley and Routt National Forest

Trivia
Steamboat Springs probably received its name in the early 1800s from French trappers, who mistakenly thought that they heard the chugging steam engine of a steamboat. In fact, they were hearing a natural mineral spring.

I n 1875, James Crawford, the first white settler of **Steamboat Springs,** arrived here from Missouri with two wagons, his family, his horses, and a few head of cattle. He was attracted to the area by a newspaper article. The author of the piece described his view from the top of the Park Mountain Range as "a wilderness of mountain peaks and beautiful valleys, dark forests and silvery streams—a deserted land except for immense herds of elk and deer and buffalo which had not yet learned by experience to shun the presence of man."

The Yampa Valley's idyllic setting and mild climate made the eventual "presence of man" inevitable. Even before Crawford built his log cabin along the west bank of Soda Creek, the Yampa Valley had sheltered Ute Indians and, later, French and English fur trappers. (Legend has it that

French fur trappers named the town Steamboat Springs because of the peculiar chugging sound from the hot springs near the river.)

Cattle ranchers had found Steamboat's emerald-green slopes ideal for fattening their herds en route to market. Hot and cold running water in the forms of three creeks, numerous hot springs, and the flow of the Yampa River lured more and more settlers to the valley.

Recreational skiing first came here in the early 1900s, when Norwegian Carl Howelson introduced the sports of ski jumping and ski racing to the community.

Before the turn of the century, they skied in "Ski Town U.S.A." facing Main Street on long boards, with a long staff, the women in long skirts. They jumped here from a giant hill before many other people thought of such things.

For years, they've taught Steamboat youngsters to ski, gratis, from kindergarten up, all through high school, and through the small local college. Men with first names like Alf, Ansten, Lars, and Ragnar showed off their telemark turns way back when, and Steamboat Springs skiers—immigrants as well as natives—showed the world what they were made of. Many Olympians cut their ski teeth here.

A Tour of Steamboat Springs

*T*he giant **Steamboat Ski Area** caters to skiers of all abilities and to four-season travelers. Massive mountains with almost countless lifts, a prestigious ski school, and a top-notch ski patrol all add to this ski area's quality. All kinds of accommodations await in or on the edge of this handsome community, which sticks to its western image: You see plenty of jeans, Stetsons, cowboy boots, and saddles.

Steamboat, also known as "Ski Town U.S.A.," is closer to Denver (153 miles) than Aspen (205 miles). From Denver, the three-hour drive follows I-70 west to the Silverthorne exit

(exit 205). Head north on SR 9 to Kremmling, and then west on US 40, which takes you over Rabbit Ears Pass and into Steamboat. Arrival by air is also possible; daily direct flights land at Yampa Valley International Airport, near Hayden, which is 22 miles from the ski area. The skiing starts in November and runs through April; open 8:30 A.M. to 4:00 P.M. daily. For more information: Steamboat Central Reservations, P.O. Box 774728, Steamboat Springs 80477-4728; (970) 879-6111 or (800) 922-2722. Fax (970) 879-0740. E-mail: info@steamboat-ski.com. Web site: www.steamboat.com.

Trivia

Ten national ski-jumping records have been set on Howelsen Hill.

Steamboat has an excellent ski school, of course, which operates 2 miles away on Mt. Werner and Storm Peak. A Ski Marching Band unfurls every February with an "oompah-oompah" during the **Steamboat Springs Winter Carnival,** one of the country's oldest ski festivals. It features skijoring, ski obstacle races, ski jumping, skiing with torches, ski parades, and ski balls. Call (970) 879–0695 for details.

At last, in the 1960s, the town was discovered by tourism, first by a giant Texas conglomerate, then by some private investors. In 1981, the real boom began.

Trivia

More Olympians—fifty-two in all—have emerged from Steamboat Springs than from any other town in the United States. The reason? World-class skiing, including the area's famed trademark, its Champagne Powder.

Millions of dollars have since been invested in new ski lifts, new trails (and reshaping old ones), and other amenities. A Swiss gondola's eight-passenger car, the Silver Bullet, carries loads of skiers an hour up Thunderhead Mountain. The downhill skier can choose from 110 different trails, including the lengthy **Why Not Trail,** which meanders toward the valley from 9,080-foot Thunderhead Mountain. You ski along gentle logging roads and hiking trails that cut through sound-muffling conifer forests. The same trails make dandy walking paths in summer.

While downhill skiing is taught on a big scale here, cross-country skiing isn't neglected. The many programs even include a Citizens Cross-Country Race Camp for would-be competitors, many of them in their fifties and sixties.

The **Scandinavian Lodge** has expensive rates, which seem commensurate with its facilities and prestige. For more information: 2883 Burgess

An Egg-citing Event

*E*very year, the ski season in Steamboat winds up its season with a fun frenzy on the slopes as participants search for three "magical eggs," each of which contains a season pass for the following year—one for an adult, one for a teen, and one for a child. The resort hands out helpful clues at 8:00 A.M., and then they're off to the races! Join in the festivities of the Annual Easter Egg Hunt. Contact the Steamboat Ski Area for more information at (800) 922–2722 or visit the Web site: www.steamboat.com.

Creek Road, Steamboat Springs 80477; (970) 879–0517 or (800) 233–8102. E-mail: info@steamboat-springs.com. Web site: www. steamboat-springs.com/scandinavian.html.

Steamboat does have springs. A walking tour downtown will take you past ten hot springs, easily identified by their pungent smell.

Trivia
Steamboat boasts more than 100 natural hot springs.

For a rustic hot springs experience, check out *Strawberry Park Natural Hot Springs,* located about 7 miles outside of downtown Steamboat Springs. With three main pools varying in temperature and gorgeous masonry construction—including five waterfalls—this special place warrants a visit. Recent additions include a stone steam house, a warm changing area, and picnic areas. Strawberry Park has a small, warm pool for Watsu (water massage) and offers conventional massage services as well (both cost extra).

Overnight reservations for cabins, a renovated train caboose, covered wagons, and tenting sites are available but should be made in advance. Strawberry Park Natural Hot Springs is open from 10:00 A.M. to 10:30 P.M. in summer and winter and 10:00 A.M. to 11:00 P.M. during the off-season. Daytime admission to the pools is $5.00 for adults and teenagers, $3.00 for children three to twelve, children younger than three free. Nightime and weekend admission is $10.00 for adults, $5.00

Downhill All the Way

*N*o, I'm not talking about skiing, but about the annual **Steamboat Springs Marathon,** which takes place in early June. Starting out at an elevation of 8,128 feet and finishing at 6,728 feet, the marathon really is mostly downhill, but don't let that fool you. Though Runner's World cited this course as one of the "10 Most Scenic Marathons of the Year" (February 1996) and one of the "Top Ten Destination Marathons in North America" (March 1999), it's still quite a challenge. I found this out when I ran my first marathon here in 1998.

After finishing, I soaked my aching body at nearby Strawberry Park Natural Hot Springs—a destination of choice for many marathoners, who were easily discerned by their stiff-legged gaits as they staggered and groaned their way down the stairs into the pools.

Sign up early for the marathon, which is limited to 500 runners. For more information call (970) 879–0880 or visit the Web site www.runningseries.com/SteamboatMarathon/ssmarathon.htm.

for teenagers thirteen to seventeen, $3.00 for children three to twelve, children younger than three free. For more information: 44200 County Road #36, Steamboat Springs 80487; (970) 879–0342. Fax (970) 879–6834. E-mail: hot@springsips.com. Web site: www.strawberryhotsprings.com.

Steamboat Springs is also home to one of the country's best automobile driving schools. But don't expect to learn how to parallel park here. The **Bridgestone Winter Driving School** is patterned after similar facilities at European ski resorts. In operation since 1983, the school is open from December 15 through March 10. The track is a snow- and ice-covered course with enough turns, loops, and straights to satisfy anyone who envisions being a race-car driver.

But this is not play. You often share your class with law enforcement officers and ambulance personnel. Although these people are professional drivers, they recognize the need for practice, and many return every year. But the novice is welcome here, too. A recent winter student was a homemaker from Atlanta, Georgia, who had never seen snow before.

For safety, the track is surrounded by high walls of soft snow. In case of a spinout—and there will be spinouts!—the snow guard walls catch the car and hold it safely. No injury to driver or machine.

All vehicles are new and supplied by the school in conjunction with Jeep/Eagle, Bridgestone, and the Weather Channel. Students are put into threatening positions and must learn how to stop on glare ice on a downhill slope and what to do when the car spins out of control. (No, you don't apply the brake for this one, but the gas—and hard! It works.) After the one-day class, you will feel confident in your ability to avoid collisions due to ice- and snow-covered roads. Costs range from $145 to $1,475. For more information, contact The Bridgestone Winter Driving School at (800) 949–7543. E-mail: mail@winterdrive.com; Web site: www.winterdrive.com. The mailing address is 1850 Ski Time Square Drive, P.O. Box 774167, Steamboat Springs 80477. Classes are available in half-day, full-day, and two-day sessions. Count on personalized small groups, with video presentations. Instructors remain in constant contact with pupils by two-way radios. These well-qualified teachers monitor every movement from their separate cars, so the students are on their own. Cars spin and skid down a $1\frac{1}{2}$-mile ice circuit. In fact, instructors claim that the more you spin, the more you learn!

Though Steamboat Springs has grown over the years (permanent year-round population is now nearly 9,000), it has retained its scenic beauty

Steamboat Water Sports

*T*he Steamboat area is renowned for its variety of water sports options. It offers river floats, churning whitewater rafting, canoeing, sailing, and more.

Anglers will love **Steamboat Lake State Park,** which allows fly, lure, and bait fishing for its cutthroat and rainbow trout year-round with a Colorado fishing license. Take US 40 west through Steamboat Springs for 2 miles, and then turn north on County Road 129 and go another 26 miles. Cost is $4.00 for a vehicle day pass. For information: Steamboat Lake State Park, P.O. Box 750, Clark 80428; (970) 879–3922. E-mail: steamboat.lake@ state.co.us. Web site: www.parks.state. co.us/steamboat.

Fishing licenses may be purchased from most sporting goods and convenience stores in Colorado.

A one-day license costs $5.25 and a five-day license costs $18.25 for both residents and non-residents. An annual fishing license costs $20.25 for residents or $40.25 for non-residents.

Whitewater rafting is great on the nearby Yampa and Elk Rivers during the summer. There are a number of guiding services available. In Steamboat Springs contact the **Steamboat Rafting Company,** P.O. Box 882987, Steamboat Springs 80488-2987; (970) 879–6699 or (888) 888–7238. E-mail: scott@steamboat-rafting.com. Web site: www.steamboat-rafting.com. Kayakers, too, can join in the fray. Contact **Mountain Sports Kayak School,** 1450 South Lincoln, P.O. Box 881986, Steamboat Springs 80488-1986; (970) 879–8794.

and western charm. Cattle ranching is still important, too. Lots of saddles and boots and Stetsons are for sale in downtown Steamboat.

Typical for this western community is the *Annual Cowboy Downhill:* Some one hundred genuine cowboys compete in a "ski rodeo" on the famous ski slopes. This involves a slalom on skis, the lassoing of pretty hostesses, and saddling a horse.

Those who come to visit or stay are drawn to many of the same qualities that caused James Crawford to settle in the valley.

Steamboat Springs is 170 miles west of Denver via US 40. For information on year-round Steamboat Springs, write or call Steamboat Springs Chamber Resort Association, P.O. Box 774408, Steamboat Springs 80488; (970) 879–0880. E-mail: info@steamboat-chamber.com. Web site: www.steamboat-chamber.com.

The *Vista Verde Guest & Ski Touring Ranch* sits at the end of a rugged road, 30 miles north of Steamboat Springs. It's one of the best such vacation places in the state. The staff is warm, helpful, eager to please, and experienced. Apart from horseback riding, this dude ranch offers supervised hiking, cycling, fly fishing, white-water rafting, and even rock-climbing instruction. Almost every Thursday balloon rides zoom the guests heavenward. In winter, you can cross-country ski here.

The summer staff consists of eighteen people who take care of the horses, the housekeeping, the office, and the kitchen, plus are hiking guides. Every spring, the application letters cascade onto owner John Munn's desk. Munn gets from 200 to 300 applications for the eighteen summer jobs.

The hiring procedure is by telephone—long interviews and reference checks. What does Munn look for? "The work ethic," he says. "The love of the outdoors. Real caring for the guests." Much of the staff is versatile and interchangeable; the Vista Verde's bookkeeper, for instance, helps clean the rooms. The staff brings strong background experience to their jobs, guarenteeing that you'll be in the care of experts.

The typical wrangler knows how to shoe horses, how to treat the sick ones, and how to please the others. He or she knows a dozen horse tricks. One Oklahoman spends so much time around the hoofed crea-tures—his real love—that he has been stepped on, backed into, and severely kicked by horses. A few years ago, three of his ribs were broken by one of his animals. The rancher spent a week in the hospital, cursing and cussing. Yet he wouldn't give it all up for anything. His nostrils love the sweet smell of hay and manure, and his ears like to pick up the com-forting, caressing sound of horses feeding.

John Munn, the owner, bought the 600-acre for-mer homestead with the environment in mind: He immediately buried the power lines and other utilities underground to enhance the beauty of the high-altitude landscape. Guests sleep in a dozen authentic log cabins. John's wife personally decorated these spacious units.

Trivia
One of North America's largest elk herds ranges near Steamboat Springs.

Shortly after dawn one morning, Vista Verde's chief wrangler and an assistant headed up the hill past the golden aspen trees to the pasture where the horses grazed. "Time for the corral!" the wrangler told them, as though the creatures could understand. Later, the horses saddled, the red-shirted dude-ranch staff helped the guests mount for a morning ride. To the staff's surprise, this group of ten new arrivals had lots of riding experience. The wrangler trotted ahead, cantering along the winding trail. The western sky was perfectly blue, and a smell of sage

Sans Skis—Summer in Steamboat

*S*ummers guarantee an adrenaline rush. The breaking in of wild horses, the barrel-racing on horseback, the sound of galloping hooves through forest clearings, are all exciting. Climbers have scaled the rock faces of Rabbit Ears Pass. And of course, you can reach the Mount Werner summits in style by gondola and then test your leg muscles against the long downhill walks—or runs—through knee-high meadows or on logging roads.

was in the air. The colored mountains ascended gently toward more forests. "Lucky you," one of the guests said to the head wrangler. "Spending your summers up here!"

For more information contact Vista Verde Guest & Ski Touring Ranch, P.O. Box 465, Steamboat Springs 80477; (970) 879–3858 or (800) 526–7433. E-mail: info@vistaverde.com. Web site: www.vistaverde.com.

Steamboat Springs is 170 miles west of Denver; if you keep driving west on US 40 past Craig and Maybell, you will eventually reach the out-of-the-way **Dinosaur National Monument.** It straddles the Utah border. You get to it via the small town of Blue Mountain, or via Dinosaur, another small town. On US 40 the signs will proclaim the "Welcome Center at Dinosaur." You soon see the visitors center; as you keep driving north, you'll understand why some Colorado folk call the area a Jurassic Park. This is dinosaur fossil bone country. Of course, not everyone is overwhelmed by skeletons of sauropods or stegosauruses or other dinosaurs. But it's hard to ignore a magnificent natural landscape of giant sandstone cliffs, gray-green sage bushes, juniper, and pinon pine. Moreover, this land is laced with hiking trails. And the spectacular Yampa River is never far away. The visitors center in Colorado for Dinosaur National Monument is open daily year-round (hours vary according to season) and requires no entry fee (but no fossils can be seen here). Exhibits and a ten-minute orientation are available for viewing. Ranger talks and walks take place in summer; call for details. For more information contact Dinosaur National Monument, 4545 East Highway 40, Dinosaur 81610-9724; (435) 789–2115. Fax (970) 374–3003. E-mail: DINO_Superintendent@nps.gov. Web site: www.nps.gov/dino. An entry fee ($10 per vehicle) is required only in Utah at the Dinosaur Quarry area.

NORTHWESTERN MOUNTAINS

**PLACES TO STAY
IN THE NORTHWESTERN
MOUNTAINS**

ESTES PARK
Holiday Inn (good loca-
tion; inexpensive to expensive); 101 South Saint Vrain
Avenue; (970) 586-2332 or
(800) 803-7837

Ponderosa Lodge (open all
year; overlooks a river;
moderate to expensive);
1820 Fall River Road;
(970) 586-4233 or
(800) 628-0512

The Stanley Hotel (famous,
historic, prestigious;
deluxe); 333 Wonderview;
(970) 586-3371 or
(800) 976-1377

YMCA of the Rockies
(housekeeping cabins;
moderate); Estes Park
Center; (970) 586-3341 or
(303) 448-1616

GRANBY
C Lazy U Ranch (the plushest ranch in Colorado, if
not the entire West;
deluxe); from Granby, 3
miles west on US 40, then 4
miles northwest on CO
125; (970) 887-3340

Devil's Thumb Ranch (for
four-season vacationers
who enjoy "roughing it";
inexpensive); P.O. Box 750,
Tabernash 80478; (800)
933-4339

GRAND LAKE
Driftwood Lodge (great
lake views; inexpensive to
expensive); 12255 US 34;
(970) 627-3654

Western Riviera Motel and
Cabins (close to lake and
town; moderate);
419 Garfield Avenue;
(970) 627-3580

STEAMBOAT SPRINGS
Alpiner Lodge (inexpen-
sive to expensive);
424 Lincoln Avenue;
(970) 879-1430 or
(800) 538-7519

Best Western Inn (first-
class motel lodging; inexpensive to deluxe);
2304 Apres Ski Way;
(970) 879-1730 or
(800) 538-7519

Sky Valley Lodge (moder-
ate); 31490 US Highway 40,
80477; (970) 879-7749 or
(800) 499-4759

Vista Verde Guest and Ski
Touring Ranch (remote
and hard to reach, but a
special treat once you get
there; deluxe); P.O. Box
465, (800) 526-7433

WINTER PARK
Alpine Vacations (scenic
location; seasonal); Box
3123, 80482 (800)
551-9943

Beaver Village Condomini-
ums (the most professional
condominium complex;
moderate to deluxe); P.O.
Box 349, 80482; (970)
726-8813 or (800)
824-8438

Hi Country Haus Resort
Condominiums (seasonal);
P.O. Box 3095, 80482, (888)
686-3325

Meadow Ridge Complex
Condominiums (overlooks
the entire valley; seasonal);
Box 3123, 80482; (800)
551-9943

The Vintage Hotel (space is
at a premium; seasonal);
100 Winter Park Road;
(303) 726-8801 or (800)
472-7017

**PLACES TO EAT
IN THE NORTHWESTERN
MOUNTAINS**

ESTES PARK
Black Canyon Inn (conti-
nental; expensive to
deluxe); 800 MacGregor
Avenue; (970) 586-9344

Estes Park Brewery (brew-
pub; moderate); 470
Prospect Village Drive;
(970) 586-5421

La Casa El Centro (Mexi-
can, Cajun, steak, and
seafood; moderate); 222
East Elkhorn Avenue; (970)
586-2807

Mama Rose's (Italian;
moderate to expensive);
338 East Elkhorn Avenue;
(970) 586-3330

Nicky's (Greek, Italian; near park entrance; inexpensive); 1350 Highway 34 West; (970) 586–5376

GRANBY
Longbranch Restaurant (German-American; eclectic menu; inexpensive to moderate); 185 East Agate; (970) 887–2209

GRAND LAKE
Grand Pizza (inexpensive); 717 Grand Avenue; (970) 627–8390

Java Spirits Café; 928 Grand Avenue; (970) 627–0304

STEAMBOAT SPRINGS
Antares (continental; expensive to deluxe); 57¹/₂ Eighth Street; (970) 879–9939

L'Apogée (French; expensive to deluxe); 911 Lincoln Avenue; (970) 879–1919

La Montaña (Mexican, Southwestern; moderate to expensive); 2500 Village Drive; (970) 879–5800

Other Attractions Worth Seeing in the Northwestern Mountains

ESTES PARK

Estes Park Area Historical Museum, *(970) 586–6256*
Web site: www.estesnet.com/Museum

Enos Mills Cabin Museum Center, *(970) 586–4706*

Big Thompson Canyon, *(970) 498–2770*
Web site: www.fs.fed.us/r2/arnf

Estes Park Ride-a-Cart, *(970) 586–6495*

Tiny Town Miniature Golf, *(970) 586–6333*

GRANBY

Arapaho National Forest, *(970) 887–4100*
Web site: www.fs.fed.us/r2/arnf

Silver Creek Ski Area, *(800) 757–7669*
Web site: www.discoversilvercreek.com

STEAMBOAT SPRINGS

Routt National Forest, *(970) 879–1870*

Tread of Pioneers Museum, *(970) 879–2214*

Howelson Ice Arena *(ice skating), (970) 879–0341*

Haymaker Golf Course, *(970) 870–1846*
Web site: www.haymakergolf.com

WINTER PARK

A Maze'n Winter Park *(two-level giant labyrinth), (888) 909–6293*

Children's Center *(ski center for children), (970) 726–1551 or (303) 316–1551*
Web site: www.skiwinterpark.com

Mazzola's Italian Restaurant (large portions; well-known; authentic Italian; moderate); 917 Lincoln Avenue; (970) 879–2405

Ore House at Pine Grove (steak, seafood, game; expensive to deluxe); 1465 Pine Grove Road; (970) 879–1190

WINTER PARK
Derailer Bar and Grill (easy access from slopes; moderate); 677 Winter Park Drive; (970) 726–5514

Gasthaus Eichler Restaurant (German, American; expensive to deluxe); 78786 US Highway 40; (970) 726–5133

Rome on the Range Restaurant & Saloon (Colorado cuisine; moderate to expensive); 78491 US Highway 40; (970) 726–1111

Northwestern Mountains
General Information Resources

ESTES PARK

Estes Park Chamber Resort Association,
500 Big Thompson Avenue, P.O. Box 3050, 80517;
(970) 586–4431 or (800) 443–7837, fax (970) 586–0144
Web site: www.estesparkresort.com

GRANBY

Greater Granby Area Chamber of Commerce,
P.O. Box 35, 80446-0035; (970) 887–2311 or (800) 325–1661,
fax (970) 887–3895
E-mail: GRCOC@rkymtnhi.com
Web site: www.rkymtnhi.com/granbycoc

GRAND LAKE

Grand Lake Area Chamber of Commerce,
P.O. Box 57, 80447-0057; (970) 627–3402, (800) 531–1019, fax (970) 627–8007
E-mail: glinfo@grandlakechamber.com
Web site: www.grandlakechamber.com

STEAMBOAT SPRINGS

Steamboat Springs Chamber Resort Association,
P.O. Box 774408, 80488; (970) 879–0880
E-mail: info@steamboat-chamber.com
Web site: www.steamboat-chamber.com

WINTER PARK

Winter Park/Fraser Valley Chamber of Commerce,
P.O. Box 3236, 80482;
(800) 903–7275 or (303) 422–0666
E-mail: chamber@winterpark-info.com
Web site: www.winterpark-info.com

Western Mountains

Beyond the Front Range

"The forests are shouting with color," John Steinbeck once wrote. It's the sudden September frost that produces the spectacle that exalts Coloradans and brings them out of their homes and offices autumn after autumn. Look into the local newspapers; follow the color photographers, the Sunday painters, the young couples. Exodus to the Rockies! See the aspen trees! The leaves suddenly turn on like so many bright lights. They dazzle. They glow among the deep green of the firs. There are entire aspen forests in these mountains.

The largest groves generally are found between elevations of 8,000 and 10,000 feet. Colors start at the higher elevations and spread their way down as the season progresses. A bright golden yellow predominates, with varying shades of brilliant reds, browns, and oranges interspersed with the green of the slower-changing leaves and the surrounding conifers.

There is a lyrical something about these "quaking" trees when you're alone among them; the golden leaves tremble in the slight breeze, make a gentle sound of applause, talk to themselves, or send messages to the wild raspberry bushes. You'll see the gold and copper all over the state from the end of September through early October. In Aspen itself, in Winter Park, along the Rampart Range Road from Colorado Springs to Sedalia, beside the Peak-to-Peak Highway between Nederland and Allenspark, west of Boulder. "Aren't the aspen beautiful?" people ask, setting out to see them before winter blows down from the Rockies. Of course, it depends on how much time you have. Six hours? A day? Two? Then consider a good circle tour: Denver, Idaho Springs, Silver Plume, Breckenridge, Fairplay, Denver. No toll roads. Easy motoring.

Begin with US 6, all the more spectacular because it's been carved out of deep canyons, where the upper rocks are highlighted by the sun. It takes you up to the little mountain community of Idaho Springs (altitude

Western Mountains

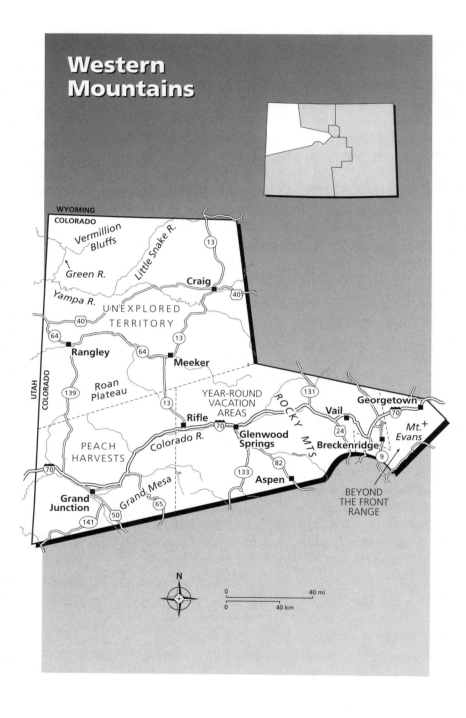

WYOMING
COLORADO

Vermillion Bluffs

Little Snake R.

Green R.

Yampa R.

13

Craig

40

UNEXPLORED TERRITORY

40

64

64

13

Rangley

Meeker

UTAH
COLORADO

139

Roan Plateau

13

YEAR-ROUND VACATION AREAS

131

Rifle

70

ROCKY MTS

Vail

Georgetown

70

PEACH HARVESTS

Colorado R.

Glenwood Springs

24

Breckenridge

Mt. Evans

9

70

82

133

Aspen

BEYOND THE FRONT RANGE

Grand Junction

Grand Mesa

65

50

141

N

0   40 mi
0   40 km

7,540 feet), on I–70, with the peaks rising on both sides. The aspen trees shine like so many lamps among the fir and spruce, and after you're through Georgetown (which is well worth a visit), you seem to be in the Alps.

The mountains go up steeply now, and the valley is narrow. For a breathtaking experience, skip the Eisenhower Memorial Tunnel—weather permitting, of course—and break off again onto SR 6, climbing up to *Loveland Pass* and the Continental Divide (11,990 feet). The views are unbeatable from up here, so take some time to get out of your car and take in the sights. Afterward, cruise down toward the Dillon Reservoir. The sun skips across these lake waters with their small marina sailboats, fishing boats, and canoes. In Frisco swing left onto SR 9, which circles this handsome reservoir. You encounter grasslands now, in shades of gold, brown, and green, which lead to the pivot of the tour—Breckenridge!

This little mining community is once more on the verge of a bonanza. In 1859, it was gold. Now it's real estate and second homes for airline people or retired corporation presidents, and skiers. Yet, you couldn't tell this boom from the looks and feeling here. Breckenridge remains congenial, unpretentious, informal, western. The children are running across the silent brown pine needles; some teenagers fish for trout in the transparent Blue River.

It's peaceful again as you drive through thick forests past beaver ponds to little-known, ever-so-gentle *Hoosier Pass.* Golden brown-yellow meadows and faded green lichened rocks provide a feast for your eyes, and there's hardly a house in sight. Impressive 14,000-foot peaks surround you—Quandary Peak, Mt. Lincoln, Mt. Sherman—as you head into Placer Valley, where the aspen trees brighten the pine woods. With a population of 500, Fairplay is the "big" town now, but you're through quickly, heading north on US 285. Suddenly, clouds darken this bright-blue sky; a quick autumn rain. The

AUTHOR'S FAVORITE ATTRACTIONS IN THE WESTERN MOUNTAINS

Glenwood Canyon,
(888) 4-GLENWOOD,
www.glenscape.com/
glncyn.htm

Mt. Evans, *(303) 567–3000,*
www.mtevans.com

Gore Range/Pass,
(970) 638–4516,
www.fs.fed.us/outernet/mrnf/
ya/yawel.htm

Town of Vail Library,
(970) 479–2184,
www.vaillibrary.com

Clark Family Orchards,
(970) 464–5385, www.
palisadecoc.com/fruit.html

Rifle Falls State Park,
(970) 625–1607, www.
parks.state.co.us/rifle_falls/
index.asp

Georgetown,
(303) 569–2840, www.
historicgeorgetown.org

Tumbling River Ranch,
(800) 654–8770,
www.tumblingriver.com

Lake Dillon Recreational
Area, (800) 530–3099,
www.usnet1.sitehosting.net/
lake_dillon/lakedill.html

Museum of Western
Colorado's Living History
Farm, (970) 434–9814,
www.mwc.mus.co.us/
crossorchards

Colorado Dangers

*C*olorado is renowned for its afternoon thunderstorms, which proliferate during the early summer months but are possible year-round. For this reason, outdoor activities—particularly those that involve a long time commitment away from safe shelter—should be undertaken only with careful planning and attention to time. If you do happen to find yourself caught in a thunderstorm, take refuge in a car (with the windows up) or a substantial building—not a shallow cave or rock outcropping. If no safe shelter is available, seek a low-lying area or trench with shrubs or trees of similar stature. Avoid lone trees, open spaces, higher ground, water, and contact with two different objects (such as rock and ground). Also maintain a 15-foot distance from others. Crouch low to the ground with both of your feet together and cover your ears. For more safety tips, visit the National Lightning Safety Institute's Web site at www. lightningsafety.com.

Flash flooding can pose a real danger in narrow canyons, even on days that begin with clear skies and sunny weather. Be sure to check weather reports for thunderstorm predictions and always have a backup plan. Disastrous flash flooding is a real danger.

As you probably know, drinking water from lakes, rivers, and streams is not exactly the same wilderness treat it once was. Unless you want to find out just how nasty a bout of giardiasis can be—think diarrhea, violent stomach cramps, and hospital visits—avoid drinking water from lakes, streams, or rivers unless you purify it first. Try to bring adequate drinking water (minimum of two liters per person per day), as well as effective water purification paraphernalia, which can be purchased from area sporting-goods stores. You can also purify water by boiling it for at least twenty minutes to kill all disease-causing organisms.

horses and cows and sheep stand in these darkening fields patiently while the water pours down. Half an hour later, along the South Platte River, the sun bursts through the trees again. At Grant, US 285 narrows and curves along the river past nice campsites that should be full but aren't. (There are few tourists after Labor Day.) All the way to Denver, the names spell nature, forest, Colorado: Pine Junction, Deer Creek, Conifer, Indian Hills, Aspen Park.

A few last golden aspen trees are followed by the russets and reds of maples and oaks. Then Morrison, where the orchards are thick with purple apples. At the lower altitude, and out of the mountains, the air warms you once more. Pleasant autumn day. After some 175 miles the Colorado circle tour ends where it began. But what a six-hour world between!

From US 6, west of Denver, follow I–70 to US 6 to Frisco, then SR 9

WESTERN MOUNTAINS

through Breckenridge to Fairplay, from where you return to Denver via US 285.

From Denver, it's a nearby trip to **Idaho Springs.**

Stroll along Idaho Springs's short main street. Step into a leather shop that features beaver hats and into a little rock store, which also sells gems and beads.

Late-hour drivers should keep in mind that the local motels, while not fancy, are among the lowest-priced in Colorado. If you reach the area around dinner time, Idaho Springs's **BeauJo's Pizza** is well-known in Colorado for its varieties and its "pizza by the pound." You can build your own pizza here as well. 1517 Miner; (303) 567–4376. Web site: www.beaujos.com. Open Sunday through Thursday from 11:00 A.M. to 9:00 P.M. and Friday and Saturday from 11:00 A.M. to 10:00 P.M.

Another dinner (or breakfast!) option is the historic, western-style **Buffalo Restaurant and Bar,** which serves up wholesome Colorado-style fare. Try any of the buffalo entrees. Salads are also fresh and tasty. 1617 Miner; (303) 567–2729. Fax: (303) 567–0273. E-mail: edm@denverbuffalo.com. Web site: www.buffalorestaurant. com. Open Monday through Friday from 8:00 A.M. to 10:00 P.M. and Saturday and Sunday from 7:00 A.M. to 10:00 P.M.

Strike Gold! At the **Phoenix Gold Mine,** located at the west end of Idaho Springs, you and your children can try your hand at what brought thousands of men to Colorado back in the 1800s . . . gold panning! The only working gold mine in Colorado that is open to the public, here you can do it all. Take a tour guided by the actual miners. Better yet, dig your own samples—you even get to keep what you score! Gold panning costs $5.00 per person, which is included in the price if you take a tour. Kids age three or younger are admitted free of charge; kids age four through eleven are charged $5.00; seniors age fifty-six or older pay $8.00; and everybody else pays $9.00.

Author's Favorite Events in the Western Mountains

Wintersköl Carnival, Aspen; mid-January; (970) 925–1940; www.aspenchamber.org/htdocs/winterskol.asp

Breckenridge Music Festival, June through August; (970) 547–3100; www.sni.net/bmi-nro

Aspen Music Festival, June through August; (970) 925–9042; www.aspenmusicfestival.com

Gold Rush Days Festival, Idaho Springs; mid-June; (303) 567–4421; www.idahospringsco.com/Index.htm

Strawberry Days, Glenwood Springs; mid-June; (888) 4–GLENWOOD; www.glenwoodchamber.com

Annual XTERRA Off-Road Triathlon, Keystone; mid-July; (800) 222–0188; www.xterra.net/keystone.htm

Peach Festival, Palisade; mid-August; (970) 464–7458; www.palisadecoc.com/calendar.html

Oktoberfest Vail, mid-September; (970) 476–1000; web.vail.net/events

Annual Fall Arts Festival, Glenwood Springs; last week in September; (888) 4–GLENWOOD; www.glenwoodchamber.com

Little Known Facts About Idaho Springs

- Some of Colorado's earliest gold strikes took place here in 1859.

- The Ute Indians were the first to discover and use its famous hot springs.

- Idaho Springs is home to the world's longest mining tunnel. The 5-mile-long tunnel once ran all the way to Central City, another gold-rush town. Unfortunately, only a portion of the tunnel remains, and it is not open to the public.

- The highway that runs to the summit of Mt. Evans from Idaho Springs is the highest paved driving road in North America.

The tours are walking tours. Open from 10:00 A.M. to 6:00 P.M. daily, weather permitting in winter.

Added bonuses: There is a picnic area for those who work up their appetites panning all that gold, and bring your camera—you're allowed to take pictures.

Note: The temperature in the mine is only 50° to 55° F, so you'll need to dress accordingly.

To get to the Phoenix Gold Mine, take I–70 eastbound to exit 239, and then take Stanley Road southwest to Trail Creek Road. For more information, call (303) 567–0422 or (800) 685–7785 or write P.O. Box 3236, Idaho Springs 80452. Web site: www.phoenixmine.com.

"It was awesome," commented one visitor. "We looked down at the passing clouds. You felt as though you'd reached the top of the world."

The traveler was referring to the highest paved auto road in the United States, which leads from Idaho Springs, west of Denver, to the top of 14,264-foot-high **Mt. Evans.** The mountain first attracted gold-hungry prospectors during the nineteenth century and was named in 1870 after Governor John Evans. A few years earlier, the famous artist Albert Bierstadt and a friend had climbed it. The climb inspired Bierstadt, whose paintings express the grandeur of this and other high Colorado peaks.

The road to the top of the mountain is usually opened in May and stays open until the first significant snowfall of the year—meaning that if you want to tackle the peak in winter, you'll need to plan accordingly by packing snowshoes or cross-country skis and having the necessary wilderness skills to do so safely. Once the road has been opened for the season, it is accessible twenty-four hours a day. Cost is $10.00 for a three-day vehicle pass, on sale at the entrance station. There is also a mechanical collection station that accepts cash ($1.00, $5.00, $10.00 bills) and credit cards; it will issue you a valid pass. Any sunny summer day will do to make your drive up to the summit, but weekdays are preferable if you want to avoid the crowds. In addition, visiting very early or very late in the day ups your odds of seeing the abundant fauna that call Mt. Evans home.

If you're starting your journey in Denver, you can choose to approach the mountain via Bergen Park and return via Idaho Springs, or vice versa. Expect to see stunning Colorado scenery along the way, including large, fertile meadows, dense lodgepole pine forests, aspen trees, ponderosa pine, Douglas fir, and thick bushes of wild raspberries, as well as the occasional chipmunk or squirrel.

Placid **Echo Lake** makes for a nice stopping point en route to the summit. Get out of the car, stretch out your legs, and perhaps enjoy a picnic lunch while you watch families angling for trout and hikers setting out for the trails that captivated Bierstadt so many years ago. If you're visiting after Thanksgiving, expect to see a vast frozen expanse—the lake freezes completely, and you can skate across it on narrow cross-country skis, reaching numerous trails that yield great views. But even in summer, it gets cool up here, so dress warmly and bring extra layers. Theoretically, for every 1,000 feet of elevation gain in the Rockies, you can compare your journey to traveling 200 miles north. Of course, this means you get to experience the cooler air in each zone on the way up, not to mention the shifting vegetation. Above Echo Lake, you can follow trails through alpine tundra, stopping to study the small grasses, sedges, herbs, and the almost microscopic plants with their teeny flowers.

If you take a close look at the ancient bristlecone pines, you will read the story of their struggle for survival in these unfriendly high-altitude settings. Each and every dwarfed bristlecone or leaning Douglas fir shows the signs of withstanding blizzards and summer storms as well as coping with blazing sunlight followed by rains. This harsh weather destroys most exposed buds and conifer seeds, limiting the trees' reproduction. Some trees are bent and twisted from the relentless wind, while others are bleached from the sun or blackened and split by lightning strikes. At timberline, the already small array of trees becomes even sparser, with only single, isolated soldiers standing to face the sky's hail cannons.

Above timberline, in Colorado's alpine life zone, the fauna changes, too. Marmots often show themselves, as well as the occasional ptarmigan.

Mountain goats are frequently seen up here, and once in a while you'll spot a bighorn sheep. ("Don't feed them," advises the U.S. Forest Service. "They sometimes bite.")

Mt. Evans' upper reaches are also dotted with lakes. At 11,700 feet, you'll spot Lincoln Lake; it's 800 feet below the highway. Then at 12,830 feet, Summit Lake awaits, complete with a short trail overlooking the picturesque Chicago Lakes, some 1,400 feet below. The Forest Service warns parents not to let their children run around in this area due to the sudden drop-offs—the highway has few guardrails.

Finally, complete the motorized journey by pulling into the parking lot at 14,130 feet. Get out of your car and hike that last 134-foot gain in altitude to the summit via a $1/4$-mile hike along a trail. Catch your breath—the air is much thinner up here than it is on the plains, so visitors from the flatlands should walk slowly and take in the scenery. From the summit, the views are tremendous.

Start your tour on I–70. Take exit 240 in Idaho Springs onto the Mt. Evans Highway (SR 103). After Echo Lake, head onto SR 5, which will take you to the summit. For a change of pace, continue west along SR 103 to Bergen Park, and then take SR 74 and I–70 to Denver. The distances are moderate—it's only 28 miles from Idaho Springs to the summit of Mt. Evans. For more information, call the Clear Creek Ranger Station at (303) 567–3000 or write to the CCRD Visitor Information Center, P.O. Box 3307, Idaho Springs 80452. E-mail: Karl@ RockyMountainNP.com. Web site: www.mtevans.com.

Trivia

Newlyweds and others can take a carriage ride and go back to a more romantic era, thanks to Rutherford Carriage Service and Picnic Pavilion; P.O. Box 574, Georgetown 80444; (303) 569–2675. Web site: www. georgetowncolorado.com/ rutherfordcarriage.htm. Open year-round.

In autumn, the wind whistles through the well-kept streets of **Georgetown,** rattling the windows of the impeccable Victorian houses. The winter snows pile up high here, and spring is slow to come at an elevation of 8,500 feet above sea level. The mountains rise so steeply on all four sides of Georgetown that even the summers are cool; the sun shines for only a few hours a day.

Yet, this community 45 miles west of Denver has more ambience, more sight-seeing, more genuine concern for its own history than most other Colorado cities. It is special in its own way. The city officials have spent six-figure sums to rebuild and preserve the pink-brick houses, the old-time saloons, the museums that conjure up the nineteenth century of gold and silver riches. The antiques shops, silversmiths, and weavers are among the best in the state. The craft shops are different, real, worth browsing in, and much better than those of Vail or other fancy ski resorts to the west.

Unlike Vail, which rose from a cow pasture, Georgetown is a historic community. And proud of it.

On a clear spring day in 1859, two prospecting brothers, George and David Griffith, struggled their way up Clear Creek searching for minerals. Unsuccessful at the other mining camps in Colorado, the two prospectors reached out for new, untried land, and this time they had luck—they found gold.

After the discovery, the Griffith brothers did a highly unusual thing for gold or silver seekers—instead of just digging up the mountain and leaving with their wealth, they brought their entire family out from Kentucky to live permanently in their valley. The tiny settlement they founded became known as George's Town, and although no more significant strikes were made, it grew steadily for five years.

Then, in 1864, assays showed an extremely high silver content. The boom was on. Over the next thirty years, the mines in and around the town produced more than $200 million worth of silver. The town became known as the Silver Queen of the Mountains—and in 1868 it was renamed Georgetown.

By 1880, some 10,000 people made the city their home. Fortunes, houses, and reputations flourished. Elaborate mansions attested to wealth. Hotels served the finest cuisine in gilt rooms with elegant furniture. An opera house brought Broadway productions and favorite classical operas to the wealthy.

All this came to an abrupt end; the silver panic of 1893 hit hard, with silver prices dropping to almost nothing. Mines, mills, and livelihoods vanished. The town became a ghost of its past glory.

Georgetown languished this way for more than six decades. Then tourism came, and interstate highways transported millions of travelers to the high mountains.

A historic transportation mode was reconstructed to bring these tourists to Georgetown. The ***Georgetown Loop Railroad*** was originally completed in 1877. The goal of the railroad company was to reach another mining boom town—Leadville.

They never made it. Instead, the workers pushed on just another 2 miles to Silver Plume, a mining camp up the valley. Even this short distance created difficult engineering problems.

Just 2 miles away, Silver Plume was 600 feet higher in elevation. To complete the spur to the next mountain stop, the rail tracks had to cover 4½ miles.

As the automobile gained popularity and the mining industry collapsed, the Loop was abandoned. The bridge and rails were used as scrap metal. The spur was forgotten and overgrown with weeds for thirty-five years.

Trivia

Two historic Georgetown homes, the Bowman-White House and the Hamill House, exemplify the city's Victorian style. See the Web site www.historic georgetown.org.

Then the Colorado Historical Society stepped in, bought the land, and set about the major task of rebuilding the tracks and the bridge. In 1984, the new Devil's Gate bridge was opened. The Georgetown Loop has been running ever since.

An eighty-minute ride takes you from historic Georgetown to Silver Plume and back, crossing the Devil's Gate trestle bridge. Views from the open cars are panoramic. Bighorn sheep may sometimes be seen in addition to other valley wildlife. In autumn, the aspens offer a gilded view of this mountain scenery. Open from late May through October 1. Call for departure times and advance reservations (highly recommended). Cost is $12.95 for anyone age sixteen or older and $8.50 for young people age three through fifteen. Children age two or younger ride free if they sit in a parent's lap. Call (303) 569–2403 or (800) 691–4386, or make reservations on-line at www.gtownloop. com. Write Georgetown Loop Railroad, Inc., P.O. Box 217 (1111 Rose Street), Georgetown 80444.

Unlike other Colorado mining towns, Georgetown was never totally destroyed by fire, so today it has more than 200 carefully preserved historic buildings.

Luckily, too, Georgetown passed a historic preservation ordinance many years ago. The local historical society is serious about its purpose. One of Georgetown's landmarks is the French-style **Hotel de Paris Museum,** full of Tiffany fixtures, lace curtains, and hand-carved furniture. (Open from Memorial Day through September 11:00 A.M. to 4:30 P.M., and on weekends from October to Memorial Day noon to 4:00 P.M. Admission is $4.00 for adults, $2.00 for children six to sixteen, and children younger than six free. Call (303) 569–2311. Web site: www.georgetowncolorado. com/museum.htm.

Georgetown has several Victorian mansions worth seeing. During the first two December weekends, a well-known Christmas market with small booths and outdoor stalls beckons. One of the best inquiry points: Polly Chandler, in Polly's Book Store, 505 Rose Street; (303) 569–3303. She really knows the town.

Georgetown enjoys a good location for travelers who plan to explore the Continental Divide in summer or Colorado ski country in winter. A one-night stay in fall or spring is equally worthwhile. Consider the ***Alpine Hideaway Bed and Breakfast*** for its coziness, attention to detail, peace and quiet, and mountain vistas. The decor here includes sheepskins, potted palm trees, dollhouses, orchids, and a fireplace in every room. Dawn Janov, the enthusiastic owner, fairly showers guests with goodies like Swiss chocolates and bedtime liqueurs. Breakfast pampering includes guava, papaya, ripe cantaloupe, kiwi slices, pancakes, quiches, and strong coffee—all left discreetly in front of your door. The Alpine Hideaway is located on a lone 8,500-foot promontory at 2045 Blue Bird Drive. Write to P.O. Box 788, Georgetown 80444 or call (800) 490–9011. E-mail: AAHideaway@aol.com. Web site: www. georgetowncolorado.com/alpinehideaway.htm. Hikers will be delighted with nearby trails to old mines; drivers can motor to the 11,600-foot Guanella Pass, which is visible from the bed-and-breakfast.

Georgetown is about an hour west of Denver via I–70. For information about Georgetown, write to the Chamber of Commerce, P.O. Box 444, Georgetown 80444–0444; (303) 569–2888 or (800) 472–8230. Fax (303) 569–2705. E-mail: markg@georgetowncolorado.com. Web site: www.georgetowncolorado.com.

Georgetown Fishing

*T**he lakes in this area are often crowded during the summer, with the exception of **Silver Dollar Lake.** A somewhat steep jaunt on foot leads off the beaten path to the lake, which yields good catches and offers peace and quiet. From Georgetown, head 8$^1/_2$ miles south on Guanella Pass Road. Turn right at the Silver Dollar Lake sign.*

Want to taste a real flavor of life in the Old West? Then plan to take your vacation at one of Colorado's dude ranches.

The horse trip leads to a sunny meadow full of wildflowers, passing a few ghost houses, with caved-in roofs and sagging walls, the wood evenly bleached by the sun. Later the party rides on. There is an excited breathlessness about the journey as it takes them across two brooks, through thickets of willows and other bushes, and then slowly down a steep, rocky slope. The riders move with caution, savoring a touch of the primitive. They are in tune with the mountain and alone with their thoughts. It is quiet except for the slight creak of the leather saddles and the clicking of the hooves.

The vacationers are far away from the high-rises and superhighways. The riders arrive for breakfast at a sunny forest clearing. Everyone sits down on long logs. The coffee steams. The cowboys fry eggs for all. The mountains say good morning.

Ask other travelers to share their experiences with you. They'll speak about the informality, the privacy, the utter friendliness of Colorado's guest ranches. What with an average of fifteen to about one hundred guests, the mood is calm and relaxed, and the owners really care about you. Families, couples, and newlyweds are pampered. If you arrive with a large party, you can write ahead for spacious quarters. At some hostelries you can also rent cabins.

The names say much: C Lazy U Ranch, Tumbling River Ranch, Peaceful Valley Lodge and Guest Ranch. They are all endearing places set in romantic, isolated Colorado locations. Some of them still breed cattle or horses.

A Colorado dude-ranch vacation is one of the most satisfying, genuine holidays available today. The air is clean, days are warm, evenings cool, and the mountain scenery absolutely spectacular.

At first primitive, the accommodations now range from rustic to deluxe ratings, such as Five Star by Mobil travel guides and Exceptional by AAA (American Automobile Association).

Colorado boasts some forty dude ranches, generally located in the scenic mountain regions. Activities are varied and informal. Life on the ranch resort is geared for the ultimate in easy relaxation. Guests are encouraged to set their own pace.

The essence of these cowboy-style vacations becomes clear when you read the greeting on a wall of one typical guest ranch on the

Wyoming–Colorado border:

Guest, you are welcome here;
Do as you please.
Go to bed when you want to
And get up at your ease.
You don't have to thank us
Or laugh at our jokes.
Say what you like,
You're one of the folks.

You may ride all day every day or merely lounge by the heated pool and take in the pure mountain air. You don't even have to swim if you don't want to. Trail rides can be a few hours to half a day or full day with a picnic. Steak-fry rides are popular, too. At night the dudes head down a pine-scented trail in the moonlight; you gaze up at the Milky Way.

A Colorado dude ranch is a small, self-contained world where you ride away from city life as well. There are lots of horse trails for novices, guided breakfast rides, ghost-town rides, and even six-day rides into the wilderness. Some dude ranches arrange river-rafting trips, or you can rent a jeep. Archery, boating, and even golf are possibilities. Chaises abound.

The phenomenon is uniquely western and especially enjoyable in the Colorado mountains, where summers are never too hot or too cold. You're therefore outdoors much of the time. While adults rest or play, children have their own supervised programs. Much of the clientele returns every year. Most stay at least a week.

How much does a dude-ranch vacation cost? Much less than you'd expect. If you settle on an average western place, you can have an unforgettable week for half or a third of what an ocean cruise would cost. Everything is included. Such vacations mean honest value; the customers can always rely on meals that are well cooked and served family style, which allows you to get acquainted with other guests. At one ranch, about a two-hour drive from Denver, the breakfasts and dinners consist of huge eat-all-you-want buffets. In the morning, you'll want to ride off some of those calories—and get some sun in the process.

The *Peaceful Valley Lodge and Guest Ranch* near Lyons is best known for its summer square-dancing activities; the dude ranch employs a caller. This establishment has a special teenage program, scout trips to ghost towns, and even English riding instruction. Lyons is easy to reach from Denver via the Boulder Turnpike; then continue via SR 7 and SR

Chapel at Peaceful Valley Lodge and Guest Ranch

72. For more information: 475 Peaceful Valley Road, Lyons 80540–8951; (303) 747–2881 or (800) 955–6343. E-mail: howdy@peacefulvalley. com. Web site: www.peacefulvalley.com. Open year-round.

The *Tumbling River Ranch* in Grant seems hewn out of native rock and local wood. At night you can hear the tumbling river under your window. The ranch stands at 9,200 feet above sea level, and, overhead, the stars stand out clearly. The ranch features not only horse activities but also a handsome outdoor pool sheltered by glass panes. The food is excellent, and you get lots of personal attention from the owners.

Grant is a short trip southwest from Denver via US 285. For more information: Tumbling River Ranch, P.O. Box 30, Grant 80448; (303) 838–5981 or (800) 654–8770. E-mail: info@tumblingriver.com. Web site: www.tumblingriver.com. Open from June 1 through September 30.

And make a note of the Colorado Dude and Guest Ranch Association for more ranches: P.O. Box 2120, Granby 80446; (303) 887–3128. E-mail: fun@coloradoranch.com. Web site: www.coloradoranch.com.

If you're driving east on Highway 6, you see the artifically created lake after you're out of the steep Glenwood Canyon, over Vail Pass, en route to Summit County. If your approach is from the west, you cross the 11,992-foot Continental Divide; then the highway suddenly straightens, and there it is —*Lake Dillon.*

With its 24½-mile shoreline, on a summer day the water can be a deep blue, dotted by white triangles of sails, and alive with small motorboats, cabin cruisers, and canoes skimming the surface. Now and then an angler fishes for rainbow trout in good privacy.

From the beaches, beyond the encircling highways, the mountains sweep upward—the domain of climbers, hikers, and horseback riders. Streams are everywhere: Blue River, Snake River, Ten Mile Creek, all agleam in the sun. The much-needed waters splash across rocks into the reservoir, flowing toward Denver, through the unseen Roberts Tunnel, not far from Dillon.

The highway has two lanes here, and if you're in a hurry, you may well sweep past the sign that reads: DILLON, ELEVATION 9156. DENVER, 78 MILES.

Trivia
In the early 1960s, the original town of Dillon—the whole town!—was moved in order to make way for the Dillon Lake reservoir.

The town is concealed by pines. But a surprise awaits the driver who heads into these woods. For all at once there is silence. The trucks rumbling toward Utah or Nebraska are no longer heard. And among the trees stands the new Dillon. The town officials and the city planners conceived it well. Buildings can be no higher than 30 feet, for instance, so that all comers can see the lake. Only natural materials—the stone and wood of the Rockies, plus glass—are permitted for the houses. The wood may be stained but not painted. The lots and homes have to keep their distance, for utmost peace. And timber was cut sparingly, for conservation's sake.

You notice other things. Dillon's signs are subdued, modest, inviting. Neon doesn't splash here; no beacons explode in the traveler's eyes. There are no unsightly shacks or dead auto carcasses. A cluster of stores—hardware, supermarket, drug—and a post office have been fashioned into a tidy shopping center. Built of native pine, it blends with the forest.

The old town was named after an early prospector. There was off-and-on gold mining, a little railroading, lumber trading, and much ranching. The first post office opened here in 1883. With the advent of the car came garages and service stations. Roads improved, and more tourists showed up "to breathe the exhilarating Rocky Mountain air," as one man put it. A longtime resident remembers the Dillon of the 1930s: "Ranchers picked up their mail here," he says, "and it was a place for a beer on Saturday night."

But on the other side of the mountains, Denver was growing, and it desperately needed more water. All through the forties and early fifties, the Denver Water Department bought up lands and ranches with water rights. Then, in 1955, Dillonites were told about the coming storage reservoir. It would inundate their town.

After many meetings and complex legal work, the machinery ground into high gear. There would be no turning back—Dillon had to move. Some of the old people left for warmer climates; others settled in nearby villages. But the young, sports-minded citizens decided to create a new Dillon on a hill of pine and evergreen. Here was a chance for a model town.

Down in the valley the old community was dismantled stick by stick. Because the water supply had to be pure, all the ancient buildings had to go. Some were cut in half and hauled elsewhere by trucks. Others had to be burned down. The Water Board uprooted telephone lines, removed old pipes, buried the last rusty tin cans. Even the peaceful graveyard, with its rococo stones and metal crosses, had to be shifted to higher ground. For a while there were still the busy swings in the school yard, and a church belfry pointed its white wooden finger into the sky. Then the school was moved, and the church found a new home in the reborn Dillon.

Slowly, the dam rose until it stood 231 feet high at some points and was capable of backing up 257,000 acre-feet of water. The Harold Roberts Tunnel, more than 23 miles long and costing $50 million, was completed to connect the reservoir with rivers flowing into Denver. Water from thawing snows and the mountain streams steadily accumulated in the reservoir behind the dam.

One August day, the waters rushed over the top and through the "glory hole" spillway into the outlet tunnel. By then nothing was left of the old Dillon town site. The roads that led to it now lay under about 150 feet of water. Unlike the fabled Atlantis, the sunken city that resurfaces, the ancient Dillon would never emerge again.

Instead of dwelling on its past, the new town has forged ahead quickly, enthusiastically redefining itself as a community rooted in nature. Tourists come to relax and experience the unique flavor of this exquisitely planned and orchestrated settlement. They can take a front row seat by renting a condo at the Lodge at Dillon Lake, known for its spectacular views. After eating at the Arapahoe Café and Pub, a charming, wood-paneled restaurant on Lake Dillon Drive, they can take a stroll through the peaceful town.

In the years ahead, Dillon and the entire vacationland around the 3,300-acre lake will witness even more development. Many agencies are involved, including the U.S. Forest Service of the Department of Agriculture; the Bureau of Land Management; the Denver Board of Water Commissioners; the Colorado Game, Fish, and Parks Department; and, of course, the town of Dillon itself. On the horizon are more motels, hotels, condos, restaurants, clothing stores, and curio and art shops.

The **Dillon Marina** hosts a number of fun community events annually, including regattas throughout the summer. For details write P.O. Box 1825, Dillon 80435 or call (970) 468–5100. E-mail: Dillonm@colorado. net. Web site: www.dillonmarina.com. The annual *Taste of Summit* takes place in the Dillon Marina Park in June. Eventgoers enjoy sampling not only Colorado-made beers and wines but also foods from all over the county. Live music, a silent auction, pontoon rides, and children's activities round out the event, which benefits the Lake Dillon Foundation for the Performing Arts. Tickets cost $14 in advance or $17

How Colorado's Ski Areas Respect the Environment

*C*ompetence is one of the Colorado ski area's earmarks. The mountain crews, the ski patrol, and the ski school are all carefully selected from some of Colorado's most experienced ski experts. Even the original forest workers fit the picture: Special crews of French-Canadian sawyers hand-cleared and close-cut stumps on most Summit County trails to avoid major disturbance of the underlying soil.

(The newer mountain developments were seeded for proper ground coverage to avoid severe erosion problems during the spring runoff.) Thanks to forestry know-how, most of the utility poles from the valley to the summits were installed by helicopter in order to avoid excessive clearing. The utility poles were given a green hue to blend in with the natural vegetation. The trails, highways, and support facilites thus coexist with nature.

on the day of the event, with children age eleven or younger admitted free. Call (970) 468–2403 for tickets.

For more information about events and attractions in Dillon during your stay, call the Dillon Event Hotline at (970) 262–3400 or write Town of Dillon, P.O. Box 8, Dillon 80435. E-mail: dillonpr@ci.dillon.co.us. Web site: www.ci.dillon.co.us/events/.

Denver is a mere seventy minutes from Lake Dillon when you use the time-saving Eisenhower Tunnel, which is a story in its own right.

"Nearly impossible!" a geologist said when a Colorado financier first suggested a long tunnel through the Continental Divide during the 1930s. "Unpredictable rock!" other geologists warned in 1941. The drilling of a pilot bore already gave a clue to the unstable rock strata of the area in the Colorado Rockies. Steel linings buckled in the exploratory shaft. For three decades tunnel builders battled the mountain some 58 miles west of Denver. Lack of money, politics, explosions, fires, and, most of all, geological problems all thwarted the builders. A tunnel engineer later summed it up better than anyone else. "We were going by the book," he said. "But the damned mountain couldn't read!"

Trivia

The utility bill for the Eisenhower Tunnel runs about $70,000 a month—each tunnel (one for east-bound and one for west-bound traffic) has 2,000 light fixtures, and each light fixture contains an eight-foot bulb!

Fortunately, the 8,941-foot-long *Eisenhower Tunnel* was eventually drilled despite the obstacles. The tunnel saves the motorist 10 miles over the twisting and turning highway that crosses Loveland Pass. Since the tunnel opened in 1973, drivers need no longer expose themselves to the fierce storms and howling winds of the pass. No more jackknifed trucks, stranded cars, or vehicles swept off the highway ledges by avalanches, rock slides, or icy curves taken too fast. One of North America's best-known mountain passes was finally tamed.

For a hundred years, since the days when railroads were first reaching across the continent, men had worked and dreamed of tunneling through the Continental Divide here, where it's narrowest.

Everyone agreed that the existing roads across the 12,000-foot-high mountain crests presented some perils and inconveniences. In the 1920s and 1930s, a motor trip was still considered a major undertaking on the 12-foot-wide Loveland Pass road. The local papers claimed that such travel resembled a stunt and called the motorists undaunted. One eye-witness reported, "Mud and a steep grade combine to balk all but the highest built cars." In summer, automobiles sometimes plummeted from the steep road, and hikers could see old hulks rusting in the valleys. The worst times were in winter, when Colorado's east and west slopes became cut off from each other. Eventually, irate citizens put placards on their auto bumpers that read, WE DEMAND A TUNNEL!

It became clear that only a tunnel would make travel possible during all seasons, besides reducing distances across the Rockies. In January 1937, a mountain community leader proposed a 10-mile tunnel. It took four years until the Colorado Highway Department began to drill a 5,483-foot pioneer bore. World War II brought the work to a halt, despite much clamor in the mountain towns and in the Colorado state capital. One November day in 1947, a large group of marchers showed up at the statehouse in Denver, calling for action. At the same time, signs appeared in Front Range cafes and restaurants that demanded a LOVELAND PASS TUNNEL NOW!

Before long the tunnel idea moved into high gear. The project was advertised and bids were to be opened. Unfortunately, only one bid was received, which brought the tunnel idea to another standstill.

In short, the mountain giant had won. No one wanted to take it on. In the pilot bore the ceilings gradually caved in, and inspectors reported gushing water and musty odors. Engineers told the press that men would have to work and live under impossible climatic conditions at an

Car Camping

*W*hen my youngest son was ten or eleven, we decided to explore the 10,000-foot level of the Continental Divide; we headed for the Rainbow Lakes, which can be accessed via a rutted, bumpy road. The famous Colorado weather was uncooperative. It rained. We had underestimated the length of the drive from Nederland, plus the long hike to the campground.

Strangely enough, the campground was empty. We were on our own. What's more, it had started to pour again. Hungry now at 8:00 P.M., we

unpacked one hamburger each, crumpled up some paper, and topped the paper with the thinnest conifer branches. Then we struck some matches, which was still permitted in that particular area at that time. No luck. The rain had gone into high gear. It poured. Under its wet onslaught, the little, moist matches refused to participate. We ate the edible: the hamburger bun, the two onion slices, an apple.

The next morning, the sun greeted us from the sky. It would be a beautiful Colorado day . . .

11,000-foot altitude and that it would be extremely difficult to transport materials to the site. Attention-seeking politicians showed up in the tunnel bore, garbed in yellow slickers, rubber boots, and impressive miner's hats. The test shaft's air quickly ended the visit.

Work progressed only slowly. The Continental Divide would not bow to the nine firms that had been welded into one contractor. Sometimes as many as 1,100 men sweated and coughed in three shifts inside the mountain. Mounted on three-tiered drilling platforms, a dozen giant drills poked into the tunnel's brain. The attack of these massive drilling machines was followed by blasts of water to wash out the fresh holes. The racket was tremendous, and bearded, hard-hatted miners wore thick plastic earmuffs lined with sponge rubber.

After just three months of penetration, workmen noticed that a large area had shifted, buckling some steel linings. Total costs soon soared above the original bids of $49 million to $100 million, with the tunnel still acting up. On February 13, 1969, miners had to run for safety as some walls 600 feet inside the west portal started to disintegrate. Dismay was equally great when the granite resisted altogether. The contractor requested permission to attack one fault zone with a specially designed shield. The five-story, twelve-drill, 22-foot monster weighed 670 tons with its tailpiece. The machine was capable of exerting a push of twenty million pounds.

The shield was first housed in a mammoth chamber near the west portal. Then came the historic day when the engineering wonder began its journey into the tunnel. The highway department's fanfare—and the newspapers' excitement—proved to be somewhat premature: The shield advanced only 70 feet in less than a month. On September 4, 1969, the device ground to a sudden standstill; its thirty-four roller bearings were stuck. The shield was redesigned to move on skids. This time, alas, the machine budged just 7 inches. The earth pressures were too much, and the expensive colossus had to be abandoned in the tunnel, where it still lies today, cemented into the walls.

No further progress was made for more than a year after this multimillion-dollar failure. The tunnel designers brought in qualified consultants at stiff fees from all over the United States—to no avail. Finished sections still threatened to fall apart. On occasion the whole mass of granite, gneiss, and schist seemed to be moving. In some areas the rock resembled clay, and dust kept squeezing through every crevice. In the collapsing areas some rock could be "nailed" to a more stable surface; in other sections, curved supports helped distribute the pressures.

Sometimes the only solution was to double the support beams. All these unforeseen emergencies and the additional materials consumed a fortune in man-hours.

There were other problems. About sixty miners walked out when a woman was hired as an engineer. Twice the workmen walked out to protest poor ventilation.

One December day a fire brought work to a complete stop. No one knows for sure how the flames started some 4,000 feet inside the western tunnel section. An acetylene torch—and some straw—may have touched off the fire. To smother it the outside air supply had to be shut off, and the smoke assaulted the men's lungs. Would gas pockets cause an explosion? The possibility seemed real enough. Almost a week passed before work could continue.

Barely three months later a $200,000 explosion rocked the concrete operation at the west entrance. This time there may have been an equipment malfunction. The mishap destroyed the huge boiler, the concrete-mixing machinery, 5,000 gallons of oil, a large propane tank, and the company ambulance.

The job had been enormous on all levels: The excavation alone had taken 524,000 cubic yards out of a mountain bent on creating mischief and causing deaths. The tunnel actually took five lives—three in accidents and two from heart attacks at the high elevation. There were more than fifty broken arms, legs, and ankles. No one could count the hours of anguish felt by the contractors, engineers, and workmen about whether the job would ever get finished. The mountain giant constantly held out its fist for more money. The original highway department estimate—made in 1937—was $1 million. The cost exceeded $115 million for one bore.

Yet, all this effort and expenditure represented a mere start, because the tunnel could at first accommodate only one lane of traffic each way. The interstate highway system must be four lanes, so a second section was dug by some 500 workers at a cost of another $225 million. The complete Eisenhower Tunnel opened for traffic on December 21, 1979. Lots of bad rock gave the engineers and drilling crews plenty of trouble.

But the job was at last accomplished. "The damned mountain finally knew the score," said one engineer. "Like it or not, we did get through!"

The Eisenhower Tunnel is 58 miles west of Denver via I–70. See the Web site www.usnet1.com/tunnel/tunnel.html for more information.

Year-Round Vacation Areas

reckenridge is the perfect Colorado frontier town—one of the few that was rebuilt and is now well preserved and thriving.

In 1859, a group of fourteen prospectors discovered gold in the Breckenridge area. A town was quickly built by miners who were hopeful that they would strike it rich. One such miner, Tom Groves, walked away a big winner when he discovered "Tom's Baby," a 136-ounce gold nugget. But, like all areas rich in minerals, the mines eventually played out. Breckenridge citizens wouldn't give up, and they found another moneymaker when Summit County's first ski area opened in 1961.

Trivia

Gold was first panned in Breckenridge's Blue River in 1859.

When a group of European journalists visited many of the state's resorts, Breckenridge seemed to delight them more than most others. Why? Here were all the earmarks of the old Gold Rush West: the little Victorian houses with their columns and crenellations; the clapboard structures of the miners, beautifully repainted; and store windows filled with antiques. Midwesterners and easterners feel the same way; they get the chance to let children (and themselves!) relive U.S. history.

The ski slopes are still named for the old mines in the area: Gold King, Wellington, Bonanza, Cashier, Silverthorn—these were the names that excited the gold hunters more than a century ago.

Breckenridge is actually one of Colorado's oldest towns. In August 1859, the first gold seekers came streaming across the Continental Divide to pan gold in the waters of the Blue River. Later, a silver lode started a second boom.

By 1861 some 5,000 people lived in and near Breckenridge. Summit County then extended as far as the Utah line and was one of seventeen counties composing Colorado Territory. It has since been whittled down to 615 square miles. Then, as now, Breckenridge was the county seat.

More than $30 million in gold was taken out of the district during its heyday. Most of that was from placer and lode mining. Later on, gold dredges came to tear up the countryside, leaving the great piles of rocks still to be seen along the Blue and Swan rivers, as well as along French Creek. Dredging came to a halt about 1942.

In the early 1960s, Breckenridge became a year-round resort, at the same time maintaining its century-old status as a former mining community.

Development moved ahead when the ski area opened in the early sixties. The runs were at first short, but fairly varied, and always aimed at families who could meet for lunch at the handsome Alpine base lodge. Soon the town attracted a number of people who built second homes in the serene forests.

Breckenridge is a good choice for the family in search of a winter vacation without pretense. Keep in mind that snowmobiling, ice fishing, easy skiing on the simply laid-out ski runs, tobogganing, snowshoeing, bowling, and sight-seeing nightly all add to satisfaction. Rates and ski lift tickets in Colorado can be expensive, however.

Do you like to snowboard? Breckenridge has 1,915 acres of snowboardable terrain. "Extreme" snowboarders can try to conquer Peak 7, which is above the timberline and offers abundant obstacles, or try Peak 8's unfathomable bowls. For a neater, well-groomed run, try Peak 9. For a messy run with lots of bumps and trees, go to Peak 10. And novices, have no fear—Breckenridge offers snowboarding lessons at every level of skill. Opening date is usually in late October or early November; the season runs until the snow is gone sometime in the spring. For more information, call the Breckenridge Resort Chamber (311 South Ridge Street, P.O. Box 1909, 80424) at (970) 453–2913. Fax: (970) 453–7238. E-mail: gobreck@gobreck.com. Web site: www.gobreck.com. You can also contact the Breckenridge Ski Resort (P.O. Box 1058, 80424) at (970) 453–5000 or (800) 789–7669. E-mail: breckguest@ vailresorts.com. Web site: www.breckenridge.com.

Breckenridge Horseback Riding

*Tired of walking? The **Kingdom of Breckenridge Stables** offers ninety-minute rides along the Breckenridge Trail, which passes some of Colorado's finest scenery. Also available is a breakfast ride, departing at 7:00 A.M. daily. The stable's most popular ride since 1983, the breakfast ride includes scrambled eggs, sausages, "Cowboy Coffee," hot chocolate, orange juice, and all-you-can-eat pancakes. Dinner rides are available as well, particularly for larger groups. Reserve all rides at least one day in advance. Ride prices range from $30 to $50, with children age five or younger paying half price for any ride.*

Call (970) 453–4438 or write P.O. Box 1816, Breckenridge 80454. E-mail: info@colorado-horses.com. Web site: www.colorado-horses.com.

Breckenridge

Mining—an important part of Colorado's past—is alive and well and can be glimpsed at the ***Country Boy Mine,*** 2 miles from downtown Breckenridge. This working mine is one of the few that offer travelers the same experience that hard-rock miners had more than one hundred years ago when the mine was established. At the Country Boy Mine you can don a hard hat and venture 1,000 feet underground, seeing what actual miners saw, feeling what real miners felt. After the tour you can try your hand at gold panning in Eureka Creek or ride the ore carts to their dump sites. Indeed, here you are the miner.

There is plenty to see at Country Boy. Wonder at the dredge boat display or wander through the museum exhibit.

From Denver take I–70 west to exit 203; drive south on Colorado 9, 10 miles into Breckenridge. Turn left on Wellington Road and stay on it until it comes to a final fork. Turn right, and then drive a mile east on

French Gulch Road. Admission costs $11.00 for anyone thirteen and older, $6.00 for children four to twelve, children three and younger free. Reservations are required. For information call (970) 453–4405. Open year-round; call for hours. P.O. Box 8569, Breckenridge 80424. Web site: www.countryboymine.com.

Breckenridge is 88 miles west of Denver via I–70 and SR 9. For more information: Breckenridge Resort Chamber, P.O. Box 1909, Breckenridge 80424; (970) 453–6018.

Where else but in Colorado would you expect to find an extensive ski museum? Founded in 1976, the **Colorado Ski Museum** in **Vail** reaches back to the old miners of the nineteenth century who raced in the Rockies surrounding their camps, competing against one another on long wooden boards, holding a long staff in one fist for braking. The museum contains a magnificent, enlarged 1859 etching of Snowshoe Thompson, the Norwegian who skied from camp to camp in severe blizzards. He delivered the mail, candy, and medicines to the marooned miners.

Here are the photos and artifacts of skiing clergymen like Father John Lewis Dyer, who brought the gospel to Colorado's historic gold towns, as well as the stories of sheepherders and trappers who braved the snows in the nineteenth century on 9-foot enormous wooden contraptions with crude leather straps holding their boots. (Some of the men used baling wire to keep the ski shovel curved during summer storage.) Mementos of the first long-ago jumpers will fascinate the viewers; photos show them taking off from knolls or flying through the air, equipment sometimes falling off high above ground.

Do you want to learn more about the first ski lifts? The Colorado Ski Museum displays the drive mechanism, pictures of the first rope tows, and photos of funny "grippers," which latched onto the moving ropes. The localized history of chairlifts, gondolas (including a gondola rescue), ski patrol toboggans, the first U.S. Army Snow Tanks, and the first ski area snow-packing and grading gear can all be seen here. Any student of ski equipment can learn much about the development of skis, bindings, boots, poles, even the first ski suits, knickerbockers, parkas, or the women's fashions of still earlier days when ladies skied in ankle-length black skirts.

The history of Colorado's famous Tenth Mountain Division is well illustrated; an entire room is devoted to the Mountain Troopers and

Ski Vail—Hut to Hut

*F*or an off-the-beaten-path ski experience, try Vail's backcountry hut-to-hut skiing. The Tenth Mountain Division Hut Association was formed in 1980 to build a backcountry ski hut system in the high mountains between Aspen, Leadville, and Vail.

Now you can reserve the huts for a fee as a take-off for day adventures or to ski from hut to hut. These shelters are within the White River and San Isabel National Forests, so stunning vistas are guaranteed. The adventure isn't for everyone, however; the Forest Service advises that the trails require at least intermediate ability. The Hut Associa-tion also requires that someone in each group be proficient in backcountry skills, such as avalanche awareness and compass reading.

The huts include woodburning stoves, propane burners, cooking and eating utensils, kitchen supplies, and mat-tresses and pillows.

Note: With average elevations of 11,000 feet, you need to prepare for high altitude.

Reservations are required; call (970) 925–5775 or write Tenth Mountain Office, 1280 Ute Avenue, Suite 21, Aspen 81612. Web site: www.huts.org.

their initial camps and wartime exploits. If the viewer is curious about methods of avalanche control, up-to-date ski racing, or the history of plush, urban, pricey Vail, it's all here in the very center of Vail, with its massive condos next door to the sleek bank, a few steps from the five-star Antlers at Vail complex, and near the ski slopes themselves. The museum features ski videos in a special viewing area. And plaques contain the pictures and biographies of Colorado Ski Hall of Fame members—a somewhat politicized assembly of engineers and entre-preneurs, ski makers, and ski teachers.

Admission is free, but the museum accepts donations. Open daily from 10:00 A.M. to 5:00 P.M. except Monday; closed during the slow May and October seasons, except on some weekends. Colorado Ski Museum, 231 South Frontage Road, Vail Village Transportation Center, Vail 81658; (970) 476–1876. Fax (970) 476–1879. E-mail: skimuse@vail.net. Web site: www. vailsoft.com/museum.

Within walking distance of the ski museum—but nicely concealed by a thick grove of fir trees—you'll find the beautifully designed ***Town of Vail Public Library.*** It was built in 1972 with native Colorado stone and woods and a grass lawn roof. A massive fireplace is lit all year. Picture windows look out into the little forest and onto the footpath that mean-ders along Gore Creek to Vail Village.

Pam Hopkins, a young local architect, won several design awards for the building. "We wanted light and endless space," she explains. "Yet we aimed for energy efficiency." The library has some 23,000 volumes, including many mountain books; several hundred magazine subscriptions; an eager reference desk department; plus cassettes and a children's department. Recently, the library began offering e-books on-line as well. Most of all, the building feels especially cozy when rain or snow glisten in the needles of the trees outside while you're warm and dry, book in hand. Library hours are 10:00 A.M. to 8:00 P.M. Monday through Thursday, 10:00 A.M. to 6:00 P.M. Friday, and 11:00 A.M. to 6:00 P.M. Saturday and Sunday. For more information write 292 West Meadow, Vail 81657 or call (970) 479–2184. Fax: (970) 479–2192. E-mail:

They Almost Blew It: Vail History

*V*ail founders never anticipated a success of such magnitude.

Although thousands of mountain troopers and skiers passed through the valley during the 1940s and 1950s, none of them saw the potential of Vail Mountain, since the best slopes were out of sight high above the highway. But Peter Seibert, an ex–Tenth Mountain man and a ski racer, knew a lot about ski areas, and he spent two years hiking, climbing, and skiing all over the Rockies to look for the ideal resort location. One day in 1957, he scaled the Vail Summit with a local prospector who lived in the valley. Upon seeing the bowls and glades and open slopes, Seibert knew he'd found the ideal site."

Seibert and some friends invested their savings. But more money was needed. Unfortunately, at that time Denver's conservative bankers wouldn't gamble on a large new ski area, with Aspen already doing well. All the same, Seibert kept looking for partners. He

turned to Michigan, Missouri, Wisconsin, Texas, and other states. He bought a snow cat and brought visitors to his magic mountain. He showed films of his powder bowls all over the country. He invited prospective investors to ski with him. One day, he finally hit a lucky streak. A Michigan oilman-skier recognized the potential and found other wealthy backers who spread Seibert's gospel. They raised $5 million, formed Vail Associates, and successfully tapped the Small Business Administration and the no-longer-reluctant Denver bankers. And they sold real estate to precisely the people who had shaken their heads the hardest.

During the summer of 1962, the bulldozers started to dig in. An excellent Milwaukee architect had drawn up the plans and now supervised the frantic building activity.

When the dust settled, there stood the first lodges, apartments, malls, homes, and lifts of Vail, Colorado.

info@vaillibrary.com. Web site: www.vaillibrary.com.

Two hours west of Denver lie some of the state's most impressive mountains—the **Gore Range.** In Vail itself you'll see the Gore Creek, especially in summer. Gore Mountain, Gore Wilderness—who in the world was Gore?

You might call him one of the more interesting visitors who ever roamed through Colorado. The best way to get acquainted with him might be north of Vail on **Gore Pass,** near Kremmling. Here a bronze plaque is visible beside the highway, at an elevation of 9,000 feet. The words on the bronze may pique your curiosity:

> HERE IN 1854 CROSSED SIR ST. GEORGE GORE. AN IRISH
> BARONET BENT ON SLAUGHTER OF GAME AND GUIDED BY JIM
> BRIDGER. FOR THREE YEARS HE SCOURED COLORADO, MON-
> TANA AND WYOMING ACCOMPANIED USUALLY BY FORTY MEN,
> MANY CARTS, WAGONS, HOUNDS, AND UNEXAMPLED CAMP
> LUXURIES.

Lord Gore's party, we learn, dispatched "more than 2000 buffalo, 1600 elk and deer, and 100 bears," among others.

Hunting was nothing new in a land where European trappers and fur traders had already searched all of Colorado for beaver. But Lord Gore set a record; besides, no one matched his style. The baronet had brought most of his retinue of hunters and even some porters from Ireland; his safari caravan eventually accumulated 112 horses, twenty-one carts, thirty wagons, and four dozen hunting dogs. He roamed the mountains for many months, shooting grizzly bear, antelope, and other animals and making elegant camp at night, complete with silver service and rare wines.

His Lordship could afford the "unexampled camp luxuries." For one thing, his income exceeded $200,000, which was quite a sum during the mid-1850s. For another, the Irish nobleman had a taste for gourmet cuisine and rare wines—and the cooks and servants to attend his needs. Lord Gore had gone to school in Oxford, and his aristocratic tastes included various mansions in Ireland and houses in East Sussex.

Lord Gore's hunt is still spoken of by schoolchildren in the area. And thanks to the Historical Society of Colorado, future visitors to the region will be reminded of the Irishman and his exploits by means of the bronze plaque.

The summit of Gore Pass and the plaque are 17 miles west of Kremmling and can be reached from Denver via US 40. The Forest Service has provided picnic grounds on the pass. You get to Vail by driving south on SR 9, then west on I–70.

Mountain flowers! What a variety of life forms! Botanists estimate that there are some 6,000 species in the Rockies alone. Who can doubt it? What a myriad of colors! Lavender, crimson, blue brushstrokes! Bright white, butter yellow, pink! The first sign of spring brings forth a rush of Easter daisies, mountain marigolds, wild sweetpeas, fairy trumpets, pink rockhill phlox, and others in many hues. Wander up in early summer to Colorado's 8,000- or 9,000-foot levels. And lo! Here, almost overnight, you'll see leafy cinquefoils, arnicas, yellow monkey flowers, and the official state flower, the blue Rocky Mountain columbine. (The latter also grows in the foothills.) In July, you'll be welcomed by the star gentians, wood lilies, the mountain aster, and several kinds of larkspur.

You cannot help but admire the hardiness of vegetation at the altitudes of the Rockies. How is it possible that the plants do not die under the battle conditions of winter storms? What makes tiny wildflowers get along with less oxygen and more radiation? How do some mountain flowers manage to spite the short summers and harsh climate above timberline? A sense of wonder must fill you at some mountaintop discoveries.

First of all, smallness helps. The tinier the leaves, the less resistance to the wind. In the summit meadows, known as tundra, you will discover miniature grasses, sedges, and herbs. You bend down to miniflowers. If you brought a magnifying glass, you'd see details of almost microscopic leaves. There are plants without any stems; others come with stems so short that the swirling air masses can't budge them. At the same time, the roots go deep down into the ground; a 2-foot root is the 2-inch plant's insurance against being ripped out by storms.

Amazing nature! Most mountain flora hold onto the day's warmth at night by closing their petals.

Mountain flowers protect themselves with tiny umbrellas or hairs, fine layers of wool, or waxy leaves that hold moisture. Mountain flowers can also adapt to the cold. In the Rockies, thousands of avalanche lilies push through the snow, thus surprising the traveler with their delicate (and edible) yellow petals.

The growing season is short in Colorado. And nature has wisely arranged for most mountain flowers to be perennials so that they need not struggle each season. Such flora develop slowly but survive for several years. Other

Vail Hikes

*M*issouri Lakes. Hikers are sometimes discouraged by evidence of a water project at the start of this trail. However, after the first mile, the trail cuts into the plush wilderness, the likes of which experienced hikers dream about. Rustic log bridges help you cross Missouri Creek on your way to the crystal-clear lakes.

Anticipate a walk of approximately five hours if you go all the way to the lakes within the Holy Cross Wilderness.

Take I–70, exit 171 to Highway 24. Drive south to Homestake Road #703. Turn right onto #704 and travel to a T in the road. The trailhead is on the left.

For more information, call the U.S. Forest Service Rangers Station at (970) 827–5175. Web site: www.econovail.com/hiking.html.

wildflowers sprout for a brief period at certain months each year. They thrive and shine under the mysterious direction of sun and season, in concert with the flora elsewhere, waiting and then multiplying.

One Swiss botanist, Fritz Egli, notes the wondrous cycle of those multiplying and then vanishing creations: "Storms sweep up the seeds, blow them away, and wherever they fall—sometimes in the most inauspicious places—a tiny new life tries to take root; just one little life, inconspicuous among millions and millions more. Yet this tiny plant clings, waits, grows, and—bringing forth flower, color, and fruit—to master all the adversities."

Visitors to the Vail area shouldn't miss seeing one of the highest public alpine gardens in North America—the ***Betty Ford Alpine Gardens,*** located at the Gerald Ford Park. The dedication took place in August 1989, in the presence of the former First Lady.

At an elevation of 8,200 feet, tourists encounter a profusion of crocus, heather, forsythia, wild roses, and other perennial mountain plants, shrubs, and trees. A total of 500 different varieties of alpine and sub-alpine plants grow in four separate microclimates.

There is no charge to visit the gardens, but donations are accepted. For more information: Betty Ford Alpine Gardens, 183 Gore Creek Drive, Vail 81657; (970) 476–0103. E-mail: alpgrdn@vail. net. Web site: www.bettyfordalpinegardens.org.

As the vacation season grinds into high gear, park personnel gird themselves for millions of summer motorists, campers, hikers, climbers, backpackers, and other visitors. Every year travelers flock in record numbers to Colorado.

Can anything be done to lessen the impact on the fragile environment? The answer is yes.

As a traveler, you can do much to improve the situation in the Colorado mountains. Begin by not picking wildflowers. (In Switzerland, tourists pay a heavy fine if they're caught gathering edelweiss and some other rare species.)

Continue by not littering. Apparently, one litterer creates another. Many local mountain clubs organize hikes for volunteer crews to pick up trash on or near hiking trails. In Estes Park, the owners of a resort periodically ride up the trails on pack horses with saddlebags to pick up empty cigarette packages and candy wrappers. At the nearby YMCA, mountain guides pick up the empty beer cans of the careless Sunday masses.

The head of a Colorado environmental group says: "Some tourists are poor stewards of the Beautiful Country. They drive spikes into trees, use privies for target practice, shatter the forest stillness with radio or TV set. They leave initials in red paint on the rock face."

Hikers can help prevent erosion by not getting off the trail. (The state is blessed with more than 1,000 walking trails, footpaths, and mountain-bike routes.) It's especially important to stay on the paths in the high-altitude "tundra" areas. The flowers and vegetation are fragile.

Please, refrain from cutting your initials into trees, a rather common and brutal practice.

If you happen to visit a western ghost town this summer, take nothing but photographs. Forget about carrying off a souvenir piece of an abandoned cabin. Future visitors will be grateful to view the complete ghost town.

The environment credo should also interest people who toss bottle caps into resort streams. Please don't. The cap may get stuck in a fish's throat. One final good rule: If you carry it in, carry it out.

Lastly, one local conservationist suggests that the state adopt a slogan that warns, "There is only *one* Colorado. Tread gently. Make it last!"

Trivia

Shrine Ridge *is an easy hike that can be accomplished in two to three hours. You climb through open meadows with abundant wildflowers, then up the steepest part of the trail to the 12,000-foot summit. While atop the mountain, look for "Lord Gore," a man-shaped rock to the northwest.*

To reach this spot, take I–70 to Vail Pass, exit 190. Proceed on Road #709 to Shrine Pass Summit. Turn left here and drive to Shrine Mountain Inn, where you can park.

The ***Lodge and Spa at Cordillera,*** in Edwards, 15 miles west of Vail, offers more sports and adventure than most first-class resorts in Colorado. While staying at this remote European castlelike lodge in winter, a guest can enjoy Alaskan dogsled rides, rent contemporary snowshoes and join a professional snowshoe guide, take lessons in cross-country skiing and skating (equipment is for rent), train for cross-country races, and get free bus service to nearby Beaver Creek for downhill skiing. In summer, the Lodge and Spa at Cordillera features guided flower hikes, mountain biking, golfing on an eighteen-hole course, swimming in an Olympic-size pool, sitting in whirlpools or in a genuine Finnish sauna, working out on Stairmasters or Lifecycles in a large gym and weight room, and pampering with massages, body wraps, and facials at the professional spa. All this plus 360-degree mountain views, fly fishing, tennis, seclusion, and privacy on 3,600 wilderness acres. This retreat is further blessed with superb accommodations for eighty-four people, and two restaurants. It's a unique, lively, luxurious setup for a moneyed clientele. (Deluxe rates.) For more information contact Lodge and Spa at Cordillera, Edwards 81632; (800) 877–3529. Web site: www. cordillera-vail.com/spa/main/index.asp.

Trivia

When all was said and done, more than 150,000 native trees, plants and shrubs had been replanted at the end of the Glenwood Canyon interstate construction in 1992. In addition, engineers had proven themselves up to the challenge of working the road around large old trees instead of chopping them down, and the freshly made rock cuts fit right in with the natural canyon scenery—they had been stained so that they'd appear weathered.

As you continue your journey along I–70 heading west, you'll suddenly find yourself surrounded by spectacular canyon walls. Welcome to ***Glenwood Canyon,*** known as "Colorado's Grand Canyon." Remarkable in and of itself, with its breathtaking geologic features and lovely scenery, the canyon is rendered even more remarkable by the fact that the interstate highway running through it was constructed with a mind to retaining the canyon's wild and natural beauty. Though it's unfortunate and perhaps even a sad commentary on humankind that such a large interstate was constructed in this incredible setting, it is nonetheless encouraging that those in charge of building the road worked hard to make it as environmentally friendly as possible.

Thus the interstate swoops and bends with the canyon, lifted up and away from the extremely popular ***Glenwood Springs Recreation Trail.*** Four rest stops along I–70 allow access to the 18-mile trail within the canyon. The trail starts behind the Yampah Spa and Vapor Caves. This paved trail and its rest areas attract not only hikers and sightseers, but also in-line skaters, cyclists, runners, rafters, and kayakers. For more information call (888) 4–GLENWOOD, or contact the Eagle Ranger District at 125 West Fifth Street, P.O. Box 720, Eagle 81631. Phone: (970) 328–6388. Fax: (970) 328–6448. E-mail: info@glenwoodsprings.net. Web site: www.glenscape.com/glncyn.htm.

Pull off of I–70 when you see signs for **Hanging Lake** if you want to catch a glimpse of this gem. Hike for $1^2/_{10}$ miles for a peaceful respite after long hours on the interstate, stretching your legs on the steep terrain as you take in the lush green foliage near the stream, the impressive redstone canyon walls, and the gushing power of Deadhorse Creek before you reach the lake itself.

Formed by a geological fault that caused the lake floor to drop down the canyon wall, Hanging Lake covers more than an acre and is up to 25 feet deep. Handrails near the top of the path provide welcome help on a steep grade. A boardwalk circles part of the lake, crossing waterfalls as they crash down from the cliff face. The summer mist from the falls is cooling. Autumn adds gilded accents as golden aspen trees mix with pines. Icicles line the lake in winter, and frozen formations stimulate the imagination. Although steep, a hike to Hanging Lake is a great side trip any time of the year.

Glenwood Springs is the gateway to some of Colorado's most dramatic and most photographed peaks, like the Maroon Bells near Snowmass or lone, spectacular Mt. Sopris, which you notice from almost everywhere in the region. The immense **White River National Forest** offers backpackers much wilderness (see www.fs.fed.us/r2/whiteriver). Anglers rave about the catches of trout (rainbows and browns) in the surround-

Kayaking the Colorado

*F*or an unforgettable experience, book a two-day novice kayak river trip with the **Boulder Outdoor Center**. The trips take you down the Colorado River as it winds through Glenwood Canyon. Though I was not at all interested in kayaking, I finally succumbed to my spouse's eager desire to try it out a couple summers ago. Accompanied by accredited instructors, we reveled in seeing the scenery of Glenwood Canyon up close as we learned how to maneuver through class II+ rapids. They even taught us how to roll! Participants must have some previous kayaking experience and be at least twelve years old. Trips run from May through September. Write 2510 North Forty-seventh Street, Boulder 80301 or call (303) 444–8420 or (800) 364–9376 for details. Fax: (303) 444–8001. E-mail: SURF@ BOC123.COM. Web site: www. boc123.com.

ing rivers—the Roaring Fork, the Frying Pan, and the Colorado. Rivers attract rafters and kayakers as well; guiding services are available in Glenwood Springs. Hiking is plentiful, and hunters flock to the region for elk, deer, grouse, and waterfowl.

What is one of the most unforgettable sights and experiences in this tourist-happy state? It's the 2-block-long ***Glenwood Hot Springs*** with happy heads of visitors bobbing in the steam, adults doing their hydrotherapy, small children riding rubber ducks, and—lo!—high mountains on all sides. Surrounded by the Rockies, with views of conifers and meadows, these thermal waters are relaxing. The Ute Indians discovered them and spoke of "miraculous healing powers." The Aspen, Colorado, mining king used these hot springs for relaxation. A famed architect, imported from Vienna, Austria, built the bathhouses here in 1890, and soon assorted American presidents came to visit Glenwood's mineral spa and "Natatorium."

Today the recreational swimming—and walking—part is kept at 85° to 95°F (29° to 32°C); hotter outdoor waters (100° to 104°F, 38° to 40°C) are also available, fed by more than 3½ million gallons. Swimmers relish the almost unlimited space in the pool, while former hospital patients or the temporarily lame—like skiers recuperating from broken legs—enjoy the medical benefits. To be sure, scientists point out

Touring Glenwood Springs

*G*lenwood Springs is 42 miles northwest of Aspen off of Colorado 82. "Glenwood," as residents call it, sits in the White River National Forest, which is a three-hour drive from Denver. Glenwood's two million acres are renowned for all manner of open-air sports. The attraction includes Flat Tops Wilderness, a huge 117,000-acre plateau north of Glenwood Springs.

Glenwood was named for its hot-spring mineral baths, which are open all year. In the 1880s, silver baron Walter Devereaux decided to convert the springs, which had been used by the Utes, into a health resort for the rich. He built the 2-block-long swimming pool, intended for the guests of the posh adjacent hotel. By the early 1900s, so many wealthy and famous people came to the spa that a rail siding was installed next to the hotel for private railroad cars. Teddy Roosevelt made Glenwood his "Summer White House" in 1901 and bear hunted in the nearby hills.

The mineral baths and vapor caves are open to visitors, with trained personnel to guide and supervise. Locals say the water is a quick cure for visitors' aching muscles and stiff joints after days in the nearby wilderness, on long hikes, or on Aspen's ski slopes.

that the hot springs contain cornucopia elements, including magnesium, calcium, sulphates, bicarbonates, phosphates, and silica.

Some travelers recline much of the day in deck chairs around the pool—Colorado's version of the *dolce vita.* No Roman bath could match Glenwood's pure air and mountain views, however.

For extra luxury, the nearby vapor baths feature massages, plus natural saunas. The pool is open daily, year-round, until 10:00 P.M., opening at 7:30 A.M. in summer and 9:00 A.M. in winter. Cost is $8.75 for anyone age thirteen or older, $5.75 for children three to twelve, children two and younger free. Contact the pool at (800) 537–7946.

Luckily, pool guests have a place to stay—in fact, they can see the steaming waters right under their windows. The 107-unit **Hot Springs Lodge** is contemporary, bright, efficient, and ideally located. Rates are not as high as you might expect. For reservations, call (970) 945–6571. For more information about the pool or lodgings, write to the Hot Springs Lodge and Pool, P.O. Box 308, Glenwood Springs 81602. Fax: (970) 947–2950. E-mail: hslodge@rof.net. Web site: www.hotspringspool.com.

Glenwood Springs may be one of the state's more interesting communities—historically, economically, scenically—yet it never gets the kind of attention accorded to Aspen (41 miles to the southeast) or overcrowded, overbuilt Vail (59 miles) or Denver (some 158 miles to the east). Buses, rental cars, and even Amtrak trains connect travelers daily from the Colorado state capital with Glenwood.

Both town and area are blessed with accommodations for every pocketbook. Economy travelers welcome the numerous campgrounds or inexpensive little cabins flanking the soothing rivers. Large and small motels abound.

You're never far from the parades with floats, carnivals, and other festivities of Glenwood's Strawberry Days, the Fall Art Festival, yearly fishing contests, various rodeos, and the quiet mountain paths under a blue sky.

Strawberry Days, now more than one hundred years old, is Glenwood Springs's oldest and most beloved annual event. The festival is thought to be Colorado's oldest civic celebration, dating back to 1898.

Early Glenwood Springs residents loved parties, and nearly everything called for a celebration. Prior to 1898 strawberry picnics celebrated the luscious harvest of berries that farmers grew in nearby fields. The event was a success, growing in attendance and extravagance every year. In 1905, it was estimated that more than 6,000 out-of-town guests plus the residents of Glenwood Springs took part in the festivities.

Today the annual Strawberry Days celebration has been extended by several days, and many new activities—including sporting events, kids' events, top-name entertainment, and a marketplace of handcrafted works—have been added. Attendance at the fair has risen to an estimated 30,000 people over the peak weekend.

Each year a new theme is chosen for the festival. For example, one theme, "Moon over the Wild Strawberries," had Native American overtones, deriving from the Seneca Indian word for the month of June, which translates to mean "Moon When the Wild Strawberries Get Ripe." The celebration usually takes place in mid-June.

The **Fall Art Festival,** held the fourth week in September, is one of the larger art shows on the Western Slope, attracting more than 400 entries. Professionals and amateurs all compete in their own levels and media. And, of course, almost everything is for sale after the judging.

While you're in Glenwood Springs, don't fail to take a leisurely stroll through the stately **Hotel Colorado,** which graces the National Register of Historic Places. The 128-room hotel is one of the oldest in the state. Indeed, it was modeled after Italy's Villa Medici and boasts a Florentine fountain in a landscaped courtyard. The hotel's renovated beige lobby must be one of the most attractive in the western United States. The myriad chandeliers, fireplaces, oil paintings, fountains, and potted palm trees hark back to the days of Royalty and the Very Rich.

Sunlight Mountain Resort

Sick of the crowds at the big resorts? Then maybe it's time to try out **Sunlight Mountain Resort.** *With more than 460 acres of terrain, plus access to plenty of Nordic trails in the adjacent White River National Forest, this resort offers a great escape. Terrific for families, almost all of the resort's ski runs come right down to the lodge. From Glenwood, head south on County Road 117. For more information, contact the resort at (970) 945–7491 or (800) 445–7931. Web site: www.sunlightmtn.com. Consider staying at the cozy Sunlight Mountain Inn, located at 10252 County Road 117 in Glenwood Springs. Call (970) 945–5225 or (800) 733–4757.*

The Hotel Colorado was financed by the silver mining of the nearby Aspen region and opened officially on June 10, 1893. The cost was a horrendous $850,000; some sixteen private railroad cars of the industrial barons drew up on a special Glenwood siding. Leading citizens from all over the world registered. European millionaires arrived in droves to stay and dine here. In 1905, President Theodore Roosevelt brought his own appetite; a typical menu encouraged the presidential visitor and his entourage to consume an eight-course repast:

Caviar Canapés
Consommé Rothschild
Veal Sweetbreads
Young Turkey
Spring Lamb
Broiled Squab
Figs
Roquefort Cheese

Actually, Roosevelt—an avid bear hunter—made the hotel his Summer White House, complete with direct telegraph connections to Washington and special couriers bringing international news to the hunting head of state.

"The Marvel of Hoteldom" attracted the likes of the Armours of packinghouse fame; the "Unsinkable" Molly Brown, who managed to survive the *Titanic*'s sinking; and President William Howard Taft, who addressed the local populace during his term. World War II transformed the hotel into a naval hospital. In more recent times moneys were spent to update the facilities, to repair leaking roofs and stalled elevators or failing steam heat. Thanks to their antiques, several suites are reminiscent of yesteryear's elegant clientele.

For more information and reservations: Hotel Colorado, 526 Pine, Glenwood Springs 81601; (970) 945–6511 or (800) 544–3998. Web site: www.hotelcolorado.com.

Trivia

Legend has it that the Teddy Bear was born at the Hotel Colorado. One time when frequent visitor President Teddy Roosevelt had a fruitless day of bear hunting, the hotel's maids sewed a stuffed bear in an effort to cheer him up. When he did succeed in hunting down a real bear, his daughter named the bear "Teddy," a name that stuck.

For more information about the Glenwood Springs area, contact the Glenwood Springs Chamber Resort Association at (888) 4–GLENWOOD or 1102 Grand Avenue, Glenwood Springs 81601; (970) 945–6589. Fax: (970)-945–1531. E-mail: info@glenwoodsprings.net. Web site: www.glenscape.com. Glenwood Springs is easily reached from Denver by rental car, bus, or train. Motorists use I–70. The distance from Denver is 158 miles.

Even by Colorado standards, the trip to **Redstone** is long and complicated, but it is worth it. The distance only enhances the charms of the little hamlet of Redstone and its historic inn and castle.

You at once see the imposing **Redstone Inn** at the end of the main street. The Tudor clock tower is an unexpected sight in this remote mountain landscape. The thirty-five rooms seem cozy and unpretentious. Rates are affordable for most people. The lobby and the restaurant are filled with antiques and a Victorian atmosphere.

Now on the National Register of Historic Places, the small Redstone hostelry was built in 1902 for unmarried coal miners. The building had steam heat and even a barber shop. Later, more than $1 million was invested in hotel facilities. A stay here, at an elevation of 7,200 feet, means pure air and a true escape from the city. In summer, horses are for rent and trout fishing is popular. The Crystal River is quiet and lovely. Hikers enjoy the area, as do backpackers. In winter, the inn serves as headquarters for sleigh rides and cross-country skiing. Contact Redstone Inn, 82 Redstone Boulevard, Redstone 81611; (800) 748–2524. Fax: (970) 963–2527. Web site: www.redstoneinn.com.

The little hamlet of Redstone is idyllic. Just a few houses, some artisan and gift shops, a cafe, and a general store.

You reach Redstone via I–70 west to Glenwood Springs, then SR 82 south out of Glenwood toward Aspen; turn right at Carbondale on SR 133—it's 18 miles to Redstone. For more information visit the Web site www.redstonecolorado.com.

If you continue along SR 82 south out of Glenwood, it won't be long until you reach the famous town of Aspen. The chairs whir upward over forest spurs and logging roads and enormous ravines that become expert ski runs in winter. From "downtown" Aspen one can see just a small portion of the whole Aspen Mountain; in fact, only a third of it is visible to those who merely stare up from their cars.

Aspen called itself at first Ute City because it was in Ute territory. Silver gave the town its big start back in the early 1880s. The first

Trivia

One nugget from the Molly Gibson Mine in Aspen weighed 1,840 pounds. It was 93 percent pure silver.

news made the prospectors head up the passes and rush to Aspen—a hard, punishing journey, even from nearby Leadville. Some men dropped dead before they could stake their first claim. Western historians still mention the stampede of that winter in 1879. They came on burro, on foot, or on horseback. A man would sometimes keel over and die on the Aspen street. Other prospectors just stuck the body into a snowbank and kept up the frantic search for silver riches. The best years were from 1885 to 1889, when mines galore—some with fascinating names like the Smuggler or Montezuma—operated above the mountain town. The smelter was booked for weeks, and silver rock would pile up everywhere.

Some miners got rich fast. "The men filled their pockets and fled," wrote one contemporary. The silver barons built the luxurious Victorian **Hotel Jerome** (330 Main Street, 800–331–7213; www. hoteljerome.com) and an opera house. They imported singers and musicians from Europe.

The crash came in 1893, however, and brought lean times. Aspen shriveled from a population of 13,000 to a mere 500. The rebirth followed in the 1930s, with skiing.

Old mining equipment was used as the first tow. After World War II, Chicago industrialist Walter Paepcke became interested in Aspen as a

Versatile Aspen

*M*ost Colorado ski centers consist of a few condos and a ski hill. By contrast, Aspen has many ski areas and Aspen is a town. At one core area you find a handsome pedestrian mall with flower boxes and benches. Moreover, Aspen's red, Old West brick buildings and the Victorian gingerbread homes are periodically restored. The antique cherry-wood bars shine, as do the contemporary Tiffany lamps and the stained-glass windows. Green plants grace many Aspen stores and cafes. Aspen outranks most North American ski resorts when it comes to the sheer number and variety of restaurants and nightlife possibilities.

There are one hundred-plus spots where one can dine or have lunch. Aspen has bistros, bars, saloons, pubs, subterranean dives, cafeterias, cafes, pastry shops, coffee houses, and several internationally famous restaurants. It's a cosmopolitan, polyglot, manifold town. Aspen is everything to every skier and, happily, to every nonskier as well; the town seems ideal for couples or families where one member or the other doesn't ski. Several hundred shops invite browsers; amusements and sports of every kind beckon.

cultural and sports colony. The pace accelerated in the little mountain town. Paepcke made good use of the granitic old opera house, and the guests stayed in the opulent Hotel Jerome, which had been built in 1889. The Aspen Music School flourished.

Some of the townspeople, however, didn't go along with the Chicagoan. When Paepcke offered them free paint for their shacks, not many old-timers took him up on it. They didn't like outsiders and wanted to be left alone. One former prospector complained to the papers that it was a "tragedy to reduce a once-great mining camp to a mere Tenderfoot Playground." Another wrote: "Gallons of printers ink to lure the tourist! And not a drop of ink to tell the world where we stood, back in the eighties shouting to the very top of Castle Peak: 'Here's the greatest ore deposit in North America!'"

In the late 1940s, many Aspen dwellings were peeling. Some stood empty. But the mountain town had uniformity. The residences and streets formed a near-perfect grid pattern. If one studies the town from Aspen Mountain, there was—and still is—a simplicity to it.

The aerial view is about the same even today. Closer inspection, however, reveals some architectural mix. Free enterprise! Aspen, rediscovered as the former mining community, grew into a 10,000-tourist-bed complex, which has meanwhile tripled.

No one seemed to agree on architectural styles, and every year downtown Aspen looked more citylike. There were the original log cabins and Victorian homes of the early miners. Contractors moved in to build new "mineshaft" condominiums, some of which block mountain views. In the more than fifty years' development, Aspen may have retained some flaws, but it also succeeded beyond all expectations as a resort. The ski facilities, what with four different ski areas and countless lifts, including the rapid Silver Queen gondola, are all extraordinary, as good as anything in the Swiss Alps. Aspen summers are a delight, with classical music, lectures, meetings, trails for hikers and bikers, rivers for anglers, areas for kiters, and an expanded airport for private pilots. Gourmets flock to the mostly overpriced Aspen restaurants; finicky guests check into ultraexpensive new hotels. And on Red Mountain, where the movie stars live, the parties go on every night.

Because of the seasonal rush, some little-known accommodations can be recommended. For otherwise hard-to-get lodging, try the *Limelite*

Fishing near Aspen, Colorado

Lodge, 228 East Cooper Avenue, Aspen 81611; (970) 925–3025 or (800) 433–0832. E-mail: info@limelite.net. Web site: www.limelite.net.

The scene is a Saturday morning in Ashcroft, a remote Colorado ghost town near Aspen. The first sun rays redden the snow. The base of nearby Castle Peak is still mauve. Nothing seems to stir in this winter landscape. Then comes complete daylight, bright, golden, topped by the flawless Colorado sky.

A few human figures assemble down the road from Ashcroft's weather-beaten buildings. Quietly, more people arrive, get together, wait for still others. All carry snowshoes, which will permit an unhurried penetration of this backcountry.

By 9:00 A.M. forty snowshoers stand ready, almost twice as many as the Colorado Mountain Club leader had expected.

Why is old-fashioned *snowshoeing* in again? The reasons are easy to understand. For one thing, snowshoeing is just winter hiking. You don't need any lessons; you learn to walk with your webbed contraptions in

Aspen Highlands

*F*ew people know that at one point in mining history—circa 1879 to 1882—Aspen had a nearby competitor named Ashcroft. Located in an adjacent valley, Ashcroft actually boasted several hotels, numerous bars, a jail, and even a newspaper. (The Ashcroft silver riches attracted silver millionaire H. A. W. Tabor and his pretty young bride.) By 1883, Aspen was famous for its silver wealth, and fortune hunters arrived by the thousands; the inhabitants of Ashcroft, meanwhile, dwindled to about 100 (from 2,600 in its heyday).

And today? Aspen is a total success as a ski resort and Ashcroft is a ghost town. A half-dozen rickety buildings stand there, bleached by sun and wind, pummeled by snow crystals, silently looking up at Castle Peak.

More than a hundred years after the silver boom and bust, Ashcroft holds some value. The modest Ashcroft Ski Touring Center offers thirty miles of cross-country trails. You reach this quiet area by driving west for a $1/2$ mile on Highway 82, and then turning on Castle Creek Road. After 12 miles, you see the cross-country trails. The center's phone number: (970) 925–1971.

minutes. Snowshoeing is healthy; that's why you find many doctors devoted to it.

A sports medicine committee of the American Academy of Surgeons made a study of energy output in various sports. According to one of the cardiologists, snowshoeing proved exceptionally good for the heart. The energy expenditure is at a safe level. Besides, you can rest during the trip and survey the scenery. For all ages, this sport means a better workout for heart and lungs, better muscle tone, better-functioning organs, better digestion, and better circulation.

Cardiologists will tell you that leg veins have valves to maintain circulation. Good muscle tone helps squeeze these veins. The valves permit the blood to go one way, back toward the heart. The better the tone of the leg muscles, the better the circulation, and the less work the heart has to do. Vigorous use of the legs is important whether it is walking, bicycling, skiing, snowshoeing, or any other exercise that uses the legs.

You can go almost anywhere on snowshoes: up the steep winter meadows of the Continental Divide, across the gentle mounds of eastern Colorado, over frozen Lake Dillon, in the dramatic deep-snow regions above Silverton and Ouray. In a survey made by the Sierra Club (which has an active snowshoe chapter), some members explained their own special motivations: "We don't disturb nature on snowshoes. We don't upset ecology."

That's what makes the sport different from skiing, especially the kind done at resorts. Colorado's snowshoers demand no cutting of trees, no bulldozing of ski boulevards, no base lodges noisy with hard-rock music. Modern ski complexes resemble mechanized cities, with lifts of all kinds, $50 ticket prices, and long lines of waiting customers. By contrast, snowshoers never have to stand in a queue; they can move whenever they please and stay warm in the process. Most skiing is now a status symbol; fashion is absent from snowshoeing.

Trivia
A 130-pound woman burns about 340 calories per hour of snowshoeing.

You need only be warm. You can therefore dress in your oldest sweater, the most beat-up windbreaker, a plain cap, an ancient faded sports shirt; no one will judge your income from the pants, either. Just make sure you're not wearing cotton, as it is worse than useless when wet. Any kind of waterproof boot will do, including the kind used for hiking. All this drives down the cost.

Snowshoe equipment is astonishingly reasonable. In a major city like Denver, for instance, you can rent a good pair of shoes with harness. What's the charge for the weekend? Fifteen dollars per day for adult sizes. At an average retail store, you can buy a pair of new snowshoes for a reasonable price.

It's a fairly simple matter to choose a pair of snowshoes. The shape and material may vary, but all the shoes consist of a frame connected to some lacing. The binding is uncomplicated.

Taking It Slow in Aspen

*C*ross-country skiing is better than average in the Aspen area. There are many options. A good place for beginners is at the Aspen Cross Country Center. Trails link a nearby golf course to the Nordic Council trail system (which is free). The center is off of Highway 82 between Aspen and Buttermilk.

Another possibility is the Snowmass Lodge & Club touring center. This facility, too, connects with the free trail system and offers a rental shop and refreshments as well. It's just off the golf course in Snowmass. For more information, call (970) 923–5600.

For a scenic tour, try Ashcroft Ski Touring. The terrain has perfect tracks for diagonal-stride skiing and skating. It also features the Pine Creek Cookhouse. Call (970) 925–1971 for more information.

Aspen Flights

Since the "Aspens" have everything, how about paragliding? The answer is, yes, paragliding, too.

With no prior experience necessary, you can soar with an experienced certified pilot from near the summit of Aspen Mountain. Scheduled on a daily basis, these summer flights are absolutely unforgettable.

*The **Aspen Paragliding School** offers a three-day course of instruction in technique and equipment. All classes are held on Eagle Hill, above Tiehack Cafe.*

For information, call (303) 925–7625 or visit the Web site serioussports.com/ aspenparagliding.

Unless you're in first-rate shape, the first trip will result in some muscle pains. Snowshoes can weigh several pounds, and every step means a workout for your legs. As you start out, the shoes feel awkward, and it will take fifteen minutes until you get used to the wide stance required for walking. (If you step normally, your own legs will be in the way.)

You'll eventually learn to raise your feet as little as possible, and after a half mile you won't step on top of your own shoes. But unlike skiing, where you must become familiar with the technique, snowshoeing requires mostly good legs. If the snow is right, you can use your leg strength—and body weight—for excellent snowshoe descents.

"The scenic rewards are great," says one enthusiast of the West. "All evidence of man is swept under a deep, sound-absorbing blanket of white. Each pine cone, every spruce branch stand out clearly. Nature is always there."

If you want to try a guided snowshoe tour with a naturalist, look no further than the Aspen Center for Environmental Studies (ACES). During the winter, two-hour Fresh Tracks Snowshoe Tours leave daily at 10:00 A.M. and 1:00 P.M. and include a gondola ride, snowshoes, instruction, a

Something Different: Aspen Dogsledding

*The free bus connects you with Snowmass. Here is the traditional spot for Alaskan-style **dogsledding at Krabloonik**. It's an expensive but exciting proposition. The same area serves hikers in summer and fall.*

For more information, call (970) 923–4342, or visit www.krabloonik.com.

guide, a snack, and a complimentary voucher for ACES Naturalist Nights program (see sidebar). Along with viewing stunning scenery in a peaceful alpine setting, tour participants learn about the various kinds of plants and animals that dwell above 10,000 feet. No experience is necessary, but warm clothes and boots are a must. Prices are $39 for adults, $25 for children and teenagers seven to seventeen and senior citizens older than sixty-five. Children younger than seven are not allowed on Fresh Tracks Snowshoe Tours. Call ACES for more information at (970) 925–5756, fax (970) 925–4819, or write 100 Puppy Smith Street, Aspen 81611. E-mail: acesone@rof.net. Web site: www2.aspen. com/dir/mac/sponsors/aces.

If snowshoeing doesn't suit your fancy, consider trying out Buttermilk. Buttermilk? One of the local farmers liked to drink it, hence the name. Buttermilk provides Aspen's easiest skiing. The hills here are gentle—a boon for the novice, and ideal for the lower-intermediate. Buttermilk's undulating terrain caters to older skiers as well. Even the nonathletic can have a ball on these tame slopes. On the other side of the same area, a few trails appeal to hardier types.

Two cafeterias—one on the summit, facing spectacular Pyramid Peak, and one at the bottom—provide perfect places for people who want to rest.

For more information on Buttermilk skiing, contact Aspen Skiing Company, P.O. Box 1248, Aspen 81612; (970) 925–1220 or toll-free (866) 889–8912. Web site: www.aspensnowmass.com.

In another world, the rapid ski lift purrs you upward to 9,000 feet, 10,000, 11,000. At 11,500 you slide off your perch and cross the clearing to a vantage point. You have done it before. But each time you catch your breath. The sight is all grandeur. The white surface ripples downward to your left and right, agleam in the morning sun. What vastness! Your skis

Naturalist Nights

A fun outing for the whole family takes place every Thursday evening at ACES from 7:00 to 8:30 P.M., January through March. Each Naturalist Night brings the outdoors a little closer with slideshows and/or movies and a magical, starlit snowshoe walk. Then you and the kids come in from the cold to the smell of piping hot chocolate and delicious desserts—all for only $5.00 for adults, $2.00 for children and teenagers seven to seventeen, children seven and younger free. Even better, if you've participated in a Fresh Tracks Tour, you can pick up a voucher and get in free!

Snowmass Summers

Snowmass summers are mellow. The rocks are warm and the moss is dry, and there is the promise of anemones, bluebells, gentian, and Indian paintbrush. The hikers move upward through the meadows. In a nearby ranch building, an arts-and-crafts school will be in session. Aspen's music festival is only twenty minutes away.

In summer, Snowmass is a center for picnickers, kayakers, jeepsters, and rock searchers. The climbers will be there, setting out for the Maroon Bells. Soon, the fishermen arrive, resplendent with nets and tackles and flies. They're ready to angle rainbow trout from many creeks. All summer, there are tenderfoot horseback riders, too. Pale city faces shielded by bold cowboy hats, they climb into the saddle and trot upward, their bodies aching for days afterward.

Then come the hunters, stalking deer in the timbered areas and in the mountain cirques.

stir impatiently. Is this descent 3 miles long? Four? More? You can tell from the tiny dots at the bottom—skiers!—that the distance is plenty enough to let you ski to your heart's content.

Suddenly, temptation gets the better of you, and you push yourself off in a flash of poles and shoot down the bowls.

Aspen, Colorado. It could also be Vail. Or Loveland Basin or Winter Park. Width and breadth are a western trademark.

Skiing remains one of Colorado's major attractions: Colorado has more resorts and ski areas than most other states, east or west.

A skilled skier aims with precision; he or she can zip around a standing novice, can pick his or her way around trees, can jump a knoll without falling. If you become good at it, you can ski as fast or as slow as you please and still stop at a moment's notice. (That's the secret, of course—the ability to come to a halt.)

Let no one tell you differently: The snow is much, much better in Colorado's Rockies. It is light, fluffy, easy-to-ski snow, the kind that obeys you. (By contrast, eastern snow means a constant struggle: You must battle ice and more ice.) Eastern landscapes are pleasing to the eyes: gentle, wooded hills; white church spires; rolling terrain. Colorado's western landscapes are grandiose. You feel a powerful impact when you look down into the valleys—far, far down—from the Crested Butte sundeck.

The state's ski meccas are justly famous. None of Colorado's ski resorts

Skier's Locomotion up Aspen Mountain

*W*hen the Aspen Skiing Corp. (now the Aspen Skiing Company) opened its first lifts on Aspen Mountain in 1947, it eliminated one of skiing's biggest drawbacks: climbing the hill.

Skiing fifty years ago was for the truly committed, because if you wanted to enjoy the slopes in winter, you had to hoof it. If skiers were lucky, they could catch a ride with miners up the back side of Aspen Mountain.

A year later, you could ascend Aspen Mountain in a single chair. The trip took more than an hour and you could get a free ticket by helping to "pack" the slopes in the morning. As many as 100 volunteers worked the slopes at the same time.

look alike; each has its special character made up of a dozen variables. Century-old mining towns like Breckenridge and Crested Butte have been revived. Aspen is immense and complex. Vail is a giant in every way, an American St. Moritz. Winter Park serves vacationers during the week and young Denverites on weekends. Loveland Basin and Keystone yield good winter days, made up in unequal portions by sun-stroked faces, pure air, and a snowscape that tugs and pulls.

If you come to this state anytime between late November and April, you should try to ski, even if you've never done it before.

Rifle Falls State Park

*B*efore you head too much farther west, consider making a side trip to **Rifle Falls State Park.** Though small, this unique gem of a state park offers visitors the unlikely opportunity to get downright tropical—or close to it! The triple waterfall plummets down 80 feet past limestone cliffs, keeping the lush vegetation moist. Dark, cool caves beckon to curious explorers, and interpretive signs help explain the phenomena. With its $4.00 per car entry fee, the park makes for a worthwhile side trip and a terrific place to have a family picnic.

From Aspen, take SR 82 north about 41 miles. In Glenwood Springs turn left onto 6th Street then left onto North River Drive, following signs to I–70 west.

Take I–70 west about 25$\frac{1}{2}$ miles to the Rifle exit. Go north on SR 13 for 3 miles. Turn right on SR 325 and drive 9$\frac{8}{10}$ miles. Call (970) 625–1607 or write Rifle Gap, 0050 County Road 219, Rifle 81650. E-mail: rifle@csn.net. Web site: parks.state.co.us/rifle_falls/ index.asp.

For more information, contact Colorado Ski Country USA, 1560 Broadway, Suite 2000, Denver 80202; (303) 837–0793. Web site: www.ski colorado.org.

Peach Harvests

Noon at **Palisade**, Colorado. The golden peach of the sun has already climbed to the top of the trees, which stand out against a poster-blue sky. You've been in the **Clark Family Peach Orchards** since seven that morning, up and down the ladders. The guys in Denver's health clubs (pumping iron indoors) should envy you out there in the fresh country air. You've gulped big amounts of it, breathing deeply. No pollution. Your nostrils take in the Elberta peach bouquet.

You reach rhythmically for the warm, ripe fruit, which you plop into a sack hanging from your shoulders. When it's full, it weighs forty or fifty pounds, enough for the waiting baskets.

Trivia

Palisade is also known for its vineyards, which are some of the best in the United States. For a flavorful outing, try out one of the free winery tours and tastings. Check out www. palisadecoc.com for details.

Your arms must stretch, your trunk must rotate, you keep bending. Your legs withstand the extra load; you rejoice in the climbing and descending from and to terra firma. In fact, you've gotten your second wind. Despite the heat, you accelerate before lunchtime. The bushels add up. The mood in the orchards is relaxed.

The pleasures of working a peach harvest should not be underestimated. When other people must slave in office cubicles in dirty cities, some folks are outdoors, in the clean, sweet-smelling orchards, getting paid for being in touch with trees and leaves and fruit. This is a pretty world for summer sport, with the colors lingering behind your eyelids for a long time.

At Palisade, on Colorado's Western Slope, you're into Elbertas. A collegian from Colorado Springs who has come to Palisade ever since he was a high schooler feels nostalgic about it. He says, "Peach time reminds me of homemade ice cream, or a secret treasure in the lunch box, a tantalizing centerpiece, or even a long drive back from the orchards amid bushels of tree-ripened Elbertas, munching on the way and saving the pits to plant."

Suddenly, it's late August, and the 310 growers in Palisade (which is 238 miles west of Denver) must round up some 4,000 harvesters to empty some 500,000 trees. The need can be so great at this juncture that the orchardists enlist the help of relatives, transients, hoboes (who arrive on freight trains), high school kids (nearby schools close for the occasion), laborers from Mexico, and university students, as well as yearly regulars headed by crew chiefs, who come to western Colorado for those two weeks.

In Colorado alone the bounty amounts to some 250,000 bushels. Because much of the harvesting is still done by hand, it takes an army of people to harvest, sort, and crate the peaches. This creates an incredible number of temporary jobs.

Negative aspects? Pay is minimal, by the bushel. Unless you're in good physical shape, you'll find it hard to scale ladders all day, to stretch your limbs until they ache. The string of your filled harvest sack bites without mercy into your shoulders or neck. You keep lugging forty-eight-pound bushels.

The work guarantees to make almost anyone lose weight. But you can't compare it to a tennis game in a breeze. In fact, some orchards—especially in those sun-baked, parched, wrinkled Colorado plateaus—get extremely hot. The canopy of trees is pierced by the sun's rays. Count on sweating a lot. You're only cool at 7:00 A.M. when you start, and in some parts of the country at 6:00 P.M. when you finish. (The Palisade Chamber of Commerce crows about the "354 days of sunshine.")

Some comers also forget about the peach fuzz. You won't feel it for a few hours, but after a day it stings. (Some people are allergic to the fuzz and break out in hives.) Talcum can help the average harvester. But it remains a problem.

Benefits? You can easily make friends, learn about other harvests, get tips on where to split to next. In Palisade, the Orchard Cafe is full of beer drinkers at night, hatching plots for the balance of the year and the coming seasons. Colorado peach harvesting is a trip that usually leads to another trip.

From Denver, drive west on I-70 toward Grand Junction until you see the Palisade turnoff. Contact Clark Family Orchards at 3887 G Road, Palisade 81526; (970) 464-5385, Web site: www. palisadecoc.com/fruit.html. Another useful contact: Palisade Chamber of Commerce, P.O. Box 729, Palisade 81526; (970) 464-7458. Fax: (970) 464-4757. Web site: www.palisadecoc.com.

If picking peaches sounds too tough for your tastes, perhaps you'd have more fun simply watching how fruit was harvested 100 years ago. You can do just that at **Cross Orchards Historic Site,** the location of the **Museum of Western Colorado's Living History Farm.** Located in Grand Junction, the farm is a site listed on the National Register of Historic Places. And a tour of the facility—especially with children—can be memorable. Here are ancient tractors and other weather-beaten farm machinery, plus old tools. Here you can see the first gas pumps (offering gasoline at fourteen cents a gallon). Costumed Cross Orchards staff members and volunteers demonstrate weaving, candle making, and blacksmithing circa 1896. A narrow-gauge railroad is still in place, and your kids are allowed to climb into the caboose.

The former Cross apple orchards can be visited from Memorial Day to Labor Day, sometimes even through October. The address is 3073 Patterson (F) Road, Grand Junction 81504; the phone number is (970) 434–9814. Fax (970) 242–3960.

Before you leave this part of Colorado, be sure to stop at the **Colorado National Monument,** known for its steep plateaus, sheer drop-offs, and craggy rock spires. If you're into cycling, a great way to experience the grandeur of this place is to ride the Rim Rock Bike Route. This 33-mile loop follows paved roads through the stark and beautiful scenery, with some challenging climbing—2,300 feet of it!

The view when you reach the top of the plateau is well worth the effort. From your open-air perch you'll absorb more of the Colorado scenery and atmosphere than those who pass you in automobiles. Use extra caution when passing through the short tunnels on this scenic ride. Take a few minutes to stop at the visitor center before your final descent into the town of Fruita. From there, Grand Junction is just a few miles away along the Colorado River. Expect the ride to take about three hours.

To reach Colorado National Monument, follow Monument Road out of downtown Grand Junction, which will take you to the entry gate. Pick up a map there. Fees are $2.00 per person or $4.00 per vehicle. For more information, call (970) 858–3617 or write Colorado National Monument, Fruita 81521. Web site: www.gjcolorado.com/cnm/.

PLACES TO STAY IN THE WESTERN MOUNTAINS

ASPEN
Aspen Mountain Lodge (moderate to expensive); 311 West Main Street; (970) 925–7650

Boomerang Lodge (one of Aspen's oldest motels; close to restaurants; expensive to deluxe); 500 West Hopkins; (970) 925–3416

Limelite Lodge (small-size inn; inexpensive to deluxe); 228 East Cooper Avenue; (800) 433–0832

BRECKENRIDGE
Bed & Breakfast on North Main Street (expensive); 303 North Main Street; (970) 453–2975 or (800) 795–2975

Evans House (moderate); 102 South French Street; (970) 453–5509

Hunt Placer Inn (expensive); 275 Ski Hill Road; (970) 453–7573

River Mountain Lodge (expensive to deluxe); 100 South Park Avenue; (970) 453–4711 or (800) 627–3766

Swan Mountain Inn (inexpensive to expensive); 16172 Colorado 9 at Swan Mountain Road; (970) 453–7903 or (800) 578–3687

DILLON
Best Western Inn (expensive); 652 Lake Dillon Drive; (970) 468–2341

Dillon Inn (moderate); 708 Anemone Trail; (970) 262–0801

Four Points Hotel (Summit County; moderate to deluxe); 560 Silverthorne Lane (Silverthorne); (888) 265–9330

Silver Inn (inexpensive); 691 Blue River Parkway; (970) 513–0104

Ski Tip Lodge (one of Colorado's first lodges; great atmosphere; a little cramped; make reservations far in advance; moderate to expensive); on Montezuma Road (Keystone); (970) 468–4202 or (800) 222–0188

GEORGETOWN
Alpine Hideaway Bed & Breakfast (has good views of Georgetown; expensive to deluxe); 2045 Blue Bird Drive; (800) 490–9011

Georgetown Motor Inn (well-established, peaceful motor inn; a modest restaurant on premises; inexpensive to moderate); 1100 Rose; (303) 569–3201, (800) 884–3201

Hardy House Inn (moderate); 605 Brownell Street; (800) 490–4802

Mad Creek Bed & Breakfast (inexpensive to moderate); 167 Park Avenue (in Empire); (303) 569–2003

GLENWOOD SPRINGS
Hot Springs Lodge (across from Glenwood pool; moderate to expensive); 415 Sixth Street; (970) 945–6571, (800) 537–7946

Hotel Colorado (historic hotel; well-restored; moderate); 526 Pine; (970) 945–6511, (800) 544–3998

Redstone Inn (inexpensive to expensive); 82 Redstone Boulevard (Redstone); (800) 748–2524

GRANT
The Tumbling River Ranch (large swimming pool; outstanding stables; a stay here guarantees a quality experience; deluxe); (800) 654-8770

IDAHO SPRINGS
H & H Motor Lodge (simple, clean motel; inexpensive to moderate); 2445 Colorado Boulevard; (303) 567-2838, (800) 445-2893

Heritage Inn (quiet motel; within walking distance of cafes; moderate); 2622 Colorado Boulevard; (303) 567-4473

PLACES TO EAT IN THE WESTERN MOUNTAINS

ASPEN
Cantina (Mexican, American; moderate to expensive); 411 East Main Street; (970) 925-3663

Paradise Bakery & Café (delicious muffins, homemade ice cream; inexpensive); 500 West Main Street; (970) 920-1444

Takah Sushi (deluxe); 420 East Hyman Avenue; (970) 925-8588

Ute City Bar and Grill (centrally located; moderate to expensive); 501 East Hyman Avenue; (970) 920-4699

Wienerstube (continental; a small restaurant; moderate to expensive); 633 East Hyman Avenue; (970) 925-3357

BRECKENRIDGE
Breckenridge Brewery (ribs, fish & chips, fajitas; moderate); 600 South Main Street; (970) 453-1550

Cafe Alpine (continental; deluxe); 106 East Adams; (970) 453-8218

Poirrier's Cajun Cafe (expensive to deluxe); 244 South Main Street; (970) 453-1877

St. Bernard Inn (steak, seafood; extremely busy in season; moderate to expensive); 103 South Main Street; (970) 453-2572

DILLON
Ristorante Al Lago (higher than average prices; veal, seafood, linguini; expensive); 240 Lake Dillon Drive; (970) 468-6111

Silverheels Southwest Grill (moderate to expensive); Wilderness Road off I-70 exit 205; (970) 468-2926

GEORGETOWN
The Happy Cooker (unpretentious, homestyle American restaurant; outdoors in summer; inexpensive to moderate); 412 Sixth Street; (303) 569-3166

GLENWOOD SPRINGS
Daily Bread Cafe (sandwiches, salads, soups; inexpensive to moderate); 729 Grand Avenue; (970) 945-6253

Dos Hombres (Mexican; moderate); 51783 Highway 6; (970) 928-0490

Florindo's (Italian; moderate to expensive); 721 Grand Avenue; (970) 945-1245

The Fireside (steak, prime rib, chicken; moderate); 51701 US 6/24; (970) 945-6613

Los Desperados (Mexican; moderate); 55 Mel Rey Road; (970) 945-6878

Mancinelli's Pizza (inexpensive); 172 West Sixth Street; (970) 928-9594

Rivers (seafood, wild game; moderate to expensive); 2525 South Grand Avenue; (970) 928-8813

IDAHO SPRINGS
BeauJo's (famous homemade pizza; moderate); 1517 Miner Street; (303) 567-4376

The Buffalo Restaurant and Bar (historical; pizza, barbecue and Mexican; not exactly a gourmet restaurant, but adequate; inexpensive to moderate); 1617 Miner Street; (303) 573-2729

VAIL

Half Moon Saloon (Mexican, American, vegetarian options; moderate); 2161 North Frontage Road West; (970) 476–4314

Left Bank (French; expensive); 183 Gore Creek Drive; (970) 476–3696

Pazzo's Pizzeria (calzones, pizza, moderate); 122 East Meadows Drive No. 9; (970) 476–9026

Sweet Basil (Italian; expensive to deluxe); 193 East Gore Creek Drive; (970) 476–2204

The Tyrolean (wild game, veal; terrific, expensive Austrian food; deluxe); 400 East Meadow Drive; (970) 476–2204

Other Attractions Worth Seeing in the Western Mountains

ASPEN

Aspen Historical Society Museum, *(970) 925–3721*

Independence Pass *(SR 82, closed in winter), no phone*

DILLON

Copper Mountain Resort Ski Area, *(800) 458–8386*

GEORGETOWN

Loveland Ski Area, *(800) 736–3SKI*

GLENWOOD

White River National Forest, *(970) 945–2521*

IDAHO SPRINGS

Colorado School of Mines, Edgar Mine, *(303) 567–2911*

Western Mountains General Information Resources

ASPEN

Aspen Chamber Resort Association,
425 Rio Grande Place, 81611; (970) 925–1940 or (800) 262–7736
Web site: www.aspenchamber.org

BRECKENRIDGE

Breckenridge Resort Chamber,
311 South Ridge Street; P.O. Box 1909, 80424; (970) 453–2913;
fax (970) 453–7238; E-mail: gobreck@gobreck.com
Web site: www.gobreck.com

GEORGETOWN

Georgetown Chamber of Commerce,
P.O. Box 444, 80444-0444; (303) 569–2888 or (800) 472–8230;
fax (303) 569–2705; E-mail: markg@georgetowncolorado.com
Web site: www.georgetowncolorado.com

GLENWOOD SPRINGS

Glenwood Springs Chamber Resort Association,
1102 Grand Avenue, 81601; (888) 4–GLENWOOD; fax (970) 945–1531
E-mail: info@glenwoodchamber.com; Web site: www.glenwoodchamber.com

IDAHO SPRINGS

City of Idaho Springs,
P.O. Box 907, 80452; (303) 567–4421; fax (303) 567–4955
E-mail: cis@idahospringsco.com; Web site: www.idahospringsco.com

PALISADE

Palisade Chamber of Commerce,
P.O. Box 729, 81526; (970) 464–7458; fax (970) 464–4757
Web site: www.palisadecoc.com

VAIL

Vail Valley Tourism and Convention Bureau,
100 East Meadow Drive, 81657; (970) 476–1000 or (800) 525–3875
Web site: www.visitvailvalley.com

Southern Colorado

Colorado Springs and Beyond

Contrary to rumors, mountain driving is not especially dangerous or tricky. According to the Colorado State Patrol, most accidents actually happen in the flat, straight stretches at high speeds.

But the stranger to winter is better off knowing a few special driving precautions and tricks. Hence, some thoughts are in order:

• When renting a car in winter, insist on special snow tires, even if the pavement is dry. Also, it's better to carry tire chains unnecessarily than to be caught without them; they are essential in blizzards. Front-wheel drive is preferable for better traction.

• Before starting out on any extended trip in wintertime, the following safety equipment should be checked: brakes, headlights and tail-lights, exhaust system, windshield wipers, defrosters, heaters, and tools. Toss in a space blanket, high-energy food that is not perishable, flares, gloves, a hat . . .

• Starting slowly on snow provides better traction and prevents spinning of wheels or skidding sideways into parked cars or other vehicles or objects. On a slick surface, start in second gear; this keeps the car's wheels from spinning.

• When driving in a fog or snowstorm, you get better visibility by using the lower headlight beam. The upper headlight beam tends to reflect back off the fog and blind you.

• Whenever visibility becomes so poor, due to fog or snow, that it is impossible to see more than a few feet ahead, it is best to pull off the road. Clean the windshield or wait until the weather eases up.

• Car heaters draw in fresh air from the outside. Vehicles should never be parked directly behind another car that has the motor running.

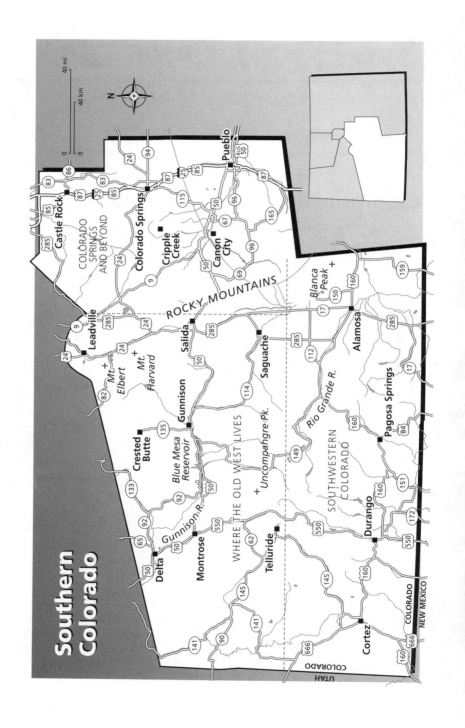

Southern Colorado

AUTHOR'S FAVORITE ATTRACTIONS IN SOUTHERN COLORADO

Great Sand Dunes National Monument, (719) 378–2312, www.nps.gov/grsa

Garden of the Gods, (719) 634–6666, www.gardenofgods.com

Seven Falls, (719) 632–0752, www.sevenfalls.com

Royal Gorge Bridge and Park, (719) 275–7507 or (888) 333–5597, www.royalgorgebridge.com

The Spa at Pagosa Springs, (970) 264–5910 or (800) 832–5523, www.subee.com/spa

Mollie Kathleen Gold Mine, (719) 689–2466, www.goldminetours.com

Mesa Verde National Park, (970) 529–4465, www.nps.gov/meve

Camp Hale, (970) 827–5715 or (970) 827–9343, www.camphale.org

Manitou and Pikes Peak Railway, (719) 685–5401, www.cograilway.com

Shelf Road, (719) 275–0631, www.co.blm.gov/rectouring.htm

- When roads are wet and the temperature drops to 32°F or below, the surface will become icy. Extreme caution is indicated. A single driver can start a chain of mass collisions on ice.

- Get the feel of the road when pavements are slippery by trying brakes occasionally while driving slowly and away from traffic.

- As the temperature rises, ice (and, to a lesser degree, snow) becomes much slicker. For example, at 20 miles per hour when the temperature is 32°F, stopping distance on ice without tire chains or snow tires is 250 feet. When the temperature is at zero, stopping distance is 110 feet. The difference of 140 feet might well cause a serious accident.

- By stopping slowly, the driver can prevent skidding and come to a safer halt. If your vehicle starts to skid or the wheels lock, release the brake pressure. Pump the brakes; that is, apply the brakes lightly and intermittently. This is especially important with old-model cars. A minimum of pressure should be used. Steady, even braking does the trick. Or do you have ABS or disc brakes? If so, just increase the pressure steadily until your car slows down.

- Keep your windshield and windows clear, making sure you can see danger in time to avoid trouble. Windshield-wiper blades should not be too worn; they should be up to the task of removing rain or snow without streaking. Also, the defroster should function efficiently. Ensure good visibility in the rear by removing the snow and ice from the back window when necessary.

- Occasionally a patch of ice will remain on a curve or other shaded spot after the rest of the road has been cleared. Be on the lookout for these ice patches.

- A thorough check of the exhaust system should be made at regular intervals; possible leaks could cause a tragedy. (Carbon monoxide poisoning is a deadly driving hazard during wintertime.) It is a good idea to leave at least one window slightly open when driving in cold weather.

• Weather and road conditions in Colorado's mountains are subject to abrupt changes. It is possible to get a report that a certain area is clear, yet you arrive there two or three hours later to find a snowstorm in progress or the highways icy and snow covered. The reverse is also true, and adverse weather conditions often clear up in a short time.

The *Devil's Head National Recreation Trail,* in the Rampart Range west of the little community of Sedalia (south of Denver), is one of the state's most scenic trails. It got its name from the red rock formations that stick out like two horns. You walk up through deep pine forests interspersed with aspen, past giant red cliffs. The trail's length—just 1³⁄₈ miles—doesn't sound like much; it climbs steeply, though, and includes a 1,000-foot vertical elevation gain. (The summit is at 9,747 feet, the parking lot at 8,800 feet.)

Along the way, you get views of the "fourteeners" (peaks over 14,000 feet high) and the Great Plains. Benches line the uphill paths for the tired. Motorized vehicles are outlawed in the ascent to Devil's Head.

Driving directions? From Denver, take Santa Fe (US 85) south to Sedalia (13 miles); turn west toward Deckers (SR 67) for 10 miles and make another left turn onto the Rampart Range Road (County Road 5); go another 10 miles until you see the Devil's Head sign. For more information: Pikes National Forest, 1920 Valley Drive, Pueblo 81008; (719) 545–8737. E-mail: gvanover@fs.fed.us. Web site: www.fs.fed.us/r2/psicc.

Trivia

The Devil's Head Lookout Tower at the end of the Devils Head National Recreation Trail rests on the highest point in the Rampart Range. It is the last operational lookout on the Front Range.

En route from Denver to Colorado Springs via the interstate, you may see a modest sign that says LARKSPUR. Few travelers have ever heard of it. Even some Denverites are unfamiliar with this hamlet.

Yet, on weekends from mid-June through July, tiny Larkspur comes alive with a bang. Cannon shots can be heard from afar. When your car draws closer to the hillside, the cannons are followed by medieval trumpets, played in unison.

For more than twenty years, the zany, lively *Colorado Renaissance Festival* has entertained summer visitors in its offbeat location above Larkspur on a wooded Colorado hillside, part theater, part learning

Colorado Renaissance Festival;
Larkspur; June and July;
(303) 688–6010;
www.coloradorenaissance.com

Pagosa Springs Winter Fest;
second weekend in February;
(800) 252–2204;
www.pagosa-springs.com

Music and Blossom Festival;
Cañon City; mid-March;
(719) 275–7200 or (800) 876–7922;
www.canoncitychamber.com

Royal Gorge Rodeo, Cañon City;
(719) 275–4784 or (719) 275–6294;
www.canoncitychamber.com

Donkey Derby, Cripple Creek;
last full weekend in June;
(877) 858–GOLD;
www.cripple-creek.co.us

**Cattlemen's Days Rodeo & County
Fair;** Gunnison; mid-July;
(970) 641–1501;
www.gunnison-co.com

Pikes Peak or Bust Rodeo;
Colorado Springs; mid-August;
(719) 635–3547;
www.coloradosprings-travel.com

Boom Days and Burro Race;
Leadville; first full weekend of August;
(719) 486–2997;
www.leadville.com/boomdays

Colorado State Fair;
Pueblo Fairgrounds; late August–
early September;
(719) 566–0530;
www.coloradosfair.com

Colorado Springs Balloon Classic;
Labor Day weekend; (719) 471–4833;
www.ballooning.org/ballooning/events/
co-springs.html

Durango Cowboy Gathering;
Durango; first week of October;
(970) 247–0312 or (800) 525–8855;
www.durango.org

experience, part petting zoo for children, part commerce. The Renaissance theme begins when you enter the walled compound and you're greeted as "My Lord" or "My Lady." Artisans galore demonstrate their craft: blacksmiths hammer away, glassblowers regale onlookers with their art, potters have brought their wheels, leather workers show their stuff. Bands of costumed musicians wander up the mountainside. Harpists, flutists, bagpipers, and minstrel singers materialize and harmonize.

Several times a day, "King Henry" and his "Court" introduce you to knights jousting on horseback at a gallop, doing tricks with their lances. The stages are busy with storytellers and merrymakers; the pubs dispense barrels of beer and huge turkey legs. Processions of celebrities—Shakespeare, Anne Boleyn—march among the visitors while, a few yards away, you can be a medieval archer or knife thrower or dart artist.

Encounter the unexpected: Youngsters ride real camels and elephants; a few steps away, jugglers and puppet masters dazzle the onlookers. A good time is had by everyone.

All this against the backdrop of—and amid—Colorado's mountains. No charge for parking weekends June through July. To reach Larkspur, take exit 172 from I–25 and follow the signs. Open 10:00 A.M. to 6:30 P.M. Saturday and Sunday. Admission costs $13.95 for adults and teenagers thirteen and older, $6.00 for children five to twelve, children four and younger free. Discount tickets can be purchased at any King Soopers (a local grocery store chain). For more information: 409F South Wilcox Street, Castle Rock 80104; (303) 688–6010. E-mail: pfrank@ coloradorenaissance.com. Web site: www.coloradorenaissance. com.

Trivia

The Air Force Academy's Cadet Chapel received a 1996 American Institute of Architects' award. The chapel conducts services for Protestant, Catholic and Jewish worshippers.

A ten-minute drive south of Larkspur, on the same little Country Road 105, you will suddenly come face-to-face with **Palmer Lake.** Almost no travel guide mentions it. Most people bypass it via speedy I–25. Palmer Lake used to be busy and important; now it's almost forgotten. A few lost souls are fishing here. Others walk around the idyllic lake on a footpath or take their young children to the small playground. Mountains rise on all sides. Traffic is minimal. It's a fine place to relax. For more information: Town Offices, P.O. Box 208, 54 Valley Crescent, Palmer Lake 80133; (719) 481–2953. E-mail: townoffices@ci. palmer-lake.co.us. Web site: www.ci.palmer-lake.co.us.

For those who like to hike or bike, the 15-mile **Santa Fe Regional Trail,** one of the largest continuous trails in El Paso County, begins at **Palmer Lake Recreation Area.** It goes through the town of Monument to the south, ending at the southern boundary of the **United States Air Force Academy.** For more information: El Paso County Parks, 2002 Creek Crossing, Colorado Springs 80906; (719) 520–6375. Fax (719) 520–6389. E-mail: prkweb@co.el-paso.co.us. Web site: www.co.el-paso. co.us/Parks.

The Air Force Academy is one of Colorado's most visited landmarks. Whether you hike, bike or drive, you should consider a stop at the academy's visitor center, located at exit 150B off I–25. A nature trail and the attractive **Cadet Chapel** appeal to the curious passerby. Eyes are invariably drawn upward by the chapel's seventeen silver-hued spires that sweep to heights of more than 150 feet. Completed in 1963, the chapel, considered to be the architectural centerpiece of the academy's campus, holds Protestant, Catholic, and Jewish services. It is open Monday through Saturday, 9:00 A.M. to 5:00 P.M.; Sundays from 1:00 to 5:00 P.M. Sunday services are open to all; call (719) 333–4515 for times.

When visiting the academy, request a map at the gate. The visitor center is open from 9:00 A.M. to 5:00 P.M. daily in winter, and until 6:00 P.M. in summer. For more information: (719) 333–8723. Web site: www.gazette.com/military/academy.html.

Not far from the U.S. Air Force Academy, you'll discover your next stop—the *ProRodeo Hall of Fame and Museum of the American Cowboy,* which presents the West's unique cowboy heritage in a facility that is both entertaining and educational. The cowboy played a vital role in opening the West to the expansion of the nineteenth century, and his reputation for courage and individualism has become part of our national folklore and has shaped the American character.

Families with children will enjoy the outdoor corral with its live animals. Inside, dioramas and exhibits of well-displayed saddles, boots, buckles, spurs, ropes, chaps, branding equipment, and other paraphernalia await examination, all telling the story of rodeo's history in this country. Rodeo as a sport comes alive through the mementos of America's major rodeo champions.

The visitor can learn about such colorful rodeo champs as bull rider Warren G. "Freckles" Brown, reputed to be the oldest man in Pro-Rodeo history to win a riding event. His long career was interrupted by a broken neck, as well as by World War II. With typical spirit during wartime parachute jumps into China, Brown put on a rodeo using army mules and native cattle and declared himself the Orient's all-around champion of 1942.

Over the years, rules and equipment were standardized, judging was streamlined, prize money increased, and the freewheeling entertainment of the 1800s evolved into the modern sport of professional rodeo.

Here the visitor can learn the fine points of saddle bronc riding and how to judge a rider's performance—and can get the jolting sensation, through film with stereo sound, of what it's like to ride a bucking Brahma bull. Other films trace the historical development of rodeo.

The ProRodeo Hall of Fame is located just north of Colorado Springs on I–25 at exit 147. Hours are 9:00 A.M. to 5:00 P.M. daily except for major holidays. A modest fee is charged to help defray expenses of the non-profit museum. Call (719) 528–4764 or write 101 Pro Rodeo Drive, Colorado Springs 80919. Web site: www.prorodeo.com.

The Garden of the Gods was once sacred ground to Native Americans.

The wonders of nature blend together at the *Garden of the Gods* in Colorado Springs to create one of the most varied natural settings in Colorado. Established as a free city park in 1909, the almost 1,370 acres are filled with silent and spectacular red sandstone rock formations, including Gateway Rocks, Cathedral Spires, and the Balanced Rock. Grasslands meet mountain forests to provide contrasts of scenic beauty. A common resident of the park is the great horned owl, whose keen, light-gathering eyes and superior hearing make it an effective nighttime hunter.

Hike, picnic, and horseback ride to fully appreciate the park's natural beauty. But most of all, bring your camera and photograph these wonders (especially at sunset or sunrise when the low sun accents the naturally colorful redstone).

The park itself is open daily from November 1 through April 30 from 5:00 A.M. to 9:00 P.M. and May 1 through October 31 from 5:00 A.M. to 11:00 P.M. The visitors center is open daily from 9:00 A.M. to 5:00 P.M. The center offers free color maps of the park and free entrance to the *Museum of Natural and Cultural History.* Arrive via exit 146 off I–25. Go west on Garden of the Gods Road, and then south on Thirtieth Street. The Visitor Center will be on your left at Gateway Road. For more information: Garden of the Gods Visitor Center, 1805 North Thirtieth Street, Colorado Springs 80904; (719) 634–6666. Web site: www.gardenofgods.com.

If you want to vacation in the lap of luxury, consider the five-star *Broadmoor,* which has 14,110-foot Pikes Peak for a backdrop. The Broadmoor actually began in the 1850s with a Silesian count. He hoped to create another Monte Carlo against the backdrop of Colorado's mountainscape. Eventually, two Philadelphians, Charles Tutt and Spencer Penrose, took over. They'd gotten rich in Cripple Creek mining and real estate; as world travelers, they knew what they wanted—a regal, Renaissance-style hotel.

Cheyenne Mountain Zoo

*A*bove the Broadmoor resort, you can visit the **Cheyenne Mountain Zoo.** *The giraffes, bears, elk, deer, penguins, and other creatures are kept in their natural environment. To reach the zoo, from I–25 go south on Nevada Avenue. Turn right on Lake Avenue. Turn onto Mirada Road and follow signs. For more information call (719) 633–9925 or visit the Web site: www.pikes-peak.com/Zoo.*

The Broadmoor's doors opened on June 29, 1918; among several nota-bles, the first to register was John D. Rockefeller, Jr. Since that day, there has been a stream of industrialists, diplomats, movie moguls, film stars, and titled ladies and gentlemen. They mingle nicely nowadays with anyone who can afford this pricey, year-round retreat. It is the largest, plushest, and most elegant in Colorado, offering every conceiv-able amenity.

The (deluxe) Broadmoor isn't for economy travelers; bring lots of trav-eler's checks or your best credit card. For more information: Broad-moor, 1 Lake Avenue, Colorado Springs 80906; (719) 634–7711 or (800) 634–7711. Fax (719) 577–5738. E-mail: reservations@broadmoor.com. Web site: www.broadmoor.com.

Seven Falls is ten driving minutes west of the Broadmoor resort. "The Grandest Mile of Scenery in Colorado" lives up to its slogan: A 1,000-foot-high granite canyon leads to seven waterfalls flanked by healthy forests of juniper, blue spruce, Douglas fir, and ponderosa pine. Not far from the dramatic, perpendicular "pillars of Hercules," you can climb several hundred steep steps to platforms from which you view these scenic wonders.

You get to Seven Falls via Cheyenne Boulevard and Mesa (exit 140B off I–25). Hours vary from 8:00 A.M. to 11:00 P.M. in midsummer to 9:00

A Tour of NORAD

*C*heyenne Mountain *houses the* bomb-proof headquarters of the **North American Aerospace Defense Com-mand, NORAD.** *Here, some 100 com-puters and more than a million miles of communications lines monitor the hori-zon for enemy missile attacks. More than 1,700 people populate a small city deep inside this hollowed-out moun-tain, where the fifteen buildings are supported by 1,319 steel springs weigh-ing 1,000 pounds each. Rock reservoirs hold 6 million gallons of water, and steel blast doors protect the complex. (In case of nuclear attack, these 25,000-pound gates can be closed in 30 seconds.)*

Please note: *Public briefings are available only on Fridays at 12:30 P.M. These briefings are free of charge and open to the public but must be booked two months in advance. Call for reser-vations and details about necessary paperwork. The 1¼-hour multimedia presentation does not take visitors into the mountain (this would be a security breach). For more information: CMOC/CSP, 1 NORAD Road, Suite 101-213, CMAFS 80914-6066, (719) 474–2238/2239. E-mail: CMAFS.Tours@ cheyennemountain.af. mil. Web site: www. cheyennemoutain. af.mil/cmoc.*

Llamas!

Short llama treks are the perfect way to see Colorado Springs and its environs; not to worry, the llama does all the real work. That's right, you explore trails lined with wildflowers, spacious meadows, and icy streams while the llama carries the packs with your lunches. All that remains for you is to breathe in the pure mountain air and take in the vistas.

One company, **Adventures Out West,** offers llama "walkabouts." Their planned hikes range from easy to challenging and last two to four hours. For more information write P.O. Box 38512, Colorado Springs 80937 or call (719) 578–0935 or (800) 755–0935. Fax (719) 444–0965. Web site: www. adventuresoutwest.com.

A.M. to 4:00 P.M. in winter; call for details. Admission costs $6.50 for adults and $4.00 for children; slightly more at night. For more information: Seven Falls Company, P.O. Box 118, Colorado Springs 80901; (719) 632–0752. Fax (719) 632–0781. Web site: www. sevenfalls.com.

The year was 1806; the discoverer of Colorado Springs's "Great Mountain" was Lieutenant Zebulon Montgomery Pike. Neither he nor any of his party got even close to the summit, due to bad weather and perhaps a lack of planning. At that time, it certainly wasn't conceivable that one of America's most unusual railroads ever constructed would carry thousands of persons to its summit.

Today, a visit to Colorado Springs can be enhanced by a trip on the country's highest railroad to the summit of famous Pikes Peak. The **Manitou and Pikes Peak Cog Railway,** which is 46,158 feet long, climbs from an elevation of 6,571 feet at the Manitou Springs station to one of 14,110 feet at the summit. This is a vertical gain of 7,539 feet, or an average of 846 feet per mile. Actually, the distance is longer than any covered by the famous cogwheel rails in Switzerland.

Trivia

Some of the bristlecone pine trees along the Manitou and Pikes Peak Cog Railway are estimated to be almost 2,000 years old, making them among the oldest living things on earth.

Along the entire route you'll be treated to a continuous panorama of scenery. At the 11,578-foot level, the trains emerge from a sea of quaking aspen into the windswept stretches of timberline and climb into the Saddle, where you get an unparalleled view of Manitou Springs and of the Garden of the Gods in the valley below. You also see the vast expanses of the Great Plains stretch toward the horizon.

132

The Manitou and Pikes Peak Cog Railroad

On clear days, it is possible to spot Denver 75 miles to the north of Colorado Springs and the dramatic Sangre de Cristo Mountains in southern Colorado. The view of the west is astounding; mile upon mile of snowcapped giants rise into the blue Colorado sky.

Be sure to leave time to peruse the offerings at Steamer Stop Shop (clothing and curios) at the Manitou Springs Station. You can grab a bite to eat at the Cog Wheel Café, also at the station, or purchase a box lunch to eat while on the train. The Cog Railway runs from April through November. Tickets run about $25 for adults, $13 for children three to eleven, children younger than three free if held on a lap throughout the ride. Reservations are required. The round-trip takes three hours and ten minutes; call for departure times. Take exit 141 (US 24) off I–25. Head west on US 24 for 4 miles to the Manitou Springs

Some Little-Known Facts About Manitou Springs

- *It was actually from Manitou Springs's mineral springs that Colorado Springs got its name.*

- *"Mantiou" is a Native American word for "Great Spirit."*

- *Native Americans attributed supernatural powers to Manitou Springs's waters and temporarily reserved the surrounding area as a sanctuary.*

Mining experts considered the creek worthless despite frequent reports of gold; still, novice prospectors, mining with pitchforks, eventually developed the "300-million-dollar cow pasture."

exit. Go west on Manitou Avenue for 1½ miles. Turn left on Ruxton Avenue. The station is ¾ mile up. For more information: Manitou and Pikes Peak Cog Railway, 515 Ruxton Avenue, P.O. Box 351, Manitou Springs 80829; (719) 685–5401. Fax (719) 685–9033. E-mail: cogtrain@iex.net. Web site: www.cograilway.com.

Back in 1891, the **Cripple Creek** gold strike proved to be the last major gold rush in North America. Within a few years, those mines in the mountains west of Colorado Springs yielded almost a billion dollars' worth of the valuable mineral. By 1900, Cripple Creek grew to some 50,000 inhabitants. The miners could patronize seventy-five saloons, forty grocery stores, seventeen churches, and eight newspapers. Every day a dozen passenger trains steamed into the depot. Eventually, 500 gold mines operated in the area. Some 8,000 men brought on a gambling, carousing, whoring boom.

Ironically, the man who discovered the first gold vein sold his claim for $500 and proceeded to drink it all away. Colorado Springs owes part of its existence to the prospectors. In time, celebrities came and went. Adventurer Lowell Thomas was born in nearby Victor, now nearly a ghost town. Groucho Marx once drove a grocery wagon in Cripple Creek. Jack Dempsey, for a brief bout a miner, trained and boxed in the region. Financier Bernard Baruch worked as a telegrapher here. Teddy Roosevelt, after a Cripple Creek visit, told the world that "the scenery bankrupts the English language." The politicians arrived in droves to see for themselves.

By and by, gold prices dropped. Production began to slip. The miners scattered. By 1920, fewer than 5,000 people lived here.

Some Little-Known Facts About Cripple Creek

• In its heyday, the Cripple Creek area produced $25 million in gold in one year.

• Famous Cripple Creek workers included Jack Johnson and Jack Dempsey. Dempsey once fought a bloody, drawn-out battle here in Cripple Creek . . . for fifty dollars.

• Speakeasy hostess "Texas" Guinan started in Cripple Creek. Perhaps this is one of the reasons why the city is now best known for its Las Vegas–style gambling.

Take a Ride on the Railroad

*F*or an unusual perspective, try viewing the area from a car on the **Cripple Creek and Victor Narrow-Gauge Railroad.** *It takes about forty-five minutes to complete the 4-mile ride behind a coal-burning steam locomotive. You travel past the area's abandoned mines. The railroad is open from mid-May through the* second week of October. Call (719) 689–2640 for departure times. The fare is $8.75 for adults, teenagers thirteen and older, and senior citizens sixty-four and older; $4.75 for children three to twelve, children two and younger free. E-mail: ccvngrr@aol.com. Web site: ccvngrailroad.webjump.com.

And today? Cripple Creek attracts hordes of summer tourists. They come for the narrow-gauge train rides. They pan for gold on Main Street. They play at the slot machines. They attend one of the summer performances put on by the ***Cripple Creek Players*** at the newly renovated ***Historic Butte Opera House.*** This building, originally constructed in 1896, has had many uses throughout its history. Before its recent renovation in the late 1990s, the building served as home to the Cripple Creek Fire Department. Extensive renovations by the city of Cripple Creek served to restore the theater's splendor. The Historic Butte Opera House now seats 174 people and boasts a 1,350-square-foot stage, state-of-the-art sound equipment and movie projectors, and a snack bar. For more information and performance dates, contact the Cripple Creek Players, P.O. Box 957, Cripple Creek 80813; (719) 689–2513 or (800) 500–2513. Web site: www.cripplecreekplayers.com.

The old railroad depot has become the ***Cripple Creek District Museum,*** along with an old assay office and the Colorado Trading and Transfer Company building, constructed in 1893. These three buildings are crammed with mementos of the mining age. Superbly kept up, the museum is well worth a visit. Hours: daily 10:00 A.M. to 5:00 P.M. Memorial Day through September; weekends for the rest of the year. Call (719) 689–2634 or (719) 689–9540. E-mail: CCDistrictMuseum@aol. com. Web site: www.cripple-creek.co.us/ccdm.html. The museum is on Bennett Avenue in Cripple Creek.

Trivia

The Cripple Creek Mining District, made up of roughly 25 towns in the Cripple Creek area, was once known as "The World's Greatest Gold Camp."

The local folks are calmly friendly despite the tourist hubbub. Cripple Creek jumps with visitors all summer. They flock to the redbrick souvenir

*Cripple Creek's Mollie
Kathleen Gold Mine, the
longest continually operating gold mine tour in the
world, boasts the only
1000-foot vertical shaft
gold mine tour in the
United States.*

and antiques shops, where a 1929 beer bottle or a 1950s glass pitcher sells as if it were a rare treasure. You can watch the donkeys on Bennett Avenue, buy cowboy boots in a real western store, and eat home-cooked food in little cafes. Main Street bustles with some shops that sell tacky merchandise. The cars jostle for a place to park.

Not many travelers venture on foot beyond the central core of this community. Yet, visual rewards await those who make the most of Cripple Creek's lovely location. It is nestled among the Colorado hillsides that climb from town (elevation: a high 9,494 feet) in every direction. Nature awaits the walker who leaves the redbrick confines and heads for the slopes of conifers and aspen trees. The mountains here are studded with old abandoned mines, which you reach by hiking up the unused roads past rusting machinery, past the old wooden mine trestles, past the piles of forgotten ore.

The *Mollie Kathleen Gold Mine* still attracts visitors, who can tour the 1,000-foot deep historic mine. Back in 1891, Mollie Kathleen Gortner moved to the area with her family, including her husband, an attorney by the name of Henry. On an excursion by herself to see a herd of elk (she'd never seen them before), Mollie Kathleen came upon an outcropping of quartz that was veined with gold. Upon attempting to file her claim in town, she was informed that as a woman, she had no right to do so. Not to be deterred, Mollie Kathleen seized the papers and signed them anyway, declaring that the issue could be taken up with her husband if there was a problem. Thus Mollie Kathleen Gortner became the first woman in the area to stake a gold claim. Her mine continued to produce gold uninterrupted for the next seventy years, with the exception of a period of time during World War II when all gold production ceased due to a nationwide ban. Today the gold that came out of the mine would be worth more than $100 million.

Appropriate for all ages (there are no steps or ladders to climb), the forty-minute tours of the Mollie Kathleen Gold Mine depart at frequent intervals during the peak season. The mine is open for tours daily from early April through early November. During the off-season, tours take place on some Fridays, Saturdays, and Sundays. Call ahead. Rates are $11.00 for adults, $5.00 for children three to eleven, children two and younger free. For more information: Mollie Kathleen Gold Mine, 1 Mile North Highway 67, P.O. Box 339, Cripple Creek 80813;

Trivia

More than half of Colorado's goods are made in Pueblo.

(719) 689–2466 or (888) 291–5689–9101. Fax (719) 689–2070. E-mail: molliegold@rmi.net. Web site: www.goldminetours.com.

Cripple Creek deserves more than a few hasty hours. At least one overnight stay makes sense.
Slot machines and other gaming devices have come to this community. Many visitors hope to strike it rich at the town's plethora of casinos, but the richness of Cripple Creek's history should not be neglected!

Cripple Creek is 45 miles west of Colorado Springs. From there it can be reached via US 24 west, then SR 67. For more information: Cripple Creek Chamber of Commerce, 367 East Bennett Avenue, Cripple Creek 80813; (719) 689–2169 or (800) 526–8777. Fax (719) 689–0512. Or contact the Cripple Creek Welcome Center at (877) 858–4653. E-mail: info@cripple-creek.co.us. Web site: www.cripple-creek.co.us.

Driving farther south, you may want to stop in *Pueblo,* a quiet, hospitable community of 105,000 souls who, in recent years, have gone historic. The citizenry is especially proud of the *Historic Arkansas Riverwalk of Pueblo (HARP) Authority.* The twenty-six acres of HARP serve as a demonstration of just how beautiful an urban waterfront can be. Pedestrian walkways and bike paths crisscross the area. A lakeside promenade for waterfowl and other wildlife exists alongside Lake Elizabeth, and the original stone wall from the Arkansas River remains intact, in keeping with HARP's historical theme. For more information: HARP, 200 West First Street, Suite 303, Pueblo 81003; (719) 595–0242. Fax (719) 583–4696. E-mail: info@puebloharp.com. Web site: www.puebloharp.com/about HARP.htm.

Trivia

In December 1999, the city of Pueblo was astonished to find seventeen trees on its Historic Arkansas Riverwalk destroyed within a matter of days. The culprit? A Colorado beaver whom officials affectionately deemed "Bandit," before they relocated the creature to a place a little farther out of town.

Pueblo, located some 40 miles south of Colorado Springs, hosts the yearly *Colorado State Fair & Exposition,* one of the biggest events in the state. Every summer, the fair promises to be an action-packed seventeen-day experience for all who visit, whether youth or adults, singles or families.

The Colorado State Fair is unique. Witness the variety of activities planned, from PRCA championship rodeo to the largest carnival and midway in the state. There are hundreds of lambs, steers, hogs, horses, and other animals to see and touch, a popular children's barnyard, parks with all

Pueblo's El Pueblo Museum

*T*he El Pueblo Museum *(324 West First Street, Pueblo; 719–583–0453) displays Native American clothing, buffalo skins, and gold panning equipment, artifacts that hark back to Colorado's early history.*

Of particular interest here, though, is the display of the thigh bone of a prehistoric mammoth. *The eons-old fossil was discovered during a reconstruction project in downtown Pueblo. After examining this old bone, you can't help but imagine this giant plodding down Main Street.*

types of free entertainment, along with scores of exhibits and creative arts, and evening performances by some of the nation's top entertainers.

General admission to the state fair is $6.00, children five and younger free. Hours run Monday through Thursday, from noon to midnight and Friday through Sunday and Labor Day from 10:00 A.M. to midnight. From I–25, take exit 97a west (Central Avenue). This will take you to Northern Avenue. Follow Northern west; the state fairgrounds will be on your right. Box office: (719) 566–0530. General information: 1001 Beulah Avenue, Pueblo 81004-2415; (719) 561–8484. Web site: www.coloradosfair.com.

Trivia

Originally, Pueblo was a crossroads for travelers, including Spaniards, fur traders, and Native Americans.

In a nearby residential district, there awaits one of Colorado's most stately bed-and-breakfasts; this mansion is known as the ***Abriendo Inn.*** This distinguished small hostelry couldn't have a better location, not far from the community college and the historic Union Avenue. The inn has only ten rooms, each a little different, but all with period furniture, old-fashioned lace curtains, canopied or brass beds, fresh flowers, oak antiques, and original art. Intriguingly, each room comes with appropriate magazines like *Victorian Homes, Country Living,* and *Architectural Digest.* The owner, Kerrelyn McCafferty Trent, happens to be an interior designer and noted gourmet whose staff serves up free evening snacks and unexpected breakfast inventions. The aristocratic atmosphere makes one think of an embassy; in fact, the inn is so perfect that it's slightly intimidating. (The grandeur is inexpensive, however; a night at the Abriendo Inn costs about one-half of Grand Hotel accommodations.) For more information: Abriendo Inn, 300 West Abriendo Avenue, Pueblo 81004; (719) 544–2703. Fax (719) 542–6544. E-mail:

Trivia

Cañon City is the county seat of Fremont County, which has nine state prison facilities and a federal prison complex with four facilities. The state and federal prisons are the largest employers in the area, together accounting for more than 3,000 workers.

abriendo@rmi.net. Web site: www.virtualcities. com/ons/co/p/cop7701. htm.

For more information on visiting the Pueblo area: Greater Pueblo Chamber of Commerce, P.O. Box 697, Pueblo 81002; (800) 233–3446. E-mail: info@pueblochamber.org. Web site: www.pueblo. org.

From Pueblo, head west on US 50 to Cañon City and its nearby attractions, including *Shelf Road.* Shelf Road makes up part of the *Gold Belt Tour,* a designated Colorado Scenic Byway. From stunning limestone cliffs that attract rock climbers from all over the world to the sheer drop-offs on the side of the road (hence the name) into lush green valleys, the views and the isolation encountered along Shelf Road are idyllic. Abundant wildlife viewing potential rounds out the area's special charm—past sightings include mule deer, foxes, hawks, American black bears, and owls.

Some of the driving is on rough roads (it's not for the faint of heart) and should be avoided in wet or icy weather; furthermore, four-wheel-drive is recommended for portions of Upper Shelf Road. However, any two-wheel-drive vehicle can enjoy some of the sights available along the portion of Shelf Road that leads out of Cañon City. The road becomes narrow once it turns to dirt, so drive carefully and slowly, watching for

Bear-ly Noticed

*W*e were driving along the Shelf Road one bright and sunny Colorado morning on our way to rock climb. My eyes lazily roved over the lush greenery of Helena Canyon several hundred feet below while I silently wondered at its isolation and wildness, despite the private road that cuts through a portion of it. Suddenly my attention was drawn to a black lumbering shape, ambling along that very road.

"A bear!" I exclaimed, filled with excitement.

My spouse slammed on the brakes and we hopped out of the car, looking down the sheer canyon walls at the bear hundreds of feet below us, yet still clearly visible. The bear, an American Black Bear, continued to snuffle its way along as we watched, until a change in the wind must have brought our scent to its attention: it raised its head, stared straight at us, and took off running in the other direction. I was filled with both amazement at the gift of watching such a being in its natural setting and an odd sense of sadness that my very presence, hundreds of yards away from this creature, could so frighten it.

oncoming traffic. Plan ahead where you are going to turn around; a good place is at mile marker 14. The entire Gold Belt Tour encompasses 131 miles of driving and takes roughly five hours. From Cañon City, venture north on Raynolds, and then head north again on Fields after Raynolds swings west. Nine miles along Fields takes you directly to Shelf Road. For more information: BLM-Royal Gorge Resource Area, 3170 East Main Street, Cañon City 81212; (719) 275–0631. Web site: www.co.blm.gov/rectouring.htm.

After a jaunt along Shelf Road, another scenic wonder awaits you at the ***Royal Gorge Bridge and Park.*** The gorge, at 1,200 feet deep, has been compared to the Grand Canyon. With its striking reds, mauves, browns, and yellows, the deep and narrow gauge stopped Lieutenant Zebulon Pike (of Pikes Peak fame) in his tracks back in 1806. He couldn't forge the gorge (and he didn't climb Pikes Peak, either).

In 1929 the Royal Gorge Bridge opened up to traffic after seven months of fatality-less construction. The bridge is able to support more than two million pounds, so don't worry about your car's weight! Seventy years later, people still flock from all over to drive across this mighty suspension bridge, allegedly the highest of its kind in the world.

The 2,200-foot-long ***Aerial Tram*** offers another viewing option as it takes visitors for a ride across the fabulous canyon. Painted a fiery red, the thirty-five-passenger tram cabin comes with a guide-conductor who assures timid passengers that the tram will not plunge into the Arkansas River, which rages and roars below. Three braking systems and an extra motor, "just in case," guarantee this. In the terminals, a total of about one hundred tons of concrete and steel anchor the conveyance's enormous cables, providing reassurance with their heftiness. In fact, a helicopter had to string the tram's pilot cable, and more than $350,000 was needed to rig up this tourist attraction.

After looking at it from above, hop aboard for a five-and-a-half-minute ride on the ***Incline Railway*** to the bottom of the gorge. Supposedly the world's steepest conveyance of its kind, the Incline Railway gives you a topsy-turvy view of the gorge as you look back up at the bridge above you. Built by the same crew who built the bridge, the railway opened in 1931 and has been operating ever since.

Families will appreciate a variety of other attractions including a carousel, a little scale-model open-air train that chugs along around the Royal Gorge Park, and a wildlife pavilion. Park admission is $14 for

Trivia

*The Royal Gorge Bridge &
Park averages about
500,000 visitors annually.*

adults and teenagers, $12 for children four to
eleven, children three and younger free. Park
hours are 8:30 A.M. until dusk daily. Admission
offers unlimited access to all park attractions,
although some attractions are seasonal. Call for
details. The Royal Gorge Bridge and Park is 12 miles west of Cañon City
on US 50. For more information: Royal Gorge Bridge Company, P.O. Box
549, Cañon City 81215; (719) 275–7507 or (888) 333–5597. E-mail:
rgb@ris. net. Web site: www.royalgorgebridge.com.

For more information about Cañon City: Cañon City Chamber of Commerce, 403 Royal Gorge Boulevard Cañon City 81212; (719) 275–2331
or (800) 876–7922. E-mail: chamber@canoncity.com. Web site: www.
canoncitychamber.com.

Perhaps after Cañon City, your route will take you farther west on US 50
to *Salida.* There are few more outdoorsy places in Colorado. Salida is
famous for white-water rafting, kayaking, and jeeping. The local folks
are friendly. In fact, the ***Tudor Rose Bed & Breakfast*** is unashamedly
relaxed and western; you're welcome to bring your own horse (stables
available; humans can stay in one of the six guest rooms, most of which
have spectacular views). The innkeeper can identify the Sangre de
Cristos and the Sawach range. As you look around you, the Tudor Rose
gets ready for your solid, western breakfast . . .

For more information: Jon and Terre Terrell, innkeepers/owners, Tudor
Rose Bed & Breakfast; P.O. Box 89, Salida 81201; (800) 379–0889. E-
mail: tudorose@amigo.net. Web site: www.virtualcities.com/ons/co/v/
cov4701.htm.

For more information on Salida: Salida, Colorado Heart of the Rockies
Chamber of Commerce, 406 West Highway 50, Salida 81201; (719)
539–2068 or (877) 772–5432. Fax (719) 539–7844. E-mail: salida@
vistaworks.com. Web site: www.fourteenernet.com/salida.

Where the Old West Lives

Camp Hale was nicknamed "Camp Hell" by the Mountain Troopers,
who first trained here, 18 miles north of Leadville. From 1942 to
1945, the camp served the famous World War II Tenth Mountain Division. Much of their tough battle preparations took place at the chilly
9,500 feet above sea level, on 6,500 mountain acres, surrounded by
12,000-foot snow giants.

The altitude and the thin air took their toll on young recruits from the Midwest; the new arrivals couldn't sleep at first and felt weak during the day. Smoke from 300 barrack chimneys and railroads hung over the camp, and you could hear a lot of coughing.

Camp Hale days often started at 4:30 A.M. with 15-mile marches through blizzards. Packs weighed eighty pounds or more, and the troopers would be pulled backward. The army skis were often so stiff that they sank into the snow. Some southern and midwestern fellows, recruited at the last minute, termed skis their "torture boards." Each time a novice lifted a leg, his muscles hurt. The arms ached, too, from the unaccustomed efforts. The Camp Hale–based mountain warfare soldiers were made to climb 12,000-foot peaks on skis while the temperature could fall to 20° below zero.

To get these men ready for combat against German *Gebirgsjäger* troops, the U.S. Army made even the basic training as realistic as possible. For a Camp Hale "Infiltration Course," the troopers had to crawl under barbed wire for an hour. Then, suddenly, machine guns with live shells shot directly over their heads. Fifty-pound charges of dynamite blew up right and left. Occasional mistakes would cause actual injuries.

Life at Camp Hale was never monotonous; the Tenth Mountain Division troops were employed to test Arctic snow vehicles and battle-station rescue toboggans. Troopers trained on large snowshoes and learned how to control avalanches. Other men worked with mules and dogs. A Scandinavian explorer was invited to teach the soldiers how to build igloos and other snow caves. Some of the camp's crack skiers and instructors were actually well-known ski racers or ski jumpers; others joined U.S. Olympic ski teams after World War II.

The training of these soldiers became even tougher in February 1944, when the Tenth Mountain men were sent on their first "D-series" maneuvers. They climbed Colorado's Tennessee Pass and moved for thirty days into the icy wilderness. The snows were so deep that supply vehicles couldn't get through. Loads were so heavy (up to ninety pounds) that only the best troopers could make it. Despite the 35°-below-zero temperatures, no fires were allowed. After devouring K-rations, the food ran out. The struggling Tenth ate almost nothing for three days. When they got back to Hale, the media counted one hundred cases of frostbite. Nearby hospitals filled with pneumonia victims.

In summer, soldiers received instruction in advanced rock-climbing techniques; they rappelled down the sheer Colorado cliffs and had to walk on suspended cables and rain-wet logs. Mountaineering knowledge would come in handy. In November 1944, the division left Camp Hale for Italy, where the troopers distinguished themselves in battling the Germans.

And the camp in Colorado? For a time Camp Hale housed German POWs. After the latter went home, the flagpoles, mule barns, and other buildings were forgotten. Suddenly, in 1947, the Pentagon brass decided to send other young soldiers to try the Colorado snows for size. Like the former Camp Hale occupants, these infantrymen pitted themselves against winter cold. When the Korean War broke out in 1950, Camp Hale served the Rangers as a special training ground. A few years later, army helicopters got their battle tests here. By then, ski troopers no longer seemed as necessary as during World War II days, and most of the military skiing moved out of Colorado and north to Alaska. On July 1, 1965, the buglers sounded a last Camp Hale retreat. Afterward, the U.S. Forest Service once more took control of the area.

During the late 1970s the Forest Service invested money and time to build the Camp Hale picnic areas, hiking paths, a wheelchair trail, and parking spaces at the onetime training camp. In May 1980, many former troopers came to the dedication of the twenty-acre *Camp Hale Memorial Campground.* It is one of the highest such sites in the United States.

Not far away from camp on Tennessee Pass, a fourteen-ton slab of granite reaches 20 feet into the sky. The stone's Roll of Honor lists the 990 comrades who gave their lives for the division. Each year on Memorial Day, hundreds of ex-troopers assemble at Tennessee Pass to remember their companions. Later they get together to talk about the old days, to swap tales, or to introduce their families to one another.

Camp Hale, now a U.S. Forest Service Campground, is 180 miles west of Denver via I–70 and SR 91. For more information: Holy Cross Ranger District, 24747 US Highway 24, P.O. Box 190, Minturn 81645; (970) 827–5715 or (970) 827–9343. E-mail: info@camphale.org. Web site: www.camphale.org.

The Tenth Mountain Division remains alive through its offbeat *Hut Association,* which consists of twenty-four mountain huts; each far-flung Colorado cabin can accommodate from six to twenty hikers, mountain bikers, or cross-country skiers. The shelters are rugged; you bring your own food and water plus a sleeping bag. The huts are reachable from such major highways as I–70 or from Tennessee Pass and

Trivia

Leadville, at 10,152 feet above sea level, is North America's highest incorporated city.

Colorado 24, among others. Distances vary: From Vail Pass, for instance, you get to the typical Shrine Mountain hut in 3 miles. All the same, you need to be fit and adequately equipped. (This includes a compass.) The alternative: Hire and pay a guide. Weekends are busiest. In any case, a reservation is essential to secure space at one of the huts. Rates are about one-half of what you'd pay for a cheap ski area motel per night. To be sure, these huts take you into Colorado's backcountry. For more information: The Tenth Mountain Division Hut Association, 1280 Ute Avenue, Aspen 81611; (970) 925–5775. Fax (970) 925–5317. Web site: www.huts.org.

Now for a story of love and power, of wealth and poverty, of joys and tragedy, of a Colorado mining town whose fortunes flourished and vanished. A story so extraordinary that it became the subject of an opera, a play, and many biographies, some of them bad ones.

The characters were bigger than life. Begin with Horace Austin Warner Tabor, a onetime Vermont stonecutter, and his straitlaced hardworking wife, Augusta. The couple gave up a Kansas homestead to try their luck first in Denver, then under Pikes Peak, then at Oro City. They arrived in **Leadville** with a rickety wagon and an old ox during the 1860s, some years after the first gold had been discovered in California Gulch.

The Tabors established themselves as best as they could—Augusta with a tiny rooming house and a small bakery, Horace with a store and later a part-time job as mayor.

The Tabors' first break came on April 20, 1878. Two destitute miners, new in town, dropped into Horace's shop. Could he help out with some tools and a basket of groceries? The accommodating mayor agreed to help for a third of whatever minerals they might find. A few days later, some hard digging produced a rich silver vein.

The Tabors were launched. By summer, that first mine—the Little Pittsburgh—lavished $8,000 a week on its owners. Before long there was $100,000 worth of silver per month; this was followed by other Tabor ventures, all successful. In time, Tabor invested in many mines, controlled a good chunk of the local bank, built the Leadville Opera House, and erected mansions in the mining town and in Denver. He owned a lot of real estate and a hotel. By 1879, Leadville had seventeen independent smelters; it took 2,000 lumberjacks to provide enough wood to fire the machinery that processed the silver riches. Thanks to Tabor's new wealth and almost daily discoveries of more ore, the immigrants flooded to Leadville in droves. Celebrities like the "Unsinkable" Molly Brown showed up, as did various Dows, Guggenheims, and Boettchers.

Marshall Sprague, a western mining authority, describes in *Money Mountain* the hustle and bustle when thousands streamed across the Continental Divide to Leadville. The road was "jammed with wagons, stages, buggies, carts. There were men pushing wheelbarrows, men riding animals, men and dogs driving herds of cattle, sheep, pigs and goats."

Tabor soon bought an additional mine—the Matchless. He prospered while Leadville grew to a city of 30,000. Oscar Wilde appeared in the famous **Tabor Opera House.** The Chicago Symphony Orchestra and the Metropolitan Opera came there, to faraway Colorado. Well-known singers, ballet dancers, actresses, and entertainers arrived to perform.

H. A. W. Tabor became a millionaire many times over. He was a tall man, mustached, kindly, and, as a local historian writes, "outgoing, gregarious, and honest as the falling rain." By contrast, Horace was married to a woman who, although she worked hard, brought Tabor no happiness. She allegedly nagged; she was described as prim and humorless. Colorado's richest man thought he deserved better.

Horace Tabor's luck changed one day in 1882. That evening the fifty-year-old silver magnate saw Elisabeth Doe-McCourt in the restaurant of Leadville's Clarendon Hotel.

"Baby" Doe was twenty-two—a beauty with shining blue eyes and curly, dark blond hair. Round-faced and charming, she'd been born into an Irish immigrant family of fourteen children. Baby Doe had just emerged from a brief, unhappy marriage with an unsupportive miner in Central City. Recently divorced, she had the good sense to look for a better partner in booming Leadville. She was a respectable young woman. And her search was crowned by success.

What began as a simple flirtation deepened into an abiding love that scandalized people in the Rockies and became the celebrated story of Colorado's opera the *Ballad of Baby Doe,* by Broadway veterans John Latouche and Douglas Moore.

Horace and Baby Doe were snubbed by Denver High Society when Tabor divorced his wife, Augusta, who allegedly received a $500,000 settlement. H. A. W. soon married his new love. The wedding took place in Washington, D.C., in the presence of President Chester Arthur and other dignitaries. Baby Doe received a $90,000 diamond necklace, and she wore a $7,500 gown.

Although young, she actually had greater substance than most of her biographers gave her credit for. She was honest and loyal, helpful to others, and interested in a variety of things. Best of all, she was in love with her much older Colorado husband. Her love was returned.

The Tabors lived the lavish life of luxury to the hilt. Most historians estimate that the Tabors spent some $100 million. Horace Tabor made few worthwhile investments. For a brief time he was elected to the U.S. Senate.

In 1893, disaster struck Leadville. Silver was replaced by paper money. The nation experienced a financial panic. The Tabors were ruined. The mines began to fail. Real estate was sold to satisfy creditors.

The couple moved to Denver, still in love. Thanks to some contacts, Horace got a postmaster's job for a short time. But the financial plunge must have been too much for him. Soon he was ailing. His final hours came on April 10, 1899, at Denver's Windsor Hotel. His wife, Baby Doe, was by his side, holding his hand.

Before Horace Tabor died, he once more spoke about his Matchless Mine in Leadville. It had long played out after yielding some $1 million during its fourteen years of operation. "Hold on to the Matchless," Tabor whispered. "It'll make millions again." His wife nodded.

Baby Doe kept her promise. She moved back to Leadville. Penniless, she lived in a shack beside the mine pit for thirty-six years. She remained faithful to Tabor.

During the winter of 1935, while in her seventies, she shopped at a local grocery for some food. The grocer gave her a ride home in his truck. Baby Doe was dressed in tatters. Her feet were sheathed in sackcloth instead of shoes. The cabin next to the Matchless Mine was squalid, but she kept a rifle in it, protecting her mine.

Leadville's altitude is more than 10,000 feet. It gets cold there on winter nights. Baby Doe Tabor was found in her shack on March 7, 1935. She had frozen to death. No one knows how long the body had been there. Ironically, there were some unopened boxes with new blankets sent by some Leadville sympathizers, which the dying woman had refused to use.

The Tabors are buried side by side in Denver. The *Ballad of Baby Doe* was added to the New York City Opera's repertoire shortly after its 1956 debut in Central City, Colorado. The role of Baby Doe was among the first that Beverly Sills sang for a company she was to head many years later.

Some Little-Known Facts About Leadville

- *Leadville is just below the timberline.*

- *Legend says that in the old days, the worth of a barrel of Leadville whiskey was as high at $1,500.*

- *Tents were once pitched on Main Street, and it was boasted that each was "the best hotel in town."*

- *"Unsinkable" Molly Brown made her fortune here; also David May, Charles Boettcher, Charles Dow, and Meyer Guggenheim.*

And how about the current Leadville? Thanks to the town's solid mining history, there is a 70,000-square-foot *National Mining Hall of Fame & Museum.* This museum should be essential for ore seekers, mining school students, and history buffs. Located in a restored Victorian schoolhouse, the facility retraces the entire Leadville history; you can also view old equipment, assorted rocks and crystals, various artifacts, and dioramas.

An addition, "The Last Chance," is a realistic replica of a hard-rock mine tunnel. Stretching more than 120 feet, the "rock" walls have exposed ore veins. Mine-gauge rail tracks are underfoot on the rock-strewn floor. Dripping water adds to the illusion of being underground in a real mine.

Admission costs $4.00 for adults and teenagers twelve and older, $2.00 for children six to eleven, children five and younger free. Hours: summer (May through October): 9:00 A.M. to 5:00 P.M. daily; winter (November through April): 10:00 A.M. to 2:00 P.M. Monday through Friday. For more information: P.O. Box 981 (120 West Ninth), Leadville 80461; (719) 486–1229. Fax (719) 486–3927. E-mail: nationalminingmuseum@bemail.com. Web site: www.leadville.com/miningmuseum.

More than 70 square blocks of Leadville have been designated as a National Historic Landmark District, making it one of the largest such districts in Colorado. You can enjoy this town's history at any time of year by going on a short historic walking tour through this district. Start your free, self-guided tour at *Ice Palace Park* in the 100 block of West Tenth. Plenty of parking can be found here. The park commemorates the ill-fated Ice Palace, built nearby in 1896. The palace, constructed of 5,000 tons of ice and 307,000 board feet of lumber, lasted only a few months before going under. From the park, you walk southeast to Harrison Avenue, where most of the tour's attractions await your exploration, including the Heritage Museum, the Hyman Block (where

A Palace of Ice

The Leadville Ice Palace was the largest such building ever constructed in North America, covering more than five acres. With its spectacular 90-foot towers, heated rooms, enormous ice sculptures. and an ice-skating rink, it was supposed to help shore up the city's floundering economy. Only a few months after opening, the unprofitable palace was forced to close its doors.

You can still experience some of the palace's original magic today by staying at the **Ice Palace Inn Bed & Breakfast.** *This building was built in 1899 using some of the original boards from the Ice Palace. For information: 813 Spruce Street Leadville 80461; (719) 486–8272 or (800) 754–2840. E-mail: icepalace@bwn.net. Web site: www.icepalaceinn.com.*

the infamous Doc Holliday shot—but failed to kill—his last victim), and the Tabor Opera House. For a map of the tour, visit the Web site www.leadville.com/walktour/ or call the Leadville/Lake County Chamber of Commerce at (800) 933–3901.

To reach Leadville from Denver, take I–70 west, turning off at SR 91 (exit 195, Copper Mountain). For more information: Leadville/Lake County Chamber of Commerce, 809 Harrison Avenue P.O. Box 861, Leadville 80461; (719) 486–3900 or (800) 933–3901. Email: leadville@ LeadvilleUSA.com. Web site: www.leadvilleusa.com.

South and west of Leadville lies ***Crested Butte,*** a sizable, scenic ski center. Thirty minutes north of Gunnison, Colorado, Crested Butte is too far from the big metropolitan cities to attract crowds. (Denver is 235 miles to the northeast.) One local inhabitant explains Crested Butte this way: "In an age plagued by problems of too many people, too many cars and roads and buildings, this kind of country has a special attraction. It seems to have been made *for* people, not *by* them."

Crested Butte aficionados speak of a feeling "that borders on reverence, a joy of simply being here." The ski area and the nearby little mining town of Crested Butte (2 miles away) give off a feeling of relaxation. The atmosphere is pastoral, sometimes even somnolent, informal, tolerant, rooted in nature.

These mountains are some of the state's most beautiful. They emanate all the power and grace of the Swiss Alps, and you seem to ski in a never-ending symphony of valleys and meadows, of crests and snowfields. Crested Butte is blessed with nicely separated terrain for

Leadville Visit

*W*hile in Leadville, well-conditioned adventurers won't want to miss a chance to hike Colorado's highest mountain, **Mt. Elbert** *(14,433 feet).*

Depending on time and ability, hikers can choose one of the Mountain's two main trails:

North Mt. Elbert Trail *is a 5-mile hike to the summit. From Sixth Street in Leadville, head south on US 24 for about 4 miles. Go west on SR 300 for ³/₄ mile, and then south (left) on Lake County Road 11 for 1¹/₄ miles. Head west (right) on Forest Road 110 for 5 miles, which will take you to the parking area at Halfmoon Campground.*

South Mt. Elbert Trail *can be serene; it is seldom crowded. It is 5¹/₂ miles to* the summit with a trailhead near Lakeview Campground. Go south on US 24, and then head west on SR 82 for about 3¹/₂ miles. Go north on Lake County 24 for just over a mile to reach the parking area, just north of the campground.

With a 4,500-foot elevation gain, both trails should be attempted only by hikers who are in good shape and are knowledgeable about safety in hiking.

For more information: San Isabel National Forest, Leadville Ranger District, 2015 North Poplar, Leadville 80461; (719) 486–0749. E-mail: gvanover@fs.fed.us. Web site: www.fs.fed.us/r2/psicc/leadvile/elbert.html.

advanced skiers (only 20 percent of the mountain), intermediates (55 percent), and beginners (25 percent). In addition, experts will find 824 acres of ungroomed terrain known as "Extreme Limits," suitable for expert skiers only. Beginners, too, are well served on this mountain.

One of the area's major assets is a gently sloping, broad, chairlift-served run on the lower mountain more than a mile long. It is excellent for novice skiers, who at many areas are confined to short, makeshift slopes with minimal lift facilities. The upper area holds myriad pleasures for more advanced skiers. One chairlift, for example, serves slopes with an average grade of 44 percent (experts find this steepness challenging, and it will scare the daylights out of average skiers).

The majority of the mountain is for the intermediate skier. This includes a many-trails complex that taps the open ski terrain of Crested Butte's north-side slopes. Here the snow comes earlier, stays longer, and is deeper and lighter than anywhere else on the mountain, with an average 33 percent grade, 1,350 vertical feet. Ideal for intermediate skiing, the Paradise Bowl reminds one of Vail's bowls and provides great joys to most visitors. Crested Butte's lift situation is adequate, thanks to its fifteen chairlifts.

Colorado's choicest cross-country adventure—indeed, a special piéce de résistance for experts—ties Crested Butte with Aspen, just 28 miles away (guides available).

The ski school has an important and reliable cross-country program for which the surrounding country seems perfectly suited. Some of the area's ski clientele have never seen snow before. The ski school is therefore a patient one. The names of some ski runs give a good clue to the customers—Houston Trail, Kansas Trail. Charters regularly fly in from states like Georgia, and you'll find some midwestern families. It is intriguing to simply sit in front of the base cafeteria and watch the mix of people, especially on weekends.

Crested Butte's ski season runs from mid-November through mid-April. The ski slopes are open from 9:00 A.M. to 4:00 P.M. Prices vary throughout the season. For more information: Crested Butte Mountain Resort, 12 Snowmass Road, Crested Butte 81225; (800) 810–7669 or (800) 544-8448. E-mail: info@cbmr.com. Web site: www.skicb.com.

The town of Crested Butte gets its character from the old mining days, and the streets are full of young and old men with beards who all look alike. On weekends you glimpse sheriffs with badges, and there are some town drunks to be taken care of. Nightlife is limited to saloons with loud banjos and other instruments, beer drinking, and talking to the multitude of ski bums. Many dogs sit in front of the clapboard buildings; dogs of various shapes leap across the pockmarked streets or show up at the lived-in ski area. Food and lodging prices range from moderate to expensive. Accommodations are available in old lodges and well-worn guest houses, plus condos for the rich. There is a glossy hotel.

Fat Tire Week in Crested Butte is a summer party on bike wheels. More than 1,000 people will show up to participate in bicycle polo, races, clinics, and tours that range from mild-mannered wildflower rides to the grinding ascent of 10,707-foot Schofield Pass. With more than 300 miles of trails, Crested Butte has a ride to satisfy every cyclist. For more information about this annual June event, contact the Crested Butte—Mt. Crested Butte Chamber of Commerce at (800) 545–4505. Web site: www.crestedbuttechamber.com.

Crested Butte was the site of the first **mountain biking** in Colorado. After a motorcycle gang had ridden their Harley Davidsons over the rough jeep road of Pearl Pass from Aspen, some "Butte" locals decided to one-up the bikers by doing the same route on bicycles.

Since then these bikes have evolved from one-speed clunkers into technological wonders of metal and gears. Crested Butte continues to celebrate this development with the ***Mountain Bike Hall of Fame and Museum.*** For more information: 120 Sopris, P.O. Box 845, Crested Butte 81224; (970) 349–6817 or (800) 454–4505. Fax (970) 349-6817. E-mail: mbikehof@crestedbutte.net. Web site: www.mountainbike.co.nz/halloffame.

Mountain bikes were designed to act like jeeps for going over rough terrain. Tires are big, fat, and knobby for climbing through gravel and maintaining traction on a steep grade. As opposed to the racing type of road bikes with skinny tires designed for maximum speed, mountain bikes come with eighteen to twenty-seven gears. This allows you to shift way down to what is called a "granny gear" and, moving at slow speeds, still be able to pedal up and over obstacles. By turning your pedals as quickly as possible—called "spinning"—you ensure that the gears absorb the load, rather than your knees.

Mountain bikes take some getting used to. Riding a trail over rocks and logs and through streams can be a bit intimidating. Be prepared to take a few falls at first.

One way to avoid crashing into obstacles like rocks is to look for a path around them instead of focusing on what is in your path. The technique of keeping your eye on the ball in tennis can be applied to mountain biking. By eyeballing that obstacle in your trail, you will hit it, too. Keep looking up the trail, not just in front of you.

To maintain traction while going down a steep hill, stand up in the pedals and stick your rear end behind the bike seat for more weight on the back tire. Also, brake most firmly with the rear brake. Using your front brake alone can abruptly stop the front tire and send you flying over the handlebars in what is called an "endo" (rear end flips over the front). It's a very undignified way to get off a bike, and it can hurt!

Required equipment includes a helmet, eye protection, cycling gloves, and shorts to prevent chafing of inner thighs. Drink from your water bottle frequently to avoid dehydration.

Most of the Colorado trails you will ride are open for public use. Cyclists are required to yield to hikers and horses. If this means you have to get off your bike and move off the trail, then do it. In many parts of the United States, failure of cyclists to yield has caused some popular trails to be closed to them.

Following on the wheels of Fat Tire Week is the **Crested Butte Wild-flower Festival.** Of course, all mountain towns have wildflowers, but the climate of sheltered valleys seems to provide more floral color here than many other Colorado places. The town also tries to make sure everyone can enjoy these delicate blooms. Days of naturalist walks, tours, photo sessions, painting classes with professional outdoor artists, evening dinners, lunch discussions, horseback tours into the higher meadows, and ski-lift rides to the top of the ski area for a leisurely walk down are some of the offerings. Variable fees for each activity help support the organizers of the event. Posters, books, and varied artwork are on sale. This is a low-key celebration of the natural mountain beauty. Many of the activities are well suited to children or to people who like to move along at a slow pace. For others, the guides will match your speed. For more information: Crested Butte Wildflower Festival, P.O. Box 216, Crested Butte 81224; (970) 349–2571. Web site: www.cbsummer.com/wildflower_capital/festival.cfm.

Crested Butte is a thirty-minute drive north of Gunnison on SR 135. For more information: Crested Butte—Mt. Crested Butte Chamber of Commerce, P.O. Box 1288, Crested Butte 81224; (970) 349–6438 or (800) 545–4505. Web site: www.crestedbuttechamber.com.

Heading west from Gunnison on US 50, your travels will take you to the spectacular **Black Canyon of the Gunnison National Park,** which became a national park in 1999. The vision of the sheer, massive rocks is stunning and unforgettable. In the sunlight, the black granite turns a mauve color. Towers, pillars, and stone blocks scintillate and make humans feel tiny. In all, the Black Canyon of the Gunnison National Park comprises some 30,385 acres. Carved by the river, the canyon is 53 miles long.

The canyon's trails are steep. They're shaded by scrub oak; on your descent toward the Gunnison River, you see white daisies, violet asters, mariposa lilies, yarrow, and lupine lilies. Chipmunks and squirrels peer out from the vegetation and the rock cracks. Golden eagles fly overhead.

The Chasm View Nature Trail measures a modest $1/3$ mile. The North Vista Trail is more ambitious, at 3 miles, and can be strenuous. A permit is required if you want to hike down all the way to the river. Rock climbing in the canyon is considered hazardous and is only for experienced climbers. (Register at the visitor center.) The national park is open in winter as well, with fewer personnel.

The entrance fee is $7.00 per vehicle or $4.00 per pedestrian (no charge

Trivia

Two thousand miles of trout-fishing streams and Colorado's largest lake are within driving range of Gunnison—excellent fishing!

for visitors age fifteen or younger). The North and South Rim stations are open daily, but access is limited in winter. To get to the South Rim take US 50 from Montrose for 15 miles to SR 347. The visitor center is at the South Rim. The North Rim is 11 miles south of Crawford via US 92 and North Rim Road, which is closed during winter.

For more information: Park Headquarters, 102 Elk Creek, Gunnison 81230; (970) 641–2337. Fax (970) 641–3127. E-mail: CURE_Vis_Mail@nps.gov. Web site: www.nps.gov/blca.

Accommodations are available nearby in Montrose at the luxurious **Best Western Red Arrow,** 1702 East Main (Highway 50 East); (970) 249–9641 or (800) 468–9323. Fax (970) 249–8380. Web site: www.bestwestern.com/reservations/us/co/main.html.

Consider the Basques who herd sheep in the western U.S. Rockies and whose homeland is the sometimes foggy Pyrenees, mountains that separate Spain from France. Colorado's Basques are not unhappy with their lot. Bernard De Voto once asked a Basque why he chose to live among sheep. "I seek the quiet heart," the shepherd answered.

The "quiet heart" of solitude can be found by these men among the meadows and knolls of their homeland as well as on the hillsides of Colorado. In the United States, they are concentrated in and around Montrose and Grand Junction. The herders are in tune with their mountains, which make a "mighty big bedroom," as they like to explain.

Most of the younger Basques are single; for them shearing time and the yearly folk festivals—with dancing, weight lifting, and wine drinking—fill a need. Many of these mountain men own their herds and let the unmarried do the herding while they stick to family life. Whether living in the western U.S. Rockies or in the Pyrenees, the Basques hold on to their own difficult-to-learn language. It resembles none other in Europe and still puzzles philologists.

Colorado's Basques wear the berets and the modest working clothes of their ancestors. Their ethnic origins remain unclear; they seem to have been in Europe longer than other groups. Anthropologists theorize that these dark-complected mountain people may have migrated to the Iberian Peninsula from the Caucasus some 2,000 years before Christ. Both the Basque sheepherders and the Basque farmers live modestly and accept their place in the Colorado high country.

Southwestern Colorado

The chute opens and Joe Alexander, champion bareback rider, holds on to the horse's riggings with one hand. The horse rears wildly, resenting the man, hooves in all directions, a bucking, pitching, twisting, snorting, wild-eyed rebel. The cowboy's hat flies high, landing in the dust.

He has been on the horse for five seconds now, and he still hangs on. He leans all the way back, ankles still spurring, his shoulder blades against the animal's spine. The man's outstretched arm hits the horse's bones. It's a human against a beast. Six seconds now. Seven. Eight.

The buzzer sounds. Alexander jumps safely onto the ground. Eight seconds of bareback riding can seem like eight hours. It still takes a strong, bold person to ride at rodeos.

These Wild West riding competitions are an important income source for some Colorado cowboys. After all, the cattle business in the United States has shrunk during the past decades. Much of the profit has been taken out. These days, ranches are fewer, and, although some of the successful ones are in southern Colorado, they're smaller than they used to be.

At one time, hundreds of men were needed to drive 6,000 or more Black Angus, Herefords, Shorthorns, and other breeds of cattle to market. Nowadays trucks often do the job. The old-time cowhand had to feed the stock in winter—a job often done by helicopters these days.

In sheer numbers the western cowpuncher has diminished, but a few large Colorado ranches still need these rugged, underpaid men to brand cattle in spring, to put up and repair fences, to rope the creatures, and to look after their health. One ranch manager for a big cattle company thirty minutes south of Denver still rounds up his stock twice a year. In the saddle for long hours, he enjoys the freedom of his 10,000 acres. He dresses the part, too. Cowboy hat, leather vest, leather belts with elaborate buckles, Levis, buckaroo boots. He says he enjoys the heat and getting dirty. Few people know that he has a law degree.

Many ranch hands have learned some veterinary skills; they know a lot about the pharmaceuticals and the vaccinations of the present-day western cattle industry. Likewise, cowboys learn about feeding, and they help with cattle sales. A few hardy cowpunchers still ride with their herds from mountain pasture to mountain pasture all summer long. The riders certainly must look after their horses. And Colorado is the state where it all happens.

This leads back to the rodeo circuit, which has become lucrative for some Colorado cowboys of all ages who can travel to the more than 1,000 competitions that go on during the year in North America. In addition, there are hundreds of nonsanctioned amateur and intercollegiate rodeos and even some for kids.

Thirty million American tourists travel to the big spectacles. For ten days each July, for instance, many of the Colorado-based cowboys and cattle flock to Calgary, in Canada's province of Alberta, where the purses keep increasing. Altogether some $5 million in prizes go to riders in the United States and Canada; at Wyoming's famous Frontier Days alone, $950,000 in rodeo winnings are split by a cast of 1,500. About 400,000 visitors are entertained here.

The top cowboys often own sizable cattle ranches themselves. The famous ones sometimes fly their own planes.

Rodeo actually began as an exciting pastime of those rough, tough cowhands who rode the range and drove the herds of beef to market. "Ride 'em cowboy" was not much more than a contest of bravery among

Southwest Colorado Overview

I n southwest Colorado, pinyons and junipers yield to spruce and aspen as elevations increase north of Durango in the San Juan Range. Surprisingly to many people, the weather here is remarkably mild year-round, despite copious snowfall at high elevations. The mountains are always cooler than the deserts, but usually comfortably so, especially in summer when days are shirt-sleeves warm, while the heat leaves with the sun and a blanket is de rigeur for sleeping at night.

As is common throughout Colorado, summer is the main tourist season in southwest Colorado, followed by the ski crowd in winter. Caution: Skiing through waist-deep, soft powder in the

high, dry air on a typical sunny winter day may be addictive. The sun always comes out after a storm, so skiers sans jackets by noon are another common sight.

Colorado's legendary outdoor world has much to do with Colorado's international popularity. The state has 1,143 mountains rising to an altitude of at least 10,000 feet above sea level—and 1,000 are 2 miles high or more. Fifty-four often snow-crowned peaks towering above 14,000 feet give the state more than six times the mountain area of Switzerland. For more information contact the Colorado Fourteeners Initiative at (303) 278–7525, ext. 115. Web site: www. coloradofourteeners.org.

cowboys of the Old West. From these unassuming beginnings, rodeo has evolved into a big business.

Some Colorado cowboys and cowgirls take care of the horses at dozens of the state's dude ranches. The latter are basically rustic, with western-style furniture against a log-cabin backdrop. The rooms often contain fur-covered sofas, rugged granite fireplaces, elk antlers on the walls, or framed words of cowboy wisdom. The cooking is plain and the food plentiful and included for the help and customer alike. There is a warm feeling about these enclaves, nesting deeply in Colorado's forests, straddling mountaintops, overlooking rivers that rush and splash. The lodges are usually built with the pine or spruce woods and the stone rock of the region. The windows will surely look out upon pretty scenes.

The cowboys at these ranches often prepare breakfast for the guests on a hillside. At one well-known vacation center, the head wrangler teaches riding to first-timers and gives equestrian advice to others. Cowboys usually lead the various outings.

Meet Leslie (Les), a typical Colorado cowboy who owns one characteristic dude ranch west of Denver. Les employs a cook who feeds the guests, a clerk who checks them in, and a lodge manager who looks after details. Les himself is mostly involved with the horses. His life has always evolved around animals.

He hates to wear suits, and he hates to go to the city (where he keeps an apartment all the same). He doesn't like fancy talk, or talk, period. He likes horses and dogs better than people, yet at this moment he leads a group of people—experienced riders all—on another daily excursion, his second one today. He is not outgoing, yet he coddles and protects his "dudes," and no lives are ever jeopardized out here.

Les loves horses more than anything. At dawn, Les had walked over to the red barn and the corral. He'd whistled. His mare, Frosty, came right out. Animal and man were one as Les rode up with the early risers, some of them very slow, typical tourists, at first fearful and uncertain. As always, two other helpers galloped ahead of the group to fry the eggs and get the pancakes ready on the griddle. The coffee boils and sends up whiffs of flavor.

Some cowboys certainly show an adaptable spirit. A few of them, for instance, also take their guests hunting for wild game in the higher mountain ranges. At one horse center, Colorado's famous, luxurious C Lazy U Ranch, two of the cowboys adjusted to the times and to fads:

They learned to cross-country ski and now take the guests on ski trips in winter.

Some wranglers don't work at these ranches; they're independent and merely operate their own stables on a busy highway, looking for other work in winter.

Inspired by western cowpokes, a whole industry has sprung up in the United States. Much of the fashion in jeans, denim jackets, and cowboy boots harks back to the Old West. (At the dude ranches, meanwhile, the city dwellers arrive garbed in western wear with large western hats.)

For amateur geologists, most sand at Colorado's Great Sand Dunes is between 0.2 and 0.3 mm in diameter, composed of 51.7 percent volcanic rock fragments, 29.1 percent quartz, 8.9 percent feldspar, 2.5 percent sandstone, 0.7 percent magnetite, 3.4 percent other minerals, and 3.7 percent other rocks.

Colorado's "cowboy artists," while no longer on horseback or herding cattle, drive jeeps into the wilderness with their easels and paints. Art galleries in Denver sell the artists' output—sceneries with wild buffalo and paintings of wild horses, high mountains, and western prairies.

Cowboy poets enjoy popularity, too. Their output can be read in newspapers; national magazines and even book publishers print their verse.

Poems hang framed on dude ranch walls. The message can be brief and wise, as this little cowboy item from an anonymous author: "Never was there a cowboy who couldn't be throwed, never a bronc who couldn't be rode."

Most of the rhymes are simple, basic, perhaps a little primitive. Example? At one western ranch, a wrangler dug deeply to express the horsey West in a poem:

> *May Your Horse Never Stumble*
> *May Your Cinch Never Break*
> *May Your Belly Never Grumble*
> *May Your Heart Never Ache.*

The poem speaks a universal language.

Still a special person, the Colorado cowboy rides on.

Before you begin your journey into the heart of southwestern Colorado on US 160, turn east and then north on SR 150 for a stop at the uniquely marvelous ***Great Sand Dunes National Monument.*** Geologists say that sand stretches such as those found here are usually the handiwork of the world's oceans. Didn't the salt water have millions of years to crush, mash, and pulverize the land? The sea pushed, licked, and retreated, eroding rocks into small particles and grinding the earth to fine silt. Moreover, winds blew sand grains from the mountains to the plains. The source of sand is sediments, eroded in time by winds and glaciers and washed into the dunes. More recently, the drying southwesterly winds carried the sands into what is today the Great Sand Dunes National Monument. Erosive forces and more winds helped fashion sand peaks that crest to heights of 750 feet above the valley floor.

The monument looks as if it were flown in from Africa's Kalahari Desert and plunked into the middle of Colorado. White men didn't discover these dunes until 1599, when Spanish explorers first crossed the sands.

According to Colorado historian Richard Grant, pictures taken in 1927 show that the main dunes have undergone very little change in the past fifty years—except that in 1932, they became a national monument! The monument encompasses 38,662 acres, offering many activities, of which hiking on the dunes seems to be most visitors' first choice. Make sure you wear shoes in the summer—the sand can reach temperatures of 140°F. Save the bare feet for wading across the soft, water-cooled sand creek.

On the other side of the stream, the dunes are incredibly massive, some rising hundreds of feet above the valley floor. Due to shadows, they are deceptively steep. The valley floor is 7,500 feet above sea level, making breathing difficult at first for those not adjusted to the altitude.

But there are few experiences that can compare with being on the dunes. It's like riding the frozen waves of a storm-blown sea. You climb to the top of a ridge, taking in a view of the gold and tan waves stretching for miles to the towering blue mountains, and then descend the trough until you are in a valley completely surrounded by immense hills of sand. These are allegedly America's tallest sand dunes. The highest dune is located opposite the visitors center, and it takes about three hours to climb to the top and return. From the summit you are presented with a sweeping vista that includes a large segment of Colorado's stunning Sangre de Cristo Mountains.

Great Sand Dune National Monument is located on SR 150 in the south-central part of the state, just 16 miles off US 160, the main east-west highway through southern Colorado. Individuals age eighteen or older pay a $3.00 entry fee. The site is open daily. The visitors center also is open daily, except for winter holidays. For more information: Great Sane Dunes National Monument, 11500 Highway 150,

Trivia

The Pagosa Springs are used for bathing, and some, at 153°F, for energy to heat houses and buildings.

Mosca 81146-9798; (719) 378–2312. Fax (719) 378–2594. E-mail: GRSA_Interpretation@nps.gov. Web site: www.nps. gov/grsa.

Because of the long distances between this and other attractions, you may want to stay in Mosca. One good choice is the *Inn at Zapata Ranch,* 4 miles south of Great Sand Dunes National Monument on SR 150. Rustic meets sophisticated here, where the antique claw-foot bathtubs in the rooms are juxtaposed by critically acclaimed ranch cuisine at the inn's restaurant. Fifteen guest rooms are available from May through October; prices range from $112 to $225 per night. For information: 5303 Highway 150, Mosca 81146; (719) 378–2356 or (800) 284–9213. Fax (719) 378–2428. Email: zapatainn@ greatsanddunes.com. Web site: www.greatsanddunes.com.

Farther west, and just south of Wolf Creek Pass on US 160 lies *Pagosa Springs.* Named for the Ute word Pahgosa, meaning "boiling water," Pagosa Springs has a ready supply of natural geothermal energy.

The Spring Inn offers eleven tubs of varying temperature for soaking cares away. The fee is a few dollars. Like any town with a natural hot springs, Pagosa claims this is the hottest natural springs in the state. For information: The Spring Inn, P.O. Box 1799, Pagosa Springs 81147; (970) 264–4168 or (800) 225–0934. Fax (970) 264–4707. E-mail: PSResort@ PagosaSprings.Net. Web site: www.websites.pagosa.net/springinn.

Another water wonder near Pagosa is *Treasure Falls.* This is the longest waterfall in the entire San Juan National Forest. To get there, follow US 160 12 miles toward the Wolf Creek summit; enjoy the magnificent alpine scenery en route. A parking area for the falls provides a safe place to leave the car away from the road. A short 1/4-mile well-worn trail takes you to Colorado's miniversion of Niagara. For more information: Pagosa Ranger District, 180 Second Street, P.O. Box 310, Pagosa Springs 81147; (970) 264–2268. Fax (970) 264–1538. E-mail: jbridges@fs.fed.us. Web site: www.fs.fed.us/r2/sanjuan.

A *man*-made wonder close to Pagosa is *Chimney Rock.* These stone ruins were home to 2,000 Anasazi Indians more than 1,000 years ago. Still intact, these ruins are well preserved and protected. A locked gate 3 miles from the ruins prevents anyone from exploring without a National Forest Service guide.

Rock house ruins built into the hillside and the round ceremonial underground structures called kivas make the place seem as if the inhabitants just left, cleaning up before they went. Named for its towering twin spires of natural stone, Chimney Rock has been compared to Machu Picchu because it nestles in the high mountains and has grand vistas from almost every vantage point. Scholars have also suggested that during the occupation of Chimney Rock, the inhabitants were all men and that Chimney Rock was a sacred site for prayer and making powerful medicine. Chimney Rock is located 17 miles west of Pagosa Springs via US 160, and then southwest on SR 151. Four times daily, the Chimney Rock Interpretive Program tour takes place. Tour costs are $5.00 for adults and teenagers twelve and older, $2.00 for children five to eleven, children four and younger free. Fees are paid at the visitors center, which is open from 9:30 A.M. to 4:00 P.M. daily during the season (May 15 through September 30).

Prepaid reservations are required for all special workshops and hikes. Costs run around $20 per person per program. For more information: Chimney Rock Interpretive Program, P.O. Box 310, Pagosa Springs 81147; (970) 883–5359 (May 15 through September 30) or (970) 385–1210 (off-season, October 1 through May 14). E-mail: chimneyrock@ chimneyrockco.org. Web site: www.chimneyrockco.org.

On the edge of the Pagosa Springs community there awaits a pleasant resort with accommodations, jeep tours, hikes, and even tennis and mountain biking. A large children's playground and an observation tower beckon, too. For more information: Fairfield Pagosa, P.O. Box 4040, Pagosa Springs 81157; (800) 523–8973. E-mail: edco@gate.net. Web site: www.condo-vacations.com/fpc.htm.

For more information about Pagosa Springs: Pagosa Springs Area Chamber of Commerce, P.O. Box 787, Pagosa Springs 81147; (800) 252–2204. E-mail: chamber@pagosa-springs.com. Web site: www.pagosa-springs. com.

Located 18 miles north of Durango on US 550, the year-round deluxe **Tamarron Resort** remains a secret to many Coloradans. This remote oasis has everything—nature, atmosphere, and amenities. Dramatic triangular rocks line one side, wooded mountains the other. In between lies an undulating 18-hole golf course, where elk herds congregate at dawn under stands of ponderosa pine. Townhouses and a stately, perfectly blending lodge rest on a 200-foot cliff. North of Tamarron, some of Colorado's most magnificent alpine scenery is visible, and legendary communities such as Ouray and Silverton await exploration.

Horseback expeditions depart each day from the stables, bringing you into the one-million-acre San Juan National Forest. Guides who are well versed in the history and ecology of the area accompany the riders through the virgin wilderness.

For the adventurous, the Tamarron Resort offers myriad active outdoor possibilities. For instance, the sports deck can arrange a river-rafting trip. Fishing trips are popular. Durango beckons with a historic narrow-gauge railroad, which winds its way over narrow mountain passes. The resort has its own jeeps for high-country tours, where you can visit old mines and wander among some fifty species of wildflowers.

For more information: Sheraton Tamarron Resort, 40292 Highway 550, Durango 81301-8663, (970) 259–2000 or (800) 678–1000. E-mail: info@tamarron.com. Web site: www.tamarron.com. Accommodations and meals are very expensive.

Built in 1892, the renovated **Rochester Hotel** in downtown **Durango** offers fifteen luxurious rooms, all decorated in an Old West motif (inspired by the many Western movies filmed nearby). The hotel is just steps away from the Durango & Silverton railway station and historic Main Avenue.

The local folks claim that a number of famous entertainers have stayed at the Rochester, including Douglas Fairbanks, Jr., for instance. For more information: Rochester Hotel, 726 East Second Avenue, Durango 81301; (970) 385–1920 or (800) 664–1920. Fax (970) 385–1967. E-mail: stay@rochesterhotel.com. Web site: www.rochesterhotel.com.

Colorful Locals

• *In the early days in Durango, there was a rowdy local gang that went by the name of the Stockton–Eskridge gang. These boys and a group of local vigilantes once fought an hour-long gun battle on the main street through town.*

• *In 1885, locals set out on an expedition to New Mexico. What did they want? Why, to "dig up Aztecs." Included in the supplies for the expeditions were five cases of tobacco, three cases of beer, ten gallons of "heavy liquids," four burro-loads of "the stuff that busted Parliament," fuse (seven reels), soap, cigars, one fish line, rubber boots, bread, lard, and a pound of bacon.*

• *Editor "Dave" Day, of the Durango* Herald-Democrat *newspaper in the 1890s, once had forty-two pending libel suits against him.*

Ah, the good old days.

The bright orange cars of the **Durango & Silverton Narrow-Gauge Railroad** seem anxious to go, as the engine chugs away waiting for passengers to board. The popular tourist attraction is America's last regularly scheduled narrow-gauge passenger train.

Once serving the miners and ranchers of Silverton and Durango, the train now caters to passengers who want to spend three and a half hours each way thundering through spectacular mountain valleys. The excursion starts in Durango, which Will Rogers described as "out of the way and glad of it." But many people come here to experience a western town in touch with today's world.

Fort Lewis College attracts international students for its academic standards and natural setting; this school specializes in geology studies. Durango supposedly has the highest per capita number of professional mountain-bike racers in the country.

Be prepared for some dust and soot. Dress accordingly.

Train reservations are required. The schedule varies according to season but the train runs year-round. Peak-season round-trip costs are $53 for adults and teenagers twelve and older, $27 for children five to eleven, children four and younger free if riding on an adult's lap. Parlor car seating is $88 and only for those 21 or older. Off-season (winter) costs are a bit less. For more information: Durango & Silverton Narrow Gauge Railroad, 479 Main Avenue, Durango 81301; (970) 247–2733 or

Ridgway

Sooner or later, a trip will find you in southwestern Colorado, ready to downhill ski in spectacular Telluride or seeking some peace in Ridgway, where you don't need much money. In fact, the simpatico Shari and Lyle Braund, the owners/hosts of the unique **Chipeta Sun Lodge and Spa** in sleepy Ridgway (Zip code 81432) will get you 50 percent off if you want to ski at nearby Telluride. The Braunds can also take you hiking, cross-country skiing, or fishing. The Sun Lodge is pure adobe, with southwestern decor, solar heating, and the clean air at 6,995 feet, as well as views of the San Juan mountain range. All this, and more reasonable prices than in the better-known places like Telluride, Ouray, or Durango.

Ridgway is located north of Durango via US 550 to SR 62. For more information: Chipeta Sun Lodge and Spa, 304 South Lena, Ridgway 81432, (970) 626–3737 or (800) 633–5868, fax (970) 626–3715. E-mail: info@chipeta.com. Web site: www.chipeta.com.

(888) 872–4607. Fax (970) 259–3570. E-mail: Info@DurangoTrain.com. Web site: www.durangotrain.com.

For more information about Durango: Durango Area Chamber Resort Association, 111 South Camino del Rio, P.O. Box 2587, Durango 81301; (800) 525–8855 or (970) 247–0312. Fax (970) 385–7884. E-mail: durango@frontier.net. Web site: www.durango.org.

The admirers of this popular state speak well about Colorado's *Mesa Verde National Park.* It is a ten-hour drive southwest of Denver and is about an hour and a half west of Durango on US 160, midway between Mancos and Cortez. More than 600,000 visitors come here per year.

Mesa Verde yields an extraordinary educational experience. A very small area here provides you with much that is of archaeological interest. Before you drive the distance, however, you should keep in mind that Mesa Verde differs substantially from other parks. There is no fishing here; nor is there boating, swimming, or rock climbing. Your pets have to be on a leash and are not allowed in the ruins. And you can see the historic, wondrous cliff dwellings only in the company of park rangers.

The 21-mile road from the park entrance curves and swings and rotates upward; its width doesn't approximate that of an interstate highway. You may have trouble if you come in a truck or try to pull a large camper.

A visit to Mesa Verde National Park should be planned with care. Earmark one or two days for the park itself and try to arrive early in the day or during the off-season. The historical scene and the colors come through especially well if you can visit Mesa Verde at dawn. The moment you see the sudden, flat-topped plateau, the cliff dwellings of a prehistoric civilization, you'll be happy that you braved the distance. No other national park can equal this one.

Begin with a visit to the park's *Chapin Mesa Archeological Museum* for clues to the mysterious Basket Weavers. These Indians left behind

Telluride

*T*elluride is renowned for its breathaking alpine beauty, but many people don't realize that Telluride lies in the center of the greatest diversity of geology and archaeology in the nation. This area, known as the Grand Circle, encompasses four states, numerous state and national parks, and a variety of topography from the Rocky Mountains to the Painted Desert.

Cliff Palace, Mesa Verde National Park

an amazing array of agricultural tools, pottery, and baskets. The tribes arrived in the area around A.D. 450 and abandoned the site in 1276. It took another 500 years for Spanish explorers to discover the old, russet blocks of stone, the turrets and primitive apartments known as cliff dwellings hanging under a canopy of glorious rock. You will never forget the Balcony House and Cliff Palace.

At its height, the Mesa Verde Plateau supported 50,000 Indians. By the close of the thirteenth century, it was completely deserted. What happened to the Anasazi—the most famous builders of southwestern cliff dwellings and the ancestors of today's Pueblo Indians—is not known. Archaeologists theorize that a thirty-year drought starting in 1246, combined with soil that had been depleted by constant use, caused successive crop failures and that the Anasazi moved farther south into New Mexico and Arizona.

The National Park Service does a good job of looking after Mesa Verde's 80-square-mile area of ponderosa pine, spruce trees, and juniper, all laced by a few paths. Not a billboard or soft-drink sign in sight.

When visiting Mesa Verde you're not too far from the Four Corners area of Colorado, Utah, New Mexico, and Arizona. This is butte country. The sky is even bluer here in the southwestern corner of the state. The plains seem to stretch wider than in the northern corners. The Colorado peaks resemble those of the Alps, with jutting slopes and deeply carved valleys. (Bring a warm change of clothes.)

After the Mesa Verde experience, your own state or province will never be the same again. Park entry fee is $10 per vehicle. The Chapin Mesa Archeological Museum is open daily at 8:00 A.M., closing at 6:30 P.M. in summer and fall and at 5:00 P.M. in winter and spring. The museum phone number is (970) 529–4631. The Far View Visitor Center is open from mid-June through late October from 8:00 A.M. to 5:00 P.M. Phone: (970) 529–5036. Mesa Verde National Park is open daily year-round. For more information: P.O. Box 8, Mesa Verde National Park 81330-0008; (970) 529–4465. Fax (970) 529–4637. E-mail: MEVE_ General_Information@nps.gov. Web site: www.nps.gov/meve.

A 50-mile drive from the historic canyons of Mesa Verde will take you to another area of Indian ruins. This is little-known **Hovenweep National Monument,** west of Cortez, Colorado, reached by traveling gravel and rough blacktop roads. You will escape the crowds when you visit these ruins.

Here the terrain is high desert plateau. Sagebrush and scattered juniper trees dot the horizon. It seems desolate, almost barren. But there was life here. A canyon opens in the plateau, and scattered cottonwood trees indicate the presence of water. A spring still flows into a small depression in the shadow of the canyon wall. This water was the center of the community 700 years ago. The towers of Hovenweep are thought to be watch towers and fortifications to protect this precious liquid resource.

With artistic skill that would rival a stonemason's today, ancient Pueblo Indians built these towers in several configurations. Round, square, and oval structures dot the canyon edge. Each rock was trimmed to fit exactly with its neighbor, and the lines of the buildings are straight and almost smooth. Small peepholes and keyhole entrances could have provided views of a possible enemy approaching or just been a way to keep an eye on the rest of the community. Standing at the structure called Hovenweep Castle, you can look east and see a tower on almost every promontory of the canyon. Hiking and interpretive trails link most of these. Allow at least a half-day to explore the exposed ruins.

The ranger station is open year-round and operates a bookstore and a small museum. Don't count on buying lunch here, because Hovenweep has no food concession. A quiet little campground with picnic tables and water beckons, however. A $3.00 entry fee per person is charged. Call for directions; the only paved entrance is from Utah. Hovenweep is open year-round from 8:30 A.M. to 4:30 P.M. (except Christmas Day). For more information: McElmo Route, Cortez 81321, (970) 562–4282. E-mail: hoveinfo@nps.gov. Web site: www.nps.gov/hove.

The **Ute Indians** are the oldest continuous residents of Colorado of the seven original tribes who still live in the southwestern part of the state today. For those with an interest in Native American culture, the city of Durango is the gateway to both the **Southern Ute and Mountain Indian Ute Reservations.**

Nearly a century ago these Indians accepted government allotments and settled on a strip of land along the Colorado–New Mexico border, near the present town of **Ignacio** (population 800). Eventually, these Utes became known as the Southern Ute Indian tribe. Claiming more than 1,000 members, the Utes have their headquarters in Ignacio.

Here they have built an Indian Country vacation complex, complete with a thirty-eight-room motel, indoor/outdoor pool, museum, and a fine arts-and-crafts shop. The tribe lives on a reservation.

In some ways the present-day Utes can hardly be distinguished from any other Americans. Sounds of their television sets, radios, and VCRs fill their modern-day urban homes. Basketball and swimming are popular reservation sports.

The ancestral home of these Native Americans once spanned most of the present state of Colorado. Although reigning over a large empire, they lacked a common Ute political organization. Instead, they formed independent bands that followed their own chiefs. The most famous groups included the Uncompahgre or Tabeguache, whose central home was the area around the present sites of Gunnison and Montrose, Colorado; the White River and Yampa bands of northwestern Colorado; the Mouache, who roamed along the front range of the Rockies in Colorado; the Capotes, who lived in the San Luis Valley of Colorado; and the Weminuche, who lived in the San Juan Basin in southwestern Colorado.

While hunting and roaming their enormous territory, the Utes often fought against other tribes, yet they remained on generally good terms with white men who trapped, traded, and prospected for gold on Indian lands.

As Anglo settlers streamed onto Colorado's eastern slope, the government, fearing trouble between Anglos and Utes, tried to persuade the Utes to move to the west of the Continental Divide. Finding it difficult to negotiate with so many chiefs, the government designated an Uncompahgre leader, Ouray—his name means "arrow"—as the Ute tribal spokesman. Chief Ouray wanted to preserve his home and Ute territory; he resisted departure from the San Luis Valley and surrounding areas. Finally, under the treaty of 1868, the Native Americans agreed to move westward.

Subsequent treaties and promises made and broken resulted in combative Indians. Trouble erupted when Utes attacked and killed U.S. soldiers in the Meeker and Thornburgh massacres, and they were later driven off their lands.

These days all is peaceful in southern Colorado, though, and the Native Americans welcome tourists, especially since legalized gambling is allowed on the reservation. Glitzy casinos offer several types of gaming and bingo.

For more information: Southern Ute Indian Tribe, P.O. Box 340, Ignacio 81137; (970) 563–3000 or (800) 876–7017. Email: sellis@southern-ute.nsn.us. Web site: www.swcolotravel.org/sute/sute.html.

**PLACES TO STAY
IN SOUTHERN COLORADO**

CAÑON CITY/ROYAL GORGE
Best Western Royal Gorge Inn (reliable motor hotel; inexpensive to moderate); 1925 Fremont Drive; (719) 275–3377 or (800) 231–7317

Cañon Inn (inexpensive to moderate); 3075 East US 50; (719) 275–8676 or (800) 525–7727

Days Inn (inexpensive); 217 North Reynolds Avenue; (719) 269–1100

COLORADO SPRINGS
The Broadmoor Resort (famous convention hotel; deluxe); 1 Lake Circle; (719) 634–7711 or (800) 634–7711

Antlers Adam's Mark (downtown, perfect for shopping; expensive to deluxe); 4 South Cascade Avenue, at Pikes Peak Avenue and Cascade Avenue; (719) 473–5600

Garden of the Gods Motel (ideal location for visiting the attraction; inexpensive to moderate); 2922 West Colorado Avenue; (719) 636–5271

Holden House (expensive); 1102 West Pikes Peak; (719) 471–3980

Old Town Guesthouse Bed and Breakfast (make reservations far in advance; expensive); 115 South Twenty-sixth Street; (719) 632–9194

Quality Inn (inexpensive to moderate); 555 West Garden of the Gods Road; (719) 593–9119

CRESTED BUTTE
Crested Butte Club (moderate to deluxe); 512 Second Street; (970) 349–6655 or (800) 815–2582

Nordic Inn (lodge; moderate to expensive); 14 Treasure Road; (970) 349–5542

Old Town Inn (motel; inexpensive to moderate); 201 North Sixth Street; (970) 349–6184

CRIPPLE CREEK
Cripple Creek Motel (inexpensive); 201 Bison; (719) 689–2491

Holiday Inn Express (motel; moderate to expensive); 601 East Galena Avenue; (719) 689–2600

Imperial Casino Hotel (historic Victorian inn; authentic Old West atmosphere; inexpensive to moderate); 123 North Third Street; (719) 689–7777 or (800) 235–2922

Independence Hotel & Casino (inexpensive); 153 Bennett Avenue; (719) 689–2744

J. P. McGill's Hotel and Casino (inexpensive to moderate); 232 Bennett Drive; (719) 689–2446

DURANGO
General Palmer Hotel (historic bed and breakfast; moderate to deluxe); 567 Main Avenue; (970) 247–4747

Iron Horse Inn (moderate); 5800 North Main Avenue; (970) 259–1010 or (800) 748–2990

Lightner Creek Hotel (expensive); 999 CR 207; 3 miles west on US 160, 1 mile on Lightner Creek Road; (970) 259–1226 or (800) 268–9804

Rochester Hotel (historic inn; first-class accommodations; close to restaurants; expensive to deluxe); 726 East Second Avenue; (970) 385–1920 or (800) 664–1920

GREAT SAND DUNES/MOSCA
Inn at Zapata Ranch (expensive to deluxe); 5303 Highway 50 (isolated location; peace and quiet); (719) 378–2356

The Great Sand Dunes Lodge (inexpensive); 7900 Highway 150N; (719) 378–2900

GUNNISON
Mary Lawrence Inn (historic bed and breakfast; moderate); 601 North Taylor Street; (970) 641–3343

Super 8 (less expensive than competition; inexpensive); 411 East Tomichi Avenue; (970) 641–3068

Water Wheel Inn (motel; inexpensive); 37478 West Highway 50; (970) 641–1650

LEADVILLE
Apple Blossom Inn (expensive); 120 West Fourth Street; (719) 486–2141 or (800) 982–9279

Ice Palace Inn Bed & Breakfast (historic bed and breakfast; moderate to expensive); 813 Spruce Street; (719) 486–8272

Timberline Motel (inexpensive); 216 Harrison Avenue; (719) 486–1876

MANITOU SPRINGS
Black Bear Inn (moderate); 5250 Pikes Peak Highway, Cascade; (719) 684–0151

El Colorado Lodge (historic cottage; inexpensive to moderate); 23 Manitou Avenue; (719) 685–5485

Red Crags Bed and Breakfast Inn (moderate to deluxe); 302 El Paso Boulevard; (719) 685–1920 or (800) 721–2248

Santa Fe Motel (historic; inexpensive); 3 Manitou Avenue; (719) 475–8185

Town-N-Country Cottages (quiet accommodations; moderate to expensive); 123 Crystal Park Road; (719) 685–5427

MESA VERDE
Far View Lodge (motel; gets busy in summer, reserve far in advance; moderate); at Navajo Hill; in the park, 15 miles from the entrance; (970) 529–4421

MONTROSE
Black Canyon (clean motel; inexpensive); 1605 East Main; (970) 249–3495 or (800) 348–3495

Country Lodge (motel; inexpensive); 1624 East Main; (970) 249–4567

Western (motel; inexpensive); 1200 East Main; (970) 249–3481 or (800) 445–7301

PAGOSA SPRINGS

Fairfield Pagosa Resort (tennis, golf, restaurant on premises; deluxe); P.O. Box 4040; (970) 731–4081

High Country Lodge (motel; inexpensive); 3821 US 160E; (970) 264–4181 or (800) 862–3707

Pagosa Lodge Resort (moderate to expensive); 3505 US 160W; (970) 731–4141 or (800) 523–7704

Spring Inn Motel (hot springs; moderate to expensive); 165 Hot Springs Boulevard; (970) 264–4168

PUEBLO

Abriendo Inn (bed and breakfast; inexpensive to moderate); 300 West Abriendo Avenue; (719) 544–2703

Best Western Inn (inexpensive to moderate) 730 North Santa Fe Avenue; (719) 543–6530

Days Inn (good value; inexpensive to moderate); 4201 North Elizabeth; (719) 543–8031

PLACES TO EAT IN SOUTHERN COLORADO

CAÑON CITY/ROYAL GORGE

Grandview Steakhouse (moderate to expensive); US 50 and Royal Gorge Road; (719) 269–3594

Merlino's Belvedere (Italian, American; moderate); 1330 Elm Avenue; (719) 275–5558

Pizza Madness (inexpensive); 509 Main Street; (719) 276–3088

COLORADO SPRINGS

Charles Court at the Broadmoor (true elegance and class; large menu; deluxe); 1 Lake Avenue; (719) 577–5774

Edelweiss (German; authentically European; moderate to expensive); 34 East Ramona Avenue; (719) 633–2220

Giuseppe's Depot (Italian, American; inexpensive to moderate); 10 South Sierra Madre; (719) 635–3111

La Casita Patio Café (Mexican; inexpensive); 1331 South Nevada Avenue; (719) 633–9616

La Petit Maison (French; deluxe); 1015 West Colorado Avenue; (719) 632–4887

Maggie Mae's (Mexican, American; inexpensive to moderate); 2405 East Pikes Peak Avenue; (719) 475–1623

CRESTED BUTTE

Donita's Cantina (Tex-Mex, Mexican; inexpensive to moderate); 332 Elk Avenue; (970) 349–6674

Crested Butte Brewery (steakhouse; moderate); 226 Elk Avenue; (970) 349–5026

La Bosquet (well-established French restaurant; expensive); 6 Red Lady Street; (970) 349–5808

CRIPPLE CREEK

The Stratton's Grill at Imperial Casino Hotel (historic; American; moderate to expensive); 123 North Third Street; (719) 689–7777

DURANGO

Ariano's (Italian; expensive); 150 East College Drive; (970) 247–8146

Henry's at the Strater (historic; regional American, moderate); 699 Main Avenue; (970) 247–4431

Lori's Family Dining (ribs; Mexican; inexpensive to moderate); 2653 Main Avenue; (970) 247–1224

Ore House (steakhouse; moderate to expensive); 147 East College Drive; (970) 247–5707

GUNNISON

Garlic Mike's (Italian; inexpensive to moderate); 2674 North Highway 135; (970) 641–2493

Quarter Circle Restaurant (American; moderate); 323 East Tomichi Avenue; (970) 641–0542

The Trough (steak, seafood, game; moderate); 2 miles west on US 50; (970) 641–3724

LEADVILLE

Columbine Cafe (American; moderate); 614 Harrison Avenue; (719) 486–3599

La Cantina (Mexican); 1942 US Highway 24; (719) 486–9021

MANITOU SPRINGS

Adam's Mountain Cafe (vegetarian; moderate); 110 Canon Avenue; (719) 685–1430

The Briarhurst Manor (continental; moderate to expensive); 404 Manitou Avenue; (719) 685–1864

Craftwood Inn (Colorado cuisine; seafood, game; expensive to deluxe); 404 El Paso Boulevard; (719) 685–9000

Mission Bell Inn (Mexican; moderate); 178 Crystal Park Road; (719) 685–9089

Stage Coach (buffalo, prime rib; moderate to expensive); 702 Manitou Avenue; (719) 685–9400

MONTROSE

Glenn Eyrie (American; expensive); 2351 South Townsend Avenue; (970) 249–9263

Jim's Texas Style BBQ (inexpensive to moderate); 1201 South Townsend; (970) 249–4809

Sakura (sushi, Japanese; moderate to expensive); 411 North Townsend; (970) 249–8230

The Whole Enchilada (Mexican; inexpensive to moderate); 44 South Grand Avenue; (970) 249–1881

PAGOSA SPRINGS

Branding Iron Bar-B-Que (western; inexpensive to moderate); 3961 East Highway 160; (970) 264–4268

Elkhorn Cafe (Mexican, American; expensive to moderate); 438C Pagosa Boulevard; (970) 264–2146

Ole Miner Steakhouse (moderate); 3825 Highway 160; (970) 264–5981

Riverside (Southwestern, American; moderate); 439 San Juan Street; (970) 264–2175

PUEBLO

Cactus Flower (Southwestern; moderate); 2149 Jerry Murphy Road; (719) 549–2009

Cafe Del Rio (continental; moderate); 5200 Nature Center Road; (719) 545–1009

Gaetano's (Italian; large portions; moderate to expensive); 910 US 50W; (719) 546–0949

La Renaissance (continental; moderate to expensive); 217 East Routt Avenue; (719) 543–6367

Nacho's (Mexican; moderate); 409 North Santa Fe; (719) 544–0733

SEDALIA

Gabriel's (historic; fine dining; deluxe); 5450 North Highway 67; (303) 688–2323

Other Attractions Worth Seeing in Southern Colorado

COLORADO SPRINGS

Flying W Ranch, (719) 598–4000
Old Colorado City, (719) 577–4112
U.S. Olympic Visitors Center, (888) 659–8687

DURANGO

Purgatory Resort, (970) 247–9000 or (800) 525–0892

GUNNISON

Alpine Tunnel, (970) 641–1501 (Chamber of Commerce)
Schofield Pass, (970) 641–1501 (Chamber of Commerce)
Tincup Old Mining Town, (970) 641–1501 (Chamber of Commerce)
Western State College of Colorado, (800) 876–5309

LEADVILLE

Leadville, Colorado & Southern Railroad Train Tour,
(719) 486–3936

MANITOU SPRINGS

Cave of the Winds, (719) 685–5444

MONTROSE

Owl Creek Pass, (970) 249–5000 or (800) 923–5515 (Chamber of Commerce)

PAGOSA SPRINGS

Navajo State Park, (970) 883–2208
Wolf Creek Pass, (970) 264–2360 or (800) 252–2204 (Chamber of Commerce)

PUEBLO

The Greenway and Nature Center of Pueblo, (719) 549–2414
University of Southern Colorado, (877) 872–9653

Southern Colorado General Information Resources

CAÑON CITY

Cañon City Chamber of Commerce,

403 Royal Gorge Boulevard 81212; (719) 275–2331 or (800) 876–7922

E-mail: chamber@canoncity.com

Web site: www.canoncitychamber.com

COLORADO SPRINGS

Colorado Springs Convention and Visitors Bureau,

104 South Cascade, Suite 104, 80903; (800) 368–4748

Web site: www.coloradosprings-travel.com

CRESTED BUTTE

Crested Butte–Mt. Crested Butte Chamber of Commerce,

P.O. Box 1288, 81224; (970) 349–6438 or (800) 545–4505

Web site: www.crestedbuttechamber.com

CRIPPLE CREEK

Cripple Creek Chamber of Commerce,

367 East Bennett Avenue, 80813; (719) 689–2169 or (800) 526–8777;

fax (719) 689–0512

Cripple Creek Welcome Center, (877) 858–4653

E-mail: info@cripple-creek.co.us

Web site: www.cripple-creek.co.us

DURANGO

Durango Area Chamber Resort Association,

111 South Camino del Rio, P.O. Box 2587, 81301; (970) 247–0312 or (800) 525–8855;

fax (970) 385–7884

E-mail: durango@frontier.net

Web site: www.durango.org

Southern Colorado General
Information Resources (cont.)

Gunnison

Gunnison Country Chamber of Commerce,

500 East Tomichi Avenue, 81230; (970) 641–1501

Web site: www.gunnison-co.com

Leadville

Leadville/Lake County Chamber of Commerce,

809 Harrison Avenue, P.O. Box 861, 80461; (719) 486–3900 or (800) 933–3901

E-mail: leadville@LeadvilleUSA.com

Web site: www.leadvilleusa.com

Manitou Springs

Manitou Springs Chamber of Commerce,

345 Manitou Avenue, 80829; (800) 642–2567

E-mail: manitou@pikes-peak.com

Web site: www.manitousprings.org

Mesa Verde

Mesa Verde National Park,

P.O. Box 8, 81330-0008; (970) 529–4465; fax (970) 529–4637

E-mail: MEVE_General_Information@nps.gov

Web site: www.nps.gov/meve

Montrose

Montrose Chamber Of Commerce,

1519 East Main Street, 81401; (970) 249–5000 or (800) 923–5515; fax (970) 249–2907

E-mail: mchamber@frontier.net

Web site: www.montrose.org/chamber2

Southern Colorado General
Information Resources (cont.)

MOSCA

Great Sane Dunes National Monument,

11500 Highway 150, 81146-9798; (719) 378–2312; fax (719) 378–2594

E-mail: GRSA_Interpretation@nps.gov

Web site: www.nps.gov/grsa

PAGOSA SPRINGS

Pagosa Springs Area Chamber of Commerce,

P.O. Box 787, 81147; (800) 252–2204

E-mail: chamber@pagosa-springs.com

Web site: www.pagosa-springs.com

PUEBLO

Greater Pueblo Chamber of Commerce,

P.O. Box 697, 81002; (800) 233–3446

E-mail: info@pueblochamber.org

Web site: www.pueblo.org

Denver and the Plains

Denver Metropolitan Area

There were the Spaniards and the Native American tribes—Utes, Cheyennes, Arapahos, and Cherokees. Then suddenly came the prospectors to that prairie wilderness 10 miles east of the mountain ramparts. The fate of a tranquil Native American village at the junction of Cherry Creek and South Platte River would be changed forever.

That summer day in 1858, the Anglo visitors found gold in these waters.

Word of the find soon spread. "The New Eldorado!" shouted the mid-western papers. That spring an estimated 150,000 people began to trek across the wide plains aboard wagons and even on foot. Only 40,000 made it or stayed; others turned back.

Gold in paying quantities was far from common. Those first months were very hard. Yet, that year a people's court was organized. The first hotel—the Denver House—opened. Publisher William N. Byers reached Denver on April 21, 1859, with a printing outfit. On April 23 he issued the first newspaper printed in Colorado. William McGaa was the

Notes on Colorado from a Longtime Denverite

I find it remarkable that I can sit at a different outdoor terrace of my house for a summer breakfast, for an al fresco lunch, and for dinner. During each meal, I can enjoy the gleam and glitter of the Rocky Mountains. More: Depending on the weather I can see Pikes Peak, the famous "Fourteener," about 75 miles to the south; I can spot Longs Peak, another Fourteener, and lastly, Mt. Evans. As I open the cereal box and watch the steaming coffee, I feel very lucky. To live in Colorado! Who could ask for more?

I remember how I came to the state. I had been living in Austria, which had gleaming mountains as well—the Alps! I opted for the Rockies instead, never to regret it.

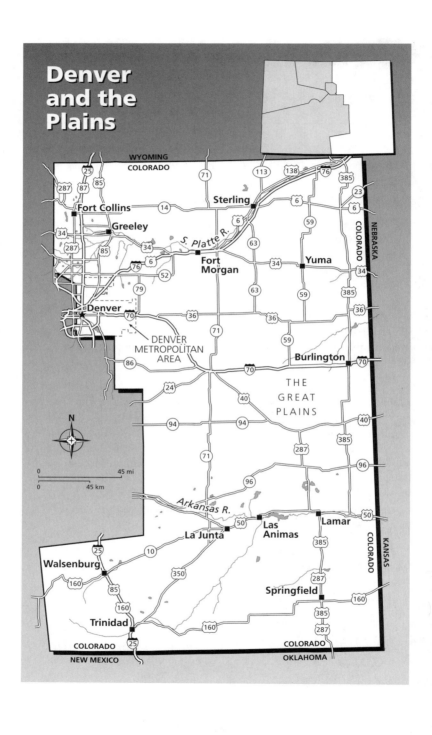

Denver
and the
Plains

WYOMING
COLORADO

25
85
287
87
85
71
113
138
76
385
23
6
6
Fort Collins
14
Sterling
6
59
34
6
Greeley
63
287
85
34
34
Yuma
34
76
6
Fort
Morgan
52
79
63
59
385
Denver
70
36
36
36
DENVER
METROPOLITAN
AREA
71
59
86
Burlington
70
24
70
40
THE
GREAT
PLAINS
40
94
94
385
N
71
287
96
96
385
0   45 mi
0   45 km
Arkansas R.
50
La Junta
50
Las
Animas
Lamar
25
385
10
Walsenburg
350
287
Springfield
160
85
160
385
160
287
Trinidad
160
25
COLORADO
COLORADO
NEW MEXICO
OKLAHOMA

S. Platte R.

COLORADO
NEBRASKA

COLORADO
KANSAS

AUTHOR'S FAVORITE ATTRACTIONS IN
DENVER AND THE PLAINS

first child born in Denver. Leavenworth and Pikes Peak Express ran the first stage to Denver. The Auraria Post Office was established.

That May, John H. Gregory discovered a vein of gold-bearing quartz near what was to become Central City. This was big news, and, at first, it nearly evacuated Denver. As mines were developed in the mountains, however, Denver grew in its coming role as an important trade center. Indeed, Horace Greeley suggested, "Go West, young man! Go West, young man!" Denver became the logical jumping-off point for the huge gold finds of Central City and Black Hawk.

Exaggerated accounts of the discovery traveled eastward, causing the Gold Rush of 1859. Thousands of fortune hunters hurried across the plains, on foot, on horseback, in wagons, some even pushing handcarts and wheelbarrows. Most of these failed to find the mineral and trudged wearily back home. But they had founded several little habitation clusters variously known as Auraria and Denver City (named after General James W. Denver, territorial governor of Kansas), and these gradually became the capital city of Colorado.

All through the late 1850s and early 1860s, a great mass of people surged back and forth in search of wealth. Conditions were primitive in these Colorado camps. Tents were eventually replaced by huts, which grew into shacks, log cabins, and finally houses.

Gold brought more fortune hunters from all over North America, but also Irish engineers, Welsh hard-rock miners, and other Europeans, 100,000 more people in all. For a period between the 1870s and 1890s, Colorado had so many Germans that the laws were printed in both German and English.

Lots of problems and calamities awaited the city.

Larimer Square,
(303) 607–1276,
www.larimersquare.com

Horsetooth Reservoir,
(970) 679–4570,
www.co.larimer.co.us/parks/
Horsetooth.htm

Brown Palace Hotel,
(800) 321–2599,
www.brownpalace.com

Governors' Mansion
(Executive Residence),
(303) 866–3681,
www.archives.state.co.us/
residenc.html

Sloan Lake,
(303) 964–2580,
www.denvergov.org/content/
template21231.asp

Lakewood's Heritage
Center, (303) 987–7850,
www.lakewood.org/parks/
belmar.html

Washington Park,
(303) 964–2580,
www.denvergov.org/content/
template21232.asp

Wellshire Inn,
(303) 759–3333,
www.wellshireinn.com

Denver Center for the
Performing Arts,
(303) 893–4000,
www.denvercenter.org

Butterfly Pavilion and
Insect Center,
(303) 469–5441,
www.butterflies.org

Early in 1863, a great fire destroyed much of the business district. The following summer the lush plains were scorched by a drought. The winter was cold beyond all previous experience. Then, in the spring of 1864, a flash flood churned along the Cherry Creek sand bed through the city, washing over houses and bridges and killing twenty people. Nearly $1 million worth of property was destroyed.

In the wake of these natural disasters, the Indians attacked. Stage stations were sacked, communication and supply lines to the East severed. Denver was left with only a week's supply of food.

But the city survived, and because of the hardships the local people developed a determination to keep on surviving. When the Union Pacific Railroad bypassed Colorado on its transcontinental route, Denver citizens raised $300,000 and built their own railroad to meet the Union Pacific at Cheyenne, Wyoming.

Soon the Kansas Pacific crossed the plains. According to historian Richard Grant, "The silver barons built elaborate mansions on Capitol Hill. Gamblers, drifters and gunmen flooded the saloons and gaming halls on Larimer and Market streets. Bat Masterson tended bar here, Soapy Smith ran the West's largest gang of thieves, crooks and con artists, and anyone who was anyone in the 'Old West' paid at least a visit to Denver's mud-filled, honky-tonk streets."

On August 1, 1876, Colorado entered the Union and was called the Centennial State in honor of the one hundredth anniversary of the Declaration of Independence.

By 1879, the Mile High City had a population of 35,000 and boasted the first telephone service in the West. Soon there was a second boom. One silver mining camp after another suddenly prospered. When the silver played out, Denver settled into a comfortable, respectable life—nearly free of gamblers, drifters, and claim jumpers.

Education now became important. In 1887, Governor Ben H. Eaton told the general assembly: "The schools of Denver are today equal to the best in the world—equal to those of Boston, Paris or Berlin. The capital of our state is the Athens of the plains, with the glory of ancient Athens."

AUTHOR'S FAVORITE EVENTS IN DENVER AND THE PLAINS

National Western Stock Show, Horse Show and Rodeo; *National Western Complex in Denver; early to mid-January; (303) 297-1166; www.nationalwestern. com/NWSS/home/index.asp*

Cherry Blossom Festival; *Sakura Square, Denver; June or July; (303) 295-1844; www.asiaxpress.com/events_enter/ eventlist.asp*

Buskerfest; *Denver; late June; (303) 478-7878; www.buskerfest.com*

Independence Stampede and Rodeo; *Greeley; late June through July 4; (800) 982-2855; www.greeleystampede.org*

Larimer County Fair and Rodeo; *Loveland; early August; (970) 669-6760; www.co.larimer.co.us/fair/lcf/index.htm*

Oktoberfest; *Larimer Square in Denver; mid-September; (303) 534-2367; www.larimersquare.com*

Great American Beer Festival; *Currigan Exhibition Hall in Denver; early October; (303) 447-0816; www.beertown.org/ GABF/gabf.htm*

Winterfest; *Larimer Square in Denver; every weekend from November 1 through January 1; (303) 534-2367; www. larimersquare.com*

WILDLIGHTS; *Denver Zoo in Denver; nightly for the month of December; (303) 376-4800; www.denverzoo.org*

Lincoln Center Showstopper Series; *Fort Collins; various evenings throughout the year; (970) 221-6735; www.fcchamber.org*

By 1910, the city had become the commercial and industrial center of the Rocky Mountain region, with a large cattle market and the largest sheep market in the world. Denver was in the process of becoming the nation's second capital, thanks to a proliferation of government offices. This situation is still true today; Denver is second only to Washington, D.C., in number of employed government workers.

Many older Denverites still harbor a nostalgic feeling about Colorado Victoriana, and some people are seriously trying to hold on to the city's remaining old mansions. There is public resistance to the wreckers sent by those who prefer the profit of more office buildings and high-rise apartment houses. Many of the noted old edifices, the Tabor Theater and the Windsor Hotel among them, had to give way to the modern glass-and-steel skyscrapers. "Part of Denver died tonight," wrote a Denverite the day another of the historic hotels was razed.

A few of the Victorian homes still exist, complete with the cherrywood dressers, mantelpieces, hat racks, and mirror frames. The historic **Brown Palace** and the **Oxford Hotel** (1600 Seventeenth Street, Denver 80202; 303–628–5400 or 800–228–3858. Fax 303–628–5413. E-mail: comments@ hotelbook.com. Web site: www.theoxfordhotel.citysearch. com/1.html) are alive and well. While in the city, you may wish to visit one of the

Trivia

Denver has 300 days of sunshine annually—more hours of sun each year than Miami Beach!

old mansions, such as the **Molly Brown House Museum,** where history is preserved.

After she became wealthy, the "Unsinkable" Molly Brown lived her flamboyant life in this mansion of native Colorado lava-stone. Following Molly's death in 1932, the building served as a rooming house. Then, at the whim of each new owner, it was remodeled or divided. Rescued in 1971 by "Historic Denver," the mansion was decorated as Molly herself had done, using old photographs Molly had taken of her home's interior. The Molly Brown House has been restored to its exaggerated, extreme opulence. It is located at 1340 Pennsylvania Street, Denver 80218; (303) 832–4092. Web site: www.mollybrown.com. Admission costs $6.00 for adults and teenagers thirteen and older, $4.00 for senior citizens sixty-five and older, $2.00 for children six to twelve, children five or younger free. Open from June 1 through August 31, Monday through Saturday from 10:00 A.M. to 4:00 P.M. and Sunday from noon to 4:00 P.M. Open from September 1 through May 31, Tuesday through Saturday from 10:00 A.M. to 4:00 P.M. and Sunday from noon to 4:00 P.M., closed Monday and major holidays.

Colorado's **Governors' Mansion** (also known as the Cheesman-Boettcher Mansion and the Executive Residence), a redbrick Colonial building with white stone trim, was built by one of the state's distinguished pioneer families, the Cheesmans. (Cheesman Park is named for them.) After serving as the home of John Evans, Colorado's second territorial governor, the property passed into the Boettcher family. Then it became part of their Boettcher Foundation, a philanthropic organization that presented it as a gift to the state of Colorado in 1960. The mansion has been the executive residence of the state's governors ever since.

Furnished with luxurious art, antiques, and furniture, the house is available for limited tours. It is located at 400 East Eighth Street in Denver. For more information about tours, contact the Colorado Historical Society's Office of Archeology and Historical Preservation, 1300 Broadway, Denver 80203; (303) 866-3681. E-mail: oahp@chs.state.co.us. Web site: www.archives.state.co.us/residenc. html.

If you enjoy visiting stately old Denver mansions, you might consider the **Pearce McAllister Cottage,** located at 1880 Gaylord Street, Denver 80206. This 1899 structure also contains the **Denver Museum of Miniatures, Dolls and Toys.** Open Tuesday through Saturday from 10:00 A.M. to 4:00 P.M. and Sunday from 1:00 to 4:00 P.M. Admission costs $3.00 for anyone age seventeen through sixty-one and $2.00

Black American West Museum & Heritage Center

*D*id you know that nearly one-third of America's working cowboys in the Old West were African-American? **The Black American West Museum** *(8 Heritage Center) offers a unique and much-needed look at the history of these and other African-Americans and the roles they played in our nation's past. The museum is housed in the former home of Denver's first African-Ameri-can doctor, Dr. Justina Ford, who delivered more than 7,000 babies during her illustrious career. Admission prices are $4.00 for adults, $3.00 for students, children two and younger free. Call for hours. For more information: 3901 California, Denver 80205, (303) 292–2566, fax (303) 382–1981. E-mail: bawmhc@aol.com. Web site: www.coax. net/people/lwf/bawmus.htm.*

for ages two to sixteen and senior citizens sixty-two and older, children one and younger free. Call (303) 322-1053 or visit the Web site: www.sni.net/start/dmmdt.

The *Grant-Humphreys Mansion* was built in 1902 and named after former Colorado governor James B. Grant. It has more than forty rooms. The mansion is open from 10:00 A.M. to 5:00 P.M. Monday through Friday; closed Saturday and Sunday. For more information: Grant-Humphreys Mansion, 770 Pennsylvania Street, Denver 80203; (303) 894–2506.

The *Byers-Evans House,* a mansion built in 1883, has been restored to its original grandeur. Admission costs $3.00 for anyone age seventeen through sixty-four, $2.50 for seniors age sixty-five or older, and $1.50 for young people age six through sixteen. Children age five or younger are admitted free. The paid admission rates rise to $5.00, $4.00, and $2.00, respectively, if you buy a combination ticket that includes admission to both the Byers-Evans House and the adjacent *Denver History Museum* housed in the mansion's carriage house. Hours of operation are 11:00 A.M. to 3:00 P.M. Tuesday through Sunday; closed Monday. For more information: Byers-Evans House, 1310 Bannock Street, Denver; (303) 620–4933 or visit the Web site www.coloradohistory.org.

The most sumptuous of all the historic buildings in this part of Denver is the castlelike *Capitol Hill Mansion,* an impeccable, deluxe bed-and-breakfast. The mansion, a landmark building listed in the National Register of Historic Places, is not far from the Governor's Mansion and the Molly Brown House. The 1891 furniture is hand-carved oak and maple. The walls are decorated with original Colorado landscape paintings. Some of the rooms come with four-posters and mountain-viewing balconies. Unlike many B&Bs, this one offers room TVs, fresh flowers, and a small refrigerator with refreshments (complimentary). For more information: Capitol Hill Mansion, 1207 Pennsylvania, Denver 80203; (303) 839–5221 or (800) 839–9329. Fax (303) 839–9046. E-mail: Info@capitolhillmansion.com. Web site: www. capitolhillmansion.com. Above-average prices.

Trivia

In 2000 Hennen's American Public Library Ratings Index honored the Denver Public Library as the number one library in the country for population centers with more than 500,000 people.

The stunning Central Library building came about as a result of the approval of a 1990 bond issue by 75 percent of Denver's voters. Designed by famed architect Michael Graves and the Denver firm of Klipp Colussy Jenks DuBois, the 540,000-square-foot library opened in 1995.

For more information: 10 West Fourteenth Avenue Parkway, Denver 80204-2731; (720) 865–1111. Open 10:00 A.M. to 9:00 P.M., Monday through Wednesday 10:00 A.M. to 5:30 P.M. Thursday through Saturday, and 1:00 to 5:00 P.M. Sunday. Web site: www.denver.lib.co.us.

Considering Colorado's booming economy and amazing environment, it's no wonder that most Denverites refuse to relocate to another city. "Move?" says one executive. "They offered me a promotion on the East Coast. But I refused. Stayed on at a lower salary." If you ask longtime Denver people why they're so partial to their city, you'll get a long string of explanations. "We ski. The mountains are close." "We love the many parks and green lawns of the homes." "Do you know a more cosmopolitan place between Los Angeles and Chicago? Denver is *it!*"

Because the mountains are only thirty minutes away from downtown, Denver attracts a young, energetic population. This dynamic energy is reflected in Denver's nightlife. The city boasts more than 2,500 restaurants, more than 150 art galleries, almost 30 theaters, 100 cinemas, an $80 million performing arts center, a convention center, and dozens of nightclubs, discos, comedy clubs, singles bars, and concert halls.

If there is one thing Denver does well (after 130 years of practice), it is the saloon. The first permanent structure in Denver was a saloon, and today there are sports bars, art bars, fern bars, outdoor cafe bars, English pubs, "Old West" saloons, rock bars, city-overlook bars, country-and-western bars, art deco bars, and even bars that don't serve alcohol. (Denver leads the nation in beer brewing, however.)

In addition to a plethora of saloons, Denver has more sporting-goods stores and ski shops per capita than most any other population center in the world and a corresponding number of

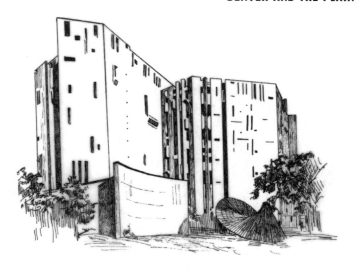

Denver Art Museum

recreation facilities that include free outdoor tennis courts, city golf courses, and the like.

At the same time, filmmakers, artists, and thinkers all gravitate toward Denver, a city that spent $6 million to build an art museum. The *Denver Public Library,* with its 4.4 million total holdings, happens to be one of the best—and most versatile—in the country. It is at the library desks that you get the feeling of Denver's wide horizons.

Denver's genuine penchant for culture shows up in several other ways. On a given evening, the visitor to the state capital could take in a play by Dylan Thomas at the boldly designed *Denver Center Theatre,* part of the *Denver Center for the Performing Arts* (DCPA). DCPA is home to two production companies—Denver Center Theatre and Denver Center Productions (DCP). DCP is responsible for importing touring Broadway shows, among other roles. DCPA also houses the *Wilbur James Gould Voice Center* (WJGVC). This unique voice center, a part of the National Center for Voice and Speech, offers free workshops to help prevent speech difficulties and works with speech- and voice-impaired individuals. WJGVC laboratories also conduct research on the human voice. For more information: DCPA: 1245 Champa Street, Denver 80204; (303) 893–4000. Tickets: (303) 893–4100 or (800) 641–1222. Web site: www.denvercenter.org.

Next door to DCPA is the 2,700-seat **Boettcher Concert Hall,** where music lovers enjoy the music of the **Colorado Symphony Orchestra,** among other performers. For ticket information call (303) 986–8742. Web site: www.coloradosymphony.org. Season runs from September through May. Boettcher Concert Hall is located at Fourteenth and Curtis Streets in Denver. The city has come of age culturally, what with its little theaters, its art cinemas, its ballets, and its chamber music ensembles.

Local interest is keen in the rest of the world. And Denver's citizens remain helpful and hospitable, especially toward tourists and guests. Just tell a Denverite that you arrived here yesterday from London or Frankfurt or Minneapolis or wherever. Doors will spring wide open.

Denverites will show off their clean city; they may want to take you to their homes, where the inevitable sprinklers deepen the green of the lawns and flower gardens.

Denver arouses special interest because of its ethnic variety. The Hispanic population is fascinating for its rich and proud heritage.

In north Denver, you find the classic Italian grocery stores that sell prosciutto, salami, black olives, and *tonno* as do those in Italy. Genuine Italian restaurants serve you homemade pasta and black olives and you drink Chianti, just as you would in Naples, Salerno, or Parma.

There is a Polish club in Denver, where the young Polish girls still wear the pretty national costumes for their national folk dances.

A small Denver contingent is German speaking, with a lasting interest in dancing *schuhplattler* and singing all the old songs. The Germans founded an appropriately named Edelweiss Club, a Goethe Club, and

Denver Firefighters Museum

*L*ooking for something a little farther off the beaten path? Check out this hands-on museum that chronicles the history of fire fighting in Denver since the construction of the first fire station in 1909. The museum is located in the well-preserved original Station No. 1 and features a wide array of fire-fighting memorabilia. Open Monday through Friday from 10:00 A.M. to 2:00 P.M.; admission is $3.00 for adults; $2.00 for children. For more information: Denver Firefighters Museum, 1326 Tremont Place, Denver 80204, (303) 892-1436. E-mail: info@firedenver. org. Web site: www.firedenver. org/museum.

the *Turnverein,* where the men do strenuous cal-isthenics and play soccer on weekends. Denver has its own German/Swiss *Delikatessen* stores, which import marinated herring from Kiel and Hamburg, Westphalian hams, and landjaeger sausages and sell their customers Nivea suntan creams, German Odol toothpaste, and *Der Stern* magazines, much as in Manhattan's Yorkville area.

There is a sizable Japanese population, with its own stores and customs and a Buddhist Temple for weddings. Vietnamese immigrants have their own shopping centers, and you will find Korean shops.

There is also Denver's enthusiasm for international dining. Well-traveled, polyglot restaurateurs like Pierre Wolfe often appear on television or radio. It should come as no surprise that the city has a number of authentic (and expensive) French eating places, such as **Normandy French Restaurant,** located at 1515 Madison Street; (303) 321–3311 (expensive). Denver's dozens of superb Asian restaurants include the ever-popular and elegant **Imperial Chinese Restaurant,** 431 South Broadway; (303) 698–2800 (expensive). E-mail: imperial@uswestmail. net. Web site: www.imperialchinese.com. Or why not enjoy an eclectic mix of the two cuisines? For a dining experience to be remembered (by both your tongue and your pocketbook), make reservations at **Papillon Café,** where new French and European cuisines blend with Asian highlights for unique meal creations. Papillon Café is located at 250 Josephine Avenue in the Cherry Creek area of Denver; (303) 333–7166. The visitor can also dine on genuine Ethiopian, Afghan, Moroccan, Greek, Armenian, Hungarian, Swiss, German, Italian, and, of course, Mexican fare.

How about the traveler from the British Isles? At the foot of the new downtown skyscrapers, **Duffy's Shamrock Restaurant** holds court with (inexpensive) Irish home cooking, followed by real Irish coffee. This pub serves a filling supper at a reasonable price (1635 Court Place; 303–534–4935).

To be sure, the city's better restaurants, its bistros and more worldly nightspots, and its extra-elegant central hotels are accustomed to and welcome the visitor from abroad.

Denver and environs attract more than ten million visitors a year. "Smile!" goes one of the state's slogans, "You live in Colorado!" And most Denverites smile a lot as they count their blessings.

For more information: Denver Metro Convention and Visitors Bureau, 1555 California, Suite 300, Denver 80202; (800) 233–6837. Fax (303) 892–1636. E-mail: corr@dmcvb.org. Web site: www.denver.org.

Of the numerous annual events that take place in Denver, the **National Western Stock Show, Rodeo, and Horse Show** is the biggest, longest, and most original—a yearly happening that radiates authenticity, excitement, and entertainment. Sixty years ago, cowboys' competitions with one another were formalized into rodeos. The stock show was born in a circus tent in 1906; the high speed of the riders, the antics of the rodeo clowns, and the pungent smells of the animals sometimes still remind you of a circus. For approximately two weeks every January, old Buffalo Bill and his Wild West entertainers seem to return to old Denver Town.

The National Western remains an important stock show, too. You can view more than 15,000 live, scrubbed, and brushed Herefords, Angus, Simmentals, Shorthorns, Longhorns, Arabian horses, Morgan horses, draft horses, miniature horses, ewes, and lambs, all in their neat pens. You watch shearing contests, breeding cattle auctions, and the judging of quarterhorse stallions. Some 600,000 visitors flock to the arenas to buy, sell, learn, and socialize. Millions of dollars exchange hands here.

"This is a cowboy convention for real-life cowboys," says one longtime Stock Show regular. "It's big business for the people who grow the stuff that ends up in our refrigerators and stomachs."

In addition to the judging and auctions, there are lectures, sales booths, meetings, and contests for the cattlemen and -women who show up here. Lots of money is in evidence. Thousand-dollar alligator boots. Hundred-dollar Stetsons. Belt buckles with diamonds. Even silver halters for the horses. A big commerce in livestock supplies, raw wool, saddles, cow tags, western art show and sale, lassoes.

New techniques are taught in feeding and breeding. In the arenas, you see riding demonstrations by horsewomen who gallop at a breakneck pace. Red-vested auctioneers and a peopled tribune asplash in color pay attention to a sale of—yes!—*llamas.*

A children's area delights the young ones with displays of baby rabbits, geese, and piglets. Each weekday some 1,200 schoolchildren are bused here to see the animals. The multifaceted spectacular not only brings aristocratic, purebred livestock to Denver. The Stock Show also regularly attracts the best of the rodeo ring, all top contenders for national championships for female barrel racing, calf roping, bull and bronco riding, steer wrestling, and many more events by more than 1,000 professional rodeo cowboys and cowgirls who are courageous and sporty. More than $400,000 in prizes are at stake.

But not all cowboys do well in Denver. A horse may refuse to buck and the rider will get nothing. A horse tosses him off after two seconds and the rider will get nothing. "They're the great American gamblers on horseback," says a western radio announcer.

Nobody gives the competitors an expense account. They pay their own way to ride at the National Western Stock Show and Rodeo. The rodeo cowboy draws no allowance, has no guaranteed annual wage. The only income comes from earnings in a fiercely competitive sport where he must win not only against other men but against the "rank" (mean) animals. And he must pay for this privilege—entry fees that can run into several hundred dollars per event per rodeo.

Most riders hail from small towns and made their first acquaintance with horses as kids. One typical bareback champ comes from Cora, Wyoming. He started as a ranch hand.

Rodeos, such as the National Western in Denver, may have well begun as a prank, a diversion for ranch hands, cowpokes. A few specialists, the "roughstring" riders who busted wild horses for a livelihood at $3.00 to $5.00 apiece, were quick to show their stuff. They were a tough bunch of men. Hardened by the summer heat and winter blizzards, used to riding through long nights, they had to deal with stampeding herds, crippled animals, and cattle rustlers. Their horses were extensions of themselves. They lived in the saddle.

Rodeo must have started during the early cattle drives and on the scattered ranches. A historian of the Denver-based Professional Rodeo Cowboys Association explains: "When their work was done, the cowboys entertained each other with roping and riding contests, showing off the skills they had sharpened during their everyday work on the range."

In the early 1880s, American ranchers began to develop the "ranch show" as a spectator sport. Already in 1888 Colorado spectators paid money to watch cowboys on bucking broncs. Within twenty years these affairs had become known as rodeos and were drawing crowds on tour in the cities of the United States.

In the early days of rodeo, the rider stayed in the saddle "until the horse was rode or the cowboy throwed." Today, the saddle bronc rider must stay aboard eight seconds, while at the same time not disqualifying himself in any number of ways. A man has to zoom out of the chute with both feet in the stirrups.

As a spectator you can see lots of thrilling action. The Stock Show grounds sprawl across 150 acres, which are only about 100 yards south of I–70. Buses get you there all day long; free shuttles run from various downtown hotels. You can also take a cab or drive. In that case, keep in mind that thousands of visiting livestock folks and rodeo fans compete for room to leave their cars, so close-in parking isn't always plentiful.

Rodeo competition takes place both afternoons and evenings. Tickets cost no more than for a movie. But wait! Have you ever been to a motion picture where you could witness a llama auction, an Australian-style sheep-shearing contest, the world's largest bull show (with one animal actually selling at $300,000), a catch-a-calf competition for teenagers? What film lets you talk to a real, true-blue Colorado rancher?

For more information: National Western Complex, 4655 Humboldt Street, Denver 80216; (303) 297–1166. Fax (303) 292–1708. E-mail: nwss@nationalwestern.com. Web site: www.nationalwestern.com.

How would you like to dine in a historic landmark and museum? How about a steaming platter of elk steak at a table under a stuffed elk, or a plate heaped with buffalo meat, with mounted buffalos staring down? The **Buckhorn Exchange** is allegedly Colorado's oldest restaurant (it celebrated its centennial in 1993). It is certainly one of the most original. Moreover, it's a saloon, a magnet for celebrities and tourists, and a moneymaker.

Supper here appeals to well-heeled meat eaters: twenty-four-ounce T-bone steaks, fourteen-ounce New York steaks, buffalo meat, baby-back ribs, Rocky Mountain oysters, rabbit—all at hefty deluxe rates in a noisy, congenial atmosphere. The saloon is upstairs, complete with a giant oak bar that was shipped here by oxcart. Nearby walls are filled with 1902 photos of hunting parties; even the men's room has historic pictures of stagecoaches.

The downstairs restaurant-museum is cluttered with more than 500 taxidermy pieces, including antelopes, deer, bears, wolverines, mountain goats, moose, weasels, zebras, and birds of all kinds, shapes, and plumage. You can look at more than a hundred rifles, pistols, and other weapons.

Even the restaurant's history has its fascinating aspects. It was begun in 1893 by owner Henry H. Zietz, a cowboy and scout with Buffalo Bill, no less; personal bodyguard of Leadville's silver millionaire H. A. W. Horace Tabor; and hunting guide of President Teddy Roosevelt, who arrived in his private train in front of the Buckhorn. The restaurant's official history relates that Henry Zietz "catered to cattlemen, miners, railroad builders, Indian chiefs, silver barons, roustabouts, gamblers, the great and the near-great." In December 1900 a masked gunman rode up to the restaurant, waved a .45, and demanded all money and valuables to be placed on the bar, "and be quick about it!" The fellow's horse had been tied to the Buckhorn's hitching post, but when the gun-man rode away at a gallop, he found himself pursued by Zietz's rifle-raising customers, who "handily dispatched the miscreant to greener pastures."

After the Zietz family's death, the restaurant-museum passed into the capable hands of several historically minded Denver investors, who put large sums into restoring the building and its contents in 1978. They also raised the prices to twentieth-century levels.

The Buckhorn's redbrick building is easy to find at 1000 Osage Street, Denver 80204. The location is between Colfax Avenue and Eighth Avenue, 5 blocks west of Santa Fe Boulevard.

The Buckhorn Exchange is open for lunch (expensive) Monday through Friday from 11:00 A.M. to 2:00 P.M., and dinner is served seven nights a week, starting at 5:00 P.M. Monday to Thursday, 4:30 P.M. Friday and Satur-day, and 4:00 P.M. Sunday. For more information or reservations call (303) 534–9505. E-mail: info@buckhorn.com. Web site: www.buckhorn.com.

The *Forney Historic Transportation Museum* is the perfect place to see some old vehicles, including 1915 Cadillacs, 1905 Fords, various old surreys, a locomobile, an ancient electric car, various carriages, bygone cycles, rail coaches, steam engines, and old airplanes. The notable exhibits include Theodore Roosevelt's Tour Car, Aly Khan's Rolls-Royce, and Amelia Earhart's Gold Bug Kissel. The children run to see the ladies' old, old dresses or the officers' military uniforms dating back to 1750 and 1800.

The Forney Historic Transportation Museum moved to a new location in early 2001. For hours, admission fees, or other information: 4303 Brighton Boulevard, Denver 80216; (303) 297–1113. E-mail: forney@info2000.net. Web site: www.forneymuseum.com.

Larimer Square is a renovated, eighteenth-century downtown oasis with a national reputation; indeed, it is the second most visited land-mark in Colorado. (The Air Force Academy is the first.)

In 1858, General William E. Larimer erected Denver's first building here. It was a mere log cabin. More than one hundred years later, a group of Colorado businesspeople founded the Larimer Square Association for the purpose of restoring the old buildings. The excitement that once was historic Larimer Street soon returned in the form of promenades, carriage rides, and quaint shops between Fourteenth and Fifteenth Streets.

In some ways Larimer Square reminds you of Ghirardelli Square in San Francisco. Or, it may make you think of Greenwich Village or New Orleans's French Quarter; others compare it to Chicago's Old Town or Toronto's Yorktown. By the same token, Larimer Square has its own visual personality; it remains an outstanding example of early Denver Victorian architecture, complete with gaslights, handwrought leaded-glass windows, stairways, historic markers, restored cornices, and handsome outdoor benches for resting and watching. In the restaurants (pricey) and shops, you find Tiffany lamps, cherrywood bars, rosewood paneling, old wallpapers, and lead ceilings.

The Square is paved with the legends of the nineteenth century. Larimer Street in Denver was once one of the most famous thoroughfares in the West. The restaurants, hotels, and theaters of its heyday were renowned. Stories of what happened when the greats, near-greats, and desperados of the West met made good newspaper copy. And tales of what went on behind closed doors in the neighborhood shocked a nation. Gambling and boozing were rampant.

Named for Denver's founder, General William E. Larimer, the street played a prominent role in the city's political and commercial history from November 16, 1858. That first day, Denver City consisted only of Larimer Street's 1400 block. As the western town grew around it, the original site became Denver's first commercial and governmental center. Here were the first post office, the first department store, the first drugstore, and the first bank and government buildings of the 1860s, 1870s, and 1880s.

As the years passed, Denver gradually moved uptown, and Larimer Street became a skid row area. Thanks to the gin mills and flophouses, the handsome Victorian buildings were forgotten, although amid the grime and dirt, their architectural beauty remained. Razing was a frequent threat.

Larimer Square is now a Landmark Preservation District. You find this important Denver tourist attraction listed in the National Register of Historic Places.

The 2-block Larimer Street area between Fourteenth and Fifteenth Streets is easily reached on foot or by free shuttle from Denver's downtown hotels. For more information: Larimer Square, 1400 Larimer Street, Suite 300, Denver 80202; (303) 607–1276. E-mail: info@ larimersquare.com. Web site: www.larimersquare.com.

Walk 1 block north of Fifteenth Street. The **Sixteenth Street Mall,** Denver's ultramodern, $76 million pedestrian thoroughfare, is the best people-watching spot in the city—a place where you can be entertained by a juggler or a classic violinst, shop in large bookstores or small exclusive boutiques, or just sit on one of hundreds of benches and watch Denver go by. A dozen fountains, festive banners, two hundred red oak trees, and a lighting system straight out of Star Wars makes this mile-long mall an attractive shopping and entertainment street. For more information contact the Denver Metro Convention and Visitors Bureau at (800) 233–6837. Web site: www.denver.org.

While there, check out the **Overland Sheepskin Co.** This western store provides a large selection of western wear, specializing in sheepskin. For more information: 1512 Larimer Street, Denver 80202; (303) 534–7717 or (888) 840–7611. Fax (303) 534–7714. E-mail: dv@overland. com. Web site: www.overland.com. Open Monday through Friday from 10:00 A.M. to 9:00 P.M., Saturday from 10:00 A.M. to 10:00 P.M., and Sunday from 10:00 A.M. to 6:00 P.M.

From its international debut in 1892 until the present, Denver's **Brown Palace Hotel** has lived up to its motto, "Where the World Registers." Indeed, this historic hotel is a classic. Nearly every U.S. president since Theodore Roosevelt has spent time here.

"The Brown," as Denverites have nicknamed it, is a remarkable example of Victorian architecture. The hotel lobby impresses the most. Upon entering, your eyes look up the six tiers of wrought-iron balconies to the stained-glass cathedral ceiling. The decorative stone on the pillars is Mexican onyx. Changing displays of historical memorabilia decorate the luxurious lobby. Old guest registers, menus, and photographs take you back to relive the role the Brown Palace played in the history of Denver.

The hotel is named for its builder, Henry Cordes Brown. As Brown watched nineteenth-century Denver grow, he saw the need for a fine hostelry for visiting easterners who came to do business with Colorado mining companies and railroads. The builder envisioned this hotel to rise from a triangular plot of land he owned near the center of the city.

Henry Cordes Brown examined and studied the blueprints of the world's deluxe hostelries before he developed his "palace."

A prominent Denver architect, Frank E. Edbrooke, designed a building in the spirit of the Italian Renaissance. Because of the geometric pattern of Brown's land, the edifice took on an unusual shape. Edbrooke gave the building a tri-frontage and then planned it so that each room faced a street. Without any interior rooms, every guest could have a view, plus morning or afternoon sunshine! The contractors, Geddes and Serrie, constructed this soon-to-be famous landmark from Colorado red granite and warm brown Arizona sandstone. James Whitehouse then carved a lovely series of medallions in the stone.

Completed in 1892, the 10-story building had 400 rooms. Fireplaces were standard for each room, as well as bathroom taps yielding artesian water straight from the hotel's wells (as they still do today). The finest achievements in steam heating and electricity were incorporated into the structure. The Brown was also noted as the second fireproof edifice in the country.

It took four years and $1 million to complete Henry Brown's luxurious dream. Cool water flowed from the taps; steam heat provided warmth. Ice machines kept the wine chilled and the produce fresh. Turkish baths, hairdressing parlors, billiard rooms—even a hotel library!— were available for guest use. Linens, china, glassware, and silver came from the finest craftsmen. Carpets and curtains in each room had special designs. Excellence abounded at every turn.

The Brown Palace opened for a banquet of the Triennial Conclave of Knights Templar and their ladies. A seven-course dinner at $10 a plate was served in the main dining room on the eighth floor. The guests viewed more than 300 miles of Rocky Mountain grandeur from the wide dining-room windows.

Denver society was formally introduced to the Brown Palace a few months later when the Tabors threw a fancy ball. In the years since, the Brown has hosted thousands of such glittering evenings.

Today the Brown Palace Hotel is listed in the National Register of Historic Places. Even in the midst of modern times, it continues to provide guests with historical authenticity, Victorian charm, and good service. The original decor has been preserved, especially in the restaurants— the hallmarks of the hotel.

It pays to make reservations several weeks in advance. The Brown

Brown Palace Hotel

Palace Hotel is at 321 Seventeenth Street, Denver 80202; (303) 297–3111 or (800) 321–2599. Fax (303) 312–5900. E-mail: marketing@ brownpalace.com. Web site: www.brownpalace.com.

The **Queen Anne Bed & Breakfast Inn** appeals to honeymooners; *Modern Bride, Bride's,* and *Bridal Guide* mention it. Because this bed-and-breakfast is so close to Denver's financial district, quiet-seeking executives also stay here.

This Victorian masterpiece dates back to 1879. Each of the ten bed chambers is different, yet all are crammed with genuine Victoriana: brass beds, canopied beds, four-poster beds, love seats, armoires, stained-glass windows, walnut tables, oak rocking chairs, and the like. (A touch of kitsch is occasionally sighted, too.)

The bed-and-breakfast ambience is carefully enhanced: a glass of sherry upon arrival, against a backdrop of piped-in chamber music;

continental breakfast served (upon request) in bed on a white wicker tray, or breakfast with other travelers at the inn, or, weather permitting, in the garden.

The location of the three-storied mansion in the Clements Historic District couldn't be better. For more information about the (expensive) accommodations, contact Queen Anne Bed & Breakfast Inn, 2147 Tremont Place, Denver 80205; (303) 296–6666, or (800) 432–4667. Fax (303) 296–2151. E-mail: travel@queenannebnb.com. Web site: www.queenannebnb.com.

How would you like to have breakfast, enjoy Sunday brunch, weekday lunch, presupper snack, or, best of all—dinner!—in a Tudor-style castle overlooking the city of Denver and a green golf course? All this has been possible for almost two decades at the **Wellshire Inn.** And you can thank a restaurateur named Leo Goto for the locale and the eating pleasures. Goto transformed a run-down clubhouse into the tasteful English chateau with its heavy wooden doors; antique, colored leaded-glass windows; sparkling chandeliers; luxurious carpets; and dramatic fireplaces. The place radiates intimacy and true elegance. Baronial splendor! Four million dollars' worth of remodeling!

Several local critics have called the Wellshire Inn "one of Denver's most beautiful restaurants." The decor is enhanced by the fresh foods—romaine lettuce, spinach, Chinese vegetables, fruit, Mediterranean greens; the entrees—Tournedos Windsor, fresh salmon filets, Italian-style Scampi, Chicken Dijon, Wellshire Chateaubriand, and Leo's famous Rack of Lamb—can only be called memorable. Scenic, pastoral views, country club atmosphere, good food, friendly service—can anyone ask for more?

For more information: Wellshire Inn, 3333 South Colorado Boulevard, Denver 80222; (303) 759–3333. E-mail: ruth@wellshireinn.com. Web site: www.wellshireinn.com. Open daily; call for details and reservations.

Few Colorado visitors—and not many Denverites—know about **Lakewood Heritage Center** at South Wadsworth and Ohio, with its park, several lakes, free guided nature walks, and some interesting 1886 buildings. Volunteers will show you a one-room schoolhouse, now used by quilters. Cheerful guides will bring to life an ancient farmhouse. You will learn how the former occupants used the butter churns and coffee grinders or heated the woodstoves. Other buildings contain drawings of Indians, a collection of shotguns, beaver pelts, and bows and arrows. This unique museum also displays 150-year-old farm machinery—

threshers, combines, tractors—along with Model Ts and even an antique fire truck. The tours take place Tuesday through Friday from 10:00 A.M. to 4:00 P.M. and Saturday and Sunday from noon to 4:00 P.M. Cost is $2.00 for adults, $1.00 for children four to twelve, children three and younger free. Groups larger than five must make advance tour reservations. For more information: Lakewood's Heritage Center, 797 South Wadsworth Boulevard, Lakewood 80227; (303) 987–7850. Web site: www.lakewood.org/parks/belmar.html.

The city of Denver has more than one hundred named parks of various sizes and shapes that stretch in every direction. It is said to be America's largest such system. Green areas abound. If you visit the *Denver Civic Center Park,* for instance, you'll at once notice the many well-tended lawns and trees. Civic Center Park is located at 100 West Fourteenth Avenue Parkway, Denver 80209.

The citizens' fondness for their greenways cannot be denied. Each year, Denverites go in for lawn contests (who has the prettiest one?). Every day, the newspapers print advice on lawn care. A wail goes up if a city father hints at the possibility of rationing the water used for sprinklers. Stores keep large stocks of fertilizer, and commerce is brisk in garden tools and boxes of petunias and geraniums that embellish the most humble Denver gardens.

On weekends, Denverites head for their public parks, which must be among the best-kept and varied in the nation. Each of the city's parks has its own charisma, its own subtle characteristics depending on location, size, and activities.

Begin with Denver's largest, 314-acre *City Park.* You can reach it from downtown in ten minutes' driving time. Keep in mind that you could spend a full summer day and evening here without a moment's boredom. A family may while away many hours, for instance, in the *Denver Zoo,* located in City Park. Hundreds of animals frolic or loaf on some 70 acres of grounds. Take the children to "Monkey Island," where monkeys swing and leap all summer (in spring you'll find these critters in the Primate House). A special glass edifice contains dozens of colorful chirping, singing, talking birds. Other natural habitat areas are for polar bears, llamas, turtles, baby elephants, rhinos, and giraffes, nearly 4,000 animals in all. A special zoo for small children is popular; here you find young ducks, lambs, chickens, and other farm animals.

The main entrance to City Park and the zoo is on East Twenty-third Avenue between Colorado Boulevard and York Street.

The zoo is open daily. Hours from April 1 through September 30 are 9:00 A.M. to 6:00 P.M., and from October 1 through March 31, 10:00 A.M. to 5:00 P.M. Admission (April 1 through September 30) is $9.00 for adults and teenagers thirteen and older, $5.00 for children four to twelve, children three and younger free. Admission (October 1 through March 31) is $7.00 for adults and teenagers thirteen and older, $4.00 for children four to twelve, children three and younger free. For more information: 2300 Steele Street, Denver 80205-4899; (303) 376–4800, fax (303) 376–4801. E-mail: zooinfo@denverzoo.org. Web site: www.denverzoo.org.

Also at City Park are a public golf course, tennis courts, flower gardens, and paddleboats that can be rented on the lakes. The **Denver Museum of Natural History** (800–925–2250, www.dmnh.org) is located here.

Washington Park—my favorite—is the place to be on a late September morning. One of Colorado's poet laureates, at age ninety, was known to walk around one of the lakes here. Actually, it has started to snow. Winter without the benefit of fall. Yesterday the sun still blazed here, and now the flakes tumble thickly. The lake steams.

Normally filled with cyclists, the park is deserted. Denver's miniblizzard air is being washed clean by the moisture. A few hardy joggers, wool caps over their ears, jog along the lake paths. The grass is still too warm for the snow to stick; the wet meadows seem greener than at any other time of the year.

The miniblizzard stops. Clouds drift overhead.

Through the park you can see some of Denver's old homes of Downing, Louisiana, and Franklin Streets. Typically, all the houses come with lawns and gardens. The latter form the visitor's first impressions.

A weekday may be the best day to stroll through Denver's Washington Park, at South Downing and East Virginia Streets, not far from East Alameda Avenue. The wide expanse of green is almost unknown to tourists, despite all the delights here. Small creeks are shaded by willows and cottonwoods. Anything and everything happens at Washington Park on weekends: Young lovers from nearby Denver University walk along the paths; elderly gentlemen play a game of boccie in slow motion on a special well-kept lawn; young champions slam tennis balls across one of the many free courts; an entire family feeds ducks and geese. Washington Park has several playgrounds for small-fry and plenty of picnic tables. Washington Park comes with ample flower beds that remind you of English gardens.

The park also boasts a large recreation center where you can swim indoors, work out in a gym with sophisticated machinery, join a basketball game, or, if you stay in town long enough, take various classes that range from puppetry to pottery. The modernistic recreation center is ideal for rainy days.

Happiness for Denverites is **Sloan Lake,** located between Sheridan Boulevard and Newton. The lakeshore and the grass often fetch an elderly clientele: pensioners, retired railroad people, old Indians— some fishing out of their automobiles, others sitting near the water—as well as young Vietnamese.

No crowds during the week. Then on summer Saturdays a crescendo of people. The climax comes on July Sundays or holidays. From the Fourth of July to Labor Day, the parking lots cannot hold all the automobiles with picnickers and their baskets; with more anglers hoping for a ten-pound carp; with teenagers ready to toss footballs, baseballs, plastic platters; with ladies and their grandchildren; with three-year-olds waving bags of bread. Orange-beaked ducks waddle eagerly ashore; wild Canada geese float with nonchalance toward the toss of popcorn.

You see father-and-son teams playing—surprise!—a game of croquet; you see water-skiers in black wet suits. Windy days produce sailboats— thirty of them? fifty?—a regatta! Sailors ply the blue Sloan Lake surface in their dinghies, Snipes, or Sunfish vessels. The joggers are always in evidence, too, and in any weather a few old, sometimes overweight couples

Denver: Some Little-Known Parks

Cheesman Park, *East Eighth Avenue and Franklin Street, is perfect for a restful hour or so; you can peruse mountain views and plan your conquest of Colorado's "Fourteeners."*

Eisenhower Park, *South Colorado Boulevard and East Dartmouth, offers a swimming pool, indoor tables for championship-type Ping-Pong players, and a hiking trail.*

Congress Park, *East Ninth Avenue and University, has an outdoor pool for lap swimming, tennis courts, and playgrounds.*

Bear Valley Park *weaves and curves along West Dartmouth near South Sheridan. A bike trail follows a small river here.*

A Quick Walk at Willow Springs Trail

*F*or tourists who're short on time, there beckons the **Willow Springs Trail.** *Access? Take Wadsworth Boulevard south to Belleview, then follow the pastoral signs west toward the reddish foothills. Belleview turns into Highway 48 and leads to the peaceful Willow Springs Country Club. Proceed uphill through the club as far as you can go, park, and head for an open gate, which bans motorized vehicles. The trail sets out past a whale-shaped rock and moves uphill through the meadows along an almost forgotten old wagon road. Leafy trees hug the little valley, and the birds sing as you tramp up and down dale. No cars or highways in sight, and Denver's brown cloud and skyscrapers are far, far below you.*

For more information: **Denver and Metro Convention & Visitors Bureau,** *225 West Colfax, Denver 80202, (303) 892–1112.*

walk around the lake—doctor's orders. On sunny days, the Rockies wink in the background.

You can enter the park from West Seventeenth Avenue or from Sheridan Boulevard and from several other points, all west of Federal Boulevard.

Actually, Denver's municipal parks stimulate plenty of outdoor life on 2,800 acres; to these you may add another city-owned 14,000 acres in the foothills. Wildflowers! Spruce trees! Pines! Meadows!

Small wonder that Denver is called "The City of Green."

For more information about Denver's parks, contact the Denver Parks and Recreation Department's Parks Division, 2300 Fifteenth Street, Denver 80202; (303) 964-2580. Web site: www.denvergov.org/dephome. asp?depid=81.

If you really want to see Denver, take a hike.

The Beaver Brook Trail, on Lookout Mountain, can be accessed from Denver by car via I–70 (take Lookout Mountain exit). Drive past Buffalo Bill's grave until you see the sign on your left, BEAVER BROOK TRAIL. You will be delighted by the varied flora and fauna and the varied terrain. Caveat: Trail can be icy in winter. For more information: Jefferson County Open Space, 700 Jefferson County Parkway, Suite 100, Golden 80401; (303) 271–5925. Fax (303) 271–5955. E-mail: outreach@co. jefferson.co.us. Web site: www.co.jefferson.co.us/dpt/openspac.

Belmar Park, at West Ohio and Wadsworth Boulevard in Lakewood, provides an hour's worth of foot trails through undulating wildflower and sedge meadows. Canada geese occupy an attractive lake; Lakewood's Heritage Center, with its old farm machinery adds a pastoral note to the landscape. Barns and sheds round out the picture. Good, too, for runners and in winter for cross-country skiers.

The nonprofit Butterfly Pavilion and Insect Center in Westminster is the only such stand-alone institution in the United States.

For more information: Lakewood Department of Community Resources; (303) 987-7800. Web site: www.lakewood.org/parks/trail.html.

Finally, before you leave the Denver Metro area entirely, delight your children (or the child inside you) with a stop at the ***Butterfly Pavilion and Insect Center,*** located in Westminster—a short jaunt up US 36 off I–25 heading north from Denver. This attraction, which opened in 1995, is one of only a dozen or so similar institutions in the United States. Borne of a need for people to gain greater understanding of arthropods, this fun "zoo" houses more than 1,200 free-flying butterflies from more than fifty species. In addition, numerous other insect species and tropical plants round out the pavilion's holdings.

Open daily from 9:00 A.M. until 5:00 P.M. year-round, the Butterfly Pavilion offers an escape from wintry weather with its climate-controlled, 7,200-square-foot tropical conservatory. Admission is $6.95 for adults, $3.95 for children four to twelve, $4.95 for senior citizens sixty-five and older, two children three and under free if accompanied by adults. The pavilion is located at 6252 West 104th Avenue, Westminster 80020. Take the Church Ranch Boulevard/104th Avenue exit off US 36 and head east on 104th. For more information: (303) 469–5441. E-mail: gwarfield@butterflies.org. Web site: www.butterflies.org.

The Great Plains

"Colorado? Ah, high peaks! Mountain towns! Skiing!" This is how many easterners, southerners, and midwesterners describe their idea of a state that has mountains on its license plates. Even Europeans know about the Rockies. The plains—especially Colorado's eastern plains, the farmer's domain—come as a surprise.

Yet, much of the land belongs to agriculture. As you drive east from Denver, Colorado Springs, Pueblo, or Trinidad, the country takes on the flat character of Kansas and Nebraska, with which Colorado shares its eastern border. The names turn rural: Punkin Center, Wild Horse, Deer Trail.

Communities like Wray, Holyoke, and Yuma all got their start through homesteading. About 94 percent of Colorado's land consists of dry or irrigated farmlands, rangeland, and forests.

Eastern Colorado was first settled during the middle and late 1880s. Little agricultural communities like Haxtun, Kiowa, and Eads sprang up. Oats, barley, wheat, and corn were planted; harvesting was done with primitive machinery. Some of the farms were the result of the early railroads selling cheap tracts of land to immigrants.

The homesteaders fought hard financial battles when the droughts hit in 1890. But the Homestead Act, which presented volunteer farmers with 160 free acres, was a big incentive in Colorado. Many of the settlers demanded few luxuries from their homesteads. They tilled, planted, harvested, and faced blizzards and hailstorms, grasshoppers, and more droughts. The worst ones hit during the 1920s.

Still, through the years, eastern Colorado produced not just corn and wheat, but also dry beans, alfalfa, potatoes, onions, rye, sorghum, and commercial vegetables. In Rocky Ford, year after year, the citizens grew watermelons and cantaloupes.

The farmers endured the summer heat and dust storms. World War II was good to the Colorado farm economy. New well-drilling techniques and irrigation improved the situation. During the 1960s wheat sales hit record figures. The 1970s brought prosperity. The export trade flourished. Land prices soared. Farmers splurged on newfangled $100,000 machinery.

When exports shrank, as everywhere in the Midwest and West, the Colorado farmers suffered. The 1980s were harsh to the eastern part of the state. Prices dropped for crops, while everything else cost more.

Yet some farmers survived. A few lucky ones—close to cities like Denver, Fort Morgan, and Sterling—switched to sod farming.

Sod creates instant lawns for suburbia, as an adjunct to the housing explosion. Near Parker you see miles and miles of green carpets, well watered, neatly rolled up, ready for shipment. New homes still go up in Englewood, Littleton, Aurora, Thornton, and Castle Rock, and each new house clamors for its swath of green, often supplied by sod farmers.

Others stay on and grow "Hard Red" winter wheat and specialty items like asparagus, flowers, peas, and sunflower seeds. A small number build greenhouses or mushroom cellars. Dry beans and millet bring profits.

Others sell out to giants, go bankrupt, or seek jobs in the city. Third-generation farmers sometimes give up; regretfully, their children move to town. Some are lucky enough to sell their land to developers of condos and shopping centers. One well-known dairy farmer plans to develop the land himself. Farmers turn into land managers for absentee agribusiness owners.

The scenery packs little excitement. Abandoned houses, an occasional silo, and fields in all directions. A grain elevator. A weighing station. Plows holding court. Small communities where one automatically slows down for the sights of feed stores or an old twelve-unit motel or the cafe with home cooking.

Many of the little hamlets in eastern Colorado seem alike. Small houses with porches. Shop windows with tools placed helter-skelter. After nine at night almost everything is closed. Main Street is so silent that you can hear the crickets in the field.

Each little town has several churches, which get busy on Sunday. Sermons crackle on your car radio. A quick glance through a picture window shows a farmer watching a television evangelist.

The inhabitants of eastern Colorado are reserved, not too friendly, perhaps distrustful, certainly preoccupied. But they have time. "Oh, sure," says one of them to an inquirer from the city. "Sure, we have problems. But there's more space to have them in."

Most visitors—and even new immigrants to Colorado—think the state consists mostly of Denver and suburbs and perhaps a few mountain towns like Vail and Aspen. They often forget northern and eastern Colorado. When Mark Twain visited in 1862, however, he reveled in the prairie and the horses. "It was a noble sport galloping over the plain in the dewy freshness of the morning," Twain wrote.

The dewy freshness is still there, along with the star-filled sky, some farms with their tilled fields, the big cottonwoods. Despite the giant interstates, the air is still pure. Unlike in Denver, where the car-caused pollution backs up against the mountains, the breezes from the northwest do a fine purification job. The cities of Fort Collins, Greeley, and Longmont have expanded; luckily, however, there is very little smokestack industry. You see new shopping malls and Holiday Inns and Kentucky Fried Chicken outposts. The tourists flock to communities such as Loveland, with its lakes and access to Rocky Mountain National Park.

In the same region, *Fort Collins* may well be the most sophisticated community in northern Colorado. With 115,000 inhabitants, it is the

Try a Yurt Vacation!

Within the **Colorado State Forest,** *70 miles west of Fort Collins, the* **Never Summer Nordic Yurt System** *offers highly unique opportunities to cyclists.*

Consider, first of all, staying in a "yurt" here. Yurts are portable, round dwellings that were first used by nomadic Mongols in Central Asia; they sleep six comfortably and are well situated as push-off sites for some great rides.

One such bike trip is the **Grass Creek Loop.** *It's a tough 16 miles round-trip. Along the way you will pass the North Michigan Reservoir and the 10,000-foot Gould Mountain.*

For more information: Never Summer Nordic, Inc., Box 1983, Fort Collins 80522; (970) 482–9411. E-mail: info@neversummernordic.com. Web site: www.neversummernordic.com/yurts.htm.

largest. Hordes of eager, serious *Colorado State University* students are here, and the visitor quickly becomes aware of wider interests. Fort Collins has several bookstores, numerous foreign-car dealers, and shops catering to the young. The distance to Denver is a manageable 66 miles.

Much of Colorado's famous corn-fed beef comes from Fort Collins. The dry climate is ideal for the Hereford and Angus cattle, and northern Colorado cattle feeders have worked out precise feeding systems. From this region the aged beef is shipped all over the world.

In recent years, the area's ranchers have adapted themselves to the times. They now raise calves that are leaner and less cholesterol-laden. Low-fat feeding methods are in. Marbled meat is out. Moreover, some of these contemporary cattlemen shun growth stimulants and avoid antibiotics.

The Fort Collins-based Colorado State University is strong on agriculture and also trains forestry students, whose tree nurseries you can visit. For more information: Colorado State University, Fort Collins 80523; (970) 491–1101. Web site: www.colostate.edu.

The city has its own symphony orchestra and a theater. "We're often under-estimated," says one Fort Collins official. "We shouldn't be. We're a microcosm of Denver, but without the air pollution and crime."

The Fort Collins region is known for its nearby fly-fishing possibilities. Among others, you might head up the drama-filled *Poudre Canyon* and the *Poudre River,* which is uniformly praised by serious anglers in search of trout. For more information: Canyon Lakes Ranger District,

Arapaho & Roosevelt National Forests, 1311 South College Avenue, Fort Collins 80524; (970) 498–2770. E-mail: lmcfadden/r2_arnfpng@ fs. fed.us. Web site: www.fs.fed.us/r2/arnf/clrd/vvc. htm.

For camping and boating, there is the **Horsetooth Reservoir** west of town. Horsetooth has 1,900 acres of water and attracts huge summer crowds with camping, boating, biking, and climbing.

To reach Horsetooth Reservoir, drive west on CR 38E (Harmony Road) from its intersection with Taft Hill Road in Fort Collins. Park permits are available from stations throughout the park; cost is $6.00 per vehicle. For more information: Larimer County Parks and Open Lands, 1800 South County Road 31, Loveland 80537; (970) 679–4570. E-mail: parksoffice@co.larimer.co.us. Web site: www.co.larimer.co.us/parks/Horsetooth.htm.

While in Fort Collins, mountain bikers will not want to be without the free map, "Tour de Fort." This pocket guide illustrates the 56 miles of local bike trails, lanes, and routes. You can pick it up at any Fort Collins bicycle shop.

Lory State Park offers great single tracks for more advanced riders. This former ranch is now a 2,400-acre park that tempts bikers with challenging mountain biking almost year-round; snow is frequent in winter, but abundant sunshine keeps the trails relatively clear.

Just beyond the park entrance at the Timber Recreation Area is the Timber Trail. This single-track route is not very technical, except loose

River Adventures in Northern Colorado

A **Wanderlust Adventure** *in Fort Collins will give you the opportunity to see the Poudre River up close and personal. Since 1982, 60,000 people have enjoyed trips run by this Fort Collins–based outfitter. From three-hour trips for the whole family to day-long and multiday paddling affairs guaranteed to give anyone a workout, Wanderlust will have a trip to fit everyone (who's old enough, that is— minimum age of seven for easiest trip). Trips run from May through August and range in price from $30 to $70 per person. For more information: A Wanderlust Adventure, 3500 Bingham Hill Road, Fort Collins 80521; (800) 745–7238 or (970) 484–1219. E-mail: patlegel@aol.com. Web site: www.awanderlustadventure.com.*

gravel adds a challenge. Take US 287 north from Fort Collins through LaPorte. Turn left at the Bellvue exit onto County Road 23N. Turn left again (23N turns). Go $1^4/_{10}$ miles and take a right on County Road 25G. The park entrance is another $1^6/_{10}$ miles away. The park is open from 8:00 A.M. to 6:00 P.M. daily. Cost is $4.00 per vehicle; $2.00 per walk-in. For more information: Lory State Park, 708 Lodgepole Drive, Bellvue 80512, (970) 493–1623. E-mail: lory.park@state.co.us. Web site: www.parks.state.co.us/lory/ index.asp.

Just south is *Loveland,* about half the size of Fort Collins, yet it has carved a national name for itself. Loveland calls itself "Colorado's Sweetheart City."

Each year many sacks of valentines are being remailed here; the senti-mental souls who send these love messages are backed by the town's civic leaders, who volunteer their time. Cupid has worked here for some four decades. Loveland's postmasters themselves often create the corny poems that appear in cachet form next to the Loveland stamp. A typical verse:

Loveland in Wintertime—or All Year Long

*L*oveland Ski Area—which is not near the city by the same name—has always been a favorite ski spot for Denverites. And for good reason. A big plus is Loveland's proximity—just 55 miles from Denver via I-70. There are no passes to cross and no Eisenhower Tunnels, either (which Loveland publicists call "a big bore").

Snowboarding sure can wake you up, and Loveland Ski Area has excellent instructors. So, if you've been skiing your whole life, try it! Skiing and snowboarding, though related, are different experiences, and it's defi-nitely worth it to discover the distinc-tion. For information on taking lessons in snowboarding from Love-land's friendly and skilled instruc-tors, call (800) 736-3754, ext. 170.

Do it before it's too late, though—the ski center shuts down in late spring, and since Loveland Ski Area does not operate hotels of offer condominiums, the area essentially shuts down when the snow melts. It's still worth a day trip, though. In summer, the slopes fill up with mountain flowers and free-lance hikers.

For more information, contact Loveland Ski Area, P.O. Box 899, Georgetown 80444, (303) 569–3203 or (800) 736–3754. Fax (303) 571–5580. E-mail: loveland@ skiloveland.com. Web site: www. skiloveland.com. Loveland Ski Area is open from November through April; lift ticket prices run from $27 to $41.

DENVER AND THE PLAINS

The day is full of gladness
And eyes with stardust shine
When Cupid works his magic
In this lovely valentine.

The Loveland Post Office patiently copes with the extra work of some 300,000 valentines with the blessing of the town officials. Local high schools paint heart signs. On the Chamber of Commerce maps, Loveland appears in the shape of a heart, and the yearly "Miss Valentine" wears hearts on her apron. The local business community has no objections; there are now even Sweetheart shops and a Sweetheart Lane. Ironically, Loveland was named after a railroad robber baron.

Actually, agriculture and tourism go on strongly here, too: you spot cornfields and sugar beets, ride horses at local stables, use local campgrounds, and visit the numerous Loveland recreation areas. And the thousands of valentines via "Cupid's Hometown" or "The Valentine Capital of the World" are a business by themselves. For more information: Loveland Chamber of Commerce, 5400 Stone Creek Circle, Suite 200, Loveland 80538; (970) 667–6311. Fax (970) 667–5211. E-mail: info@loveland.org. Web site: www.loveland.org.

The city of **Greeley** (founded by Horace Greeley, the newspaper publisher) is a few miles to the east of Loveland. Greeley was meant to become an agricultural colony, too, and succeeded. All around the town's perimeter you see sugar-beet fields, barley, and other crops.

Much of the local sight-seeing harks back to agriculture. At the **Centennial Village,** the curators have erected a sod house, a homesteader's wagon house, and a one-room rural school. In addition, Centennial Village has graceful Victorian homes. In all, some thirty structures take the visitor through the history of the High Plains, spanning the years 1860 to 1930. Open mid-April through mid-October; call for hours. Admission is $3.50 for adults and teenagers thirteen and older, $3.00 for senior citizens sixty and older, $2.00 for children six to twelve, children five and younger free. For more information: 1475 A Street, Greeley 80631; (970) 350–9220. Fax (970) 350–9700. E-mail: dillc @ci.greeley.co.us. Web site: www.greeleycvb.com/centennial.html.

Visit the **Meeker Memorial Museum,** formerly the home of Nathan Meeker. It contains many of his furnishings and the plow that turned

Trivia

Horace Greeley's original concept for his namesake town was a utopian agricultural colony modeled after the Oneida, New York, experimental settlement.

the first sod in the Union Colony. It's listed in the National Register of Historic Places. Open from mid-April through mid-October; walk-in visitors are free. Call for hours. For more information: 1324 Ninth Avenue, Greeley 80631; (970) 350–9220. E-mail: dillc@ci.greeley.co.us. Web site: www.ci.greeley.co.us/Culture/museums.html.

Another point of interest in the area: the *University of Northern Colorado,* Greeley (501 Twentieth Street, Greeley 80639; 888–700–4862; E-mail: unc@mail.unco.edu; Web site: www.univnorthco.edu). The late James Michener was one of UNC's famous alumni; this institution has grown to some 11,000 full-time students, plus 6,000 part-timers who take continuing education courses.

To be sure, James Michener was inspired to write his bestselling novel *Centennial* through his familiarity and on-location research in Greeley and surroundings.

Michener's ficticious pioneers built their town of Centennial on the Platte River. The story is one of struggle, success, failure, and, above all, endurance. Perhaps the closest thing to his invented Centennial is the near–ghost town of *Keota,* Colorado, 40 miles northeast of Greeley. Michener returned to Keota more than a dozen times to absorb its atmosphere and talk with postmaster Clyde Stanley.

Stanley had lived in Keota most of his seventy years. He had seen the eager farmers come, only to be displaced by drought and dust storms. He watched the town dwindle from 129 people in 1929 to 6 in 1970. Michener dedicated the book to Stanley, "who introduced me to the prairie." To visit Keota today, take exit 269 off I–25 (near Fort Collins). Head east on Highway 14 approximately 50 miles past the town of Briggsdale to County Road 103. Go north 5 miles to Keota. See the Web site www.ghosttowns.com/states/co/keota.html for details.

Not many people—or even Michener's readers—realize that the famous author had good reasons to turn to Greeley and northwestern Colorado for his research. In 1936, at the age of twenty-nine and not yet a writer, Michener taught in Greeley at what was to become the University of Northern Colorado.

He never regretted his decision. "In Greeley, I grew up spiritually, emotionally, intellectually," he later noted in John P. Hayes's *James A. Michener: A Biography.*

Those Western Doings in the Greeley Area

*T*he **Greeley Independence Stampede** *is held the first week of July, with six rodeos, parades, fireworks, as well as events on all downtown plazas. The rodeos are at Island Grove Park, Fourteenth Avenue and "A" Street. The* **Weld County Fair** *takes place the first week in August, with horse shows and livestock displays, plus various contests.*

For more information: Greeley/Weld Chamber of Commerce, 902 Seventh Avenue, Greeley 80631; (970) 352–3566. Fax (970) 352–3572. E-mail: info@greeleychamber.com. Web site: www.greeleychamber.com.

While there, Michener became friends with Floyd Merrill, Greeley's newspaper editor. The pair set out on almost weekly ventures into the surrounding country. At least three times a month, Merrill and the future best-selling author took off for exploration of the intricate irrigation systems that produced Colorado's vegetables and fruit, sometimes to the mountains. "We would look down into valleys crowded with blue spruce and aspen, and quite often out onto the prairie east of town where majestic buttes rose starkly from the barren waste," Michener relates in Hayes's biography.

Merrill also taught the young professor to use a camera. Michener credits the photos he took in Colorado with keeping his images of the West alive and vital long enough for *Centennial* to be conceived.

Already well known in 1970, the author returned to Colorado, determined to write an exhaustive story of the western experience. He explored the natural and social history of the region.

And he made northeastern Colorado famous.

One of the landmarks in his book *Centennial* is the fictitious "Rattlesnake Buttes." "They were extraordinary, these two sentinels of the plains. Visible for miles in each direction, they guarded a bleak and sad empire," Michener wrote.

These promontories exist and are known as the ***Pawnee Buttes,*** part of the Pawnee National Grassland. Administered by the Forest Service, the grasslands encompass nearly 200,000 acres.

The wind here is nearly constant. The terrain made history in the 1930s when drifts of wind-driven topsoil piled up like snow over fences, closing roads and killing crops. This Pawnee grassland was born from tragedy.

A gravel road goes to the Buttes trailhead. From there, a 1½-mile path takes you on foot or by mountain bike to the first butte, the western one. The eastern butte lies ¼ mile east. From a plateau the trail drops to the prairie floor, crossing open pastureland, then dropping again into a deep ravine. Cream-colored chalk cliffs form the promontories. Call it a short-grass prairie here, somewhat like a tundra. The steadily moving air masses keep growths low to the ground. Prickly pear cactus, blue gramma grass, sagebrush, and buffalo grass grow no higher then 6 inches.

Lack of water and trees do not prevent many species of birds from flourishing in this country. Lark buntings—the Colorado state bird, with its distinctive white wing patches against a black body—thrive here. So do horned larks, meadowlarks, kestrels, mountain plovers, common nighthawks, and long-billed curlews—some of the 200 species recorded here. A 36-mile self-guided birding tour is a great ride over the prairie in a high-clearance car or on a mountain bike. Cattle share this area with pronghorn antelope and windmill-powered water tanks for stock. For information, contact Pawnee National Grassland, 660 O Street, Greeley 80631; (970) 353–5004. E-mail: /sbauer/r2_arnfpng@fs.fed.us. Web site: www.fs.fed.us/arnf/png.

The eastern plains of Colorado saw much travel activity and bloodshed in the early days of this country. Indians, trappers, traders, settlers, Mexicans, and the Spanish used what was called the Santa Fe Trail, which followed along the Arkansas River for many miles.

The Bent, St. Vrain and Company, a frontier trading and retailing business, built and owned *Bent's Old Fort* near what is now La Junta. The fort was a trading place for Mexicans, Indians, and trappers. Mexico got quality manufactured goods from the United States. The Indians got cookware, metal, rifles, and other goods. Trappers obtained supplies, a market for their furs, and the company of other people following lonely months of hunting. The Bent, St. Vrain and Company traded with all these folks and among themselves. Furs and buffalo robes were sold back east.

In the mid-1800s, Bent's Old Fort was caught between resentful Indians and the whites who were moving in on them. The Indian wars began and the trade faded away. Charles Bent was killed in a revolt in Taos, New Mexico. St. Vrain left to do business further south. Cholera spread through the Indian tribes. William Bent, the remaining partner, left, a disillusioned and disappointed man. For a time, Bent's Old Fort fell into ruins.

Designated by the National Park Service as a National Historic Site, Bent's Old Fort has been rebuilt almost exactly as it was constructed originally. Authentic materials and tools were used in the reconstruction. Today, the adobe structure remains a monument to past and present-day craftspeople whose skill and patience built and rebuilt it again.

Just outside La Junta, Bent's Old Fort stands as it did almost one hundred years ago. To preserve the authentic atmosphere of this trade center, visitor parking is $1/4$ mile from the building. The long paved walk toward the fort, with its backdrop of cottonwood trees by the Arkansas River, takes you into history.

In deference to realism, there are no concessions for food, drink, or curios. In fact, you begin to believe the only bathroom may be the one rebuilt as part of the fort. But not to worry. Tucked into a corner are modern toilets and water fountains. A small bookstore exhibits numerous historical volumes.

The building is truly a fort. Four high walls surround a central courtyard. Entrance is through an archway with huge wooden doors. The two levels in the fort contain mostly community rooms, including the well room, trade room, dining area and kitchen, wash house, warehouses, and blacksmith's and laborer's modest quarters. Other accommodations are on the second level, providing more privacy and ventilation. Corrals at the back were for military horses and some cattle.

Uniformed park employees are often on hand to answer questions. But to get into the spirit of the place, join one of the $2.00-per-person guided tours conducted by an individual dressed in period clothes. These "interpreters" stay in character, thanks to the authentic costumes. Their tour will be informative and will make you feel like you lived here in the 1880s. Scheduled special events go on all year, such as the Fur Trade Encampment, a mountain-man type of rendezvous in July.

For more information: Bent's Old Fort, National Historic Site, 35110 Highway 194 East, La Junta 81050-9523; (719) 383–5010. Fax (719) 385–5031. E-mail: BEOL_Superintendent@nps.gov. Web site: www.nps.gov/beol. Open every day except Thanksgiving, Christmas, and New Year's Day. Open June 1 through August 31 from 8:00 A.M. to 5:30 P.M.; September 1 through May 31 from 9:00 A.M. to 4:00 P.M. From US 50 in La Junta take Highway 109 north 1 mile to Highway 194. Go east on Highway 194 for 6 miles to the fort.

For a trip even further back into history—150 million years further back—visit *Picket Wire Canyonlands* in *Comanche National Grasslands* about 25 miles south of La Junta. Picket Wire opened to the public in 1991. The attractions? The clear footprints of dinosaurs on a solidified limestone shelf just a few feet over the Purgatory River, as well as rock art and pioneer ruins.

Though the area is considered extremely fragile, mountain biking and hiking are allowed in Picket Wire. From a parking area near a cattle pen, an 8-mile ranch road takes the biker/hiker across a high mesa, then drops suddenly into the canyon. As you follow along, the relics of abandoned adobe houses, a church, a graveyard, and ranch buildings hold up against the dry climate.

This area gets very hot in summer, and rattlesnakes are a real hazard. This is, however, an ideal trip on a mountain bike. Would-be hikers should consider this 17-mile round-trip. Using a bike you can zip along the dusty road and catch glimpses of the current inhabitants: a coyote, kestrels, orioles. Snakes are supposed to nap in the tall grass. The dinosaur tracks are marked by small signs pointing the way. Right next to the river, you come to a shelf of limestone that looks like someone mucked around in it while it was wet. On further examination you discover that these muddlings are dinosaur tracks. You may have to clean the dirt and sand out to truly determine that these are dinosaur tracks. The brontosaurus left big holes like you'd expect from an elephant, yet much bigger. The meat-eating allosaurus left distinctive three-toed, wicked-looking footprints.

It's hot in this Colorado country. Take plenty of water and a hat to put on after you take off your bike helmet. Expect to spend about three hours for the round-trip. But also expect to be alone. There are no human inhabitants of this area now. Overnight camping is prohibited.

Petroglyphs dot the rock canyon walls. These rock etchings aren't identified by signs; you just have to find them on your own. If time is important, do this trip for the dinosaur tracks. Try to walk in their footprints, left more than 150 million years ago. Contact Comanche National Grassland, 1420 East Third Street, La Junta 81050; (719) 384–2181. Fax (719) 384–7647. E-mail: gvanover@fs.fed.us. Web site: www.ruralnet. net/~vipgrafx/misc/cng1.html.

DENVER

Brown Palace Hotel (excellent downtown location; deluxe); 321 Seventeenth Street; (303) 297–3111 or (800) 321–2599

Capitol Hill Mansion (good for business people; you can reach downtown with ease; moderate to expensive); 1207 Pennsylvania Street; (303) 839–5221 or (800) 839–9329

Castle Marne Bed & Breakfast (moderate to expensive); 1572 Race Street; (303) 331–0621 or (800) 926–2763

Oxford Hotel (close to Union Station; expensive to deluxe); 1600 Seventeenth Street; (303) 628–5400 or (800) 228–5838

Queen Anne Bed & Breakfast Inn (bed and breakfast; not in Denver's best area; moderate to deluxe); 2147 Tremont Place; (303) 296–6666 or (800) 432–4667

Victoria Oaks Inn (moderate); 1575 Race Street; (303) 355–1818 or (800) 662–6257

FORT COLLINS

Best Western Inn (inexpensive); 914 South College Avenue; (970) 484–1984

Edwards House (historic bed and breakfast; expensive); 402 West Mountain Avenue; (970) 493–9191

Helmshire Inn (moderate to expensive); 1204 South College Avenue; (970) 493–4683

Holiday Inn (moderate); 3836 East Mulberry Street; (970) 484–4660

GREELEY

Best Western Inn (inexpensive to moderate); 701 Eighth Street; (970) 353–8444

Country Inn and Suites by Carlson (inexpensive to moderate); 2501 West Twenty-ninth Street; (970) 330–3404

Sod Buster Bed and Breakfast Inn (historic inn; expensive); 1221 Ninth Avenue; (888) 300–1221 or (970) 392–1221

LOVELAND

Budget Host Exit 254 Inn (inexpensive); 2716 Southeast Frontage Road; (970) 667–5202

Cattail Creek Bed & Breakfast Inn (expensive); 2665 Abarr Drive; (970) 667–7600 or (800) 572–2466

Lovelander Bed & Breakfast Inn (moderate to expensive); 217 West Fourth Street; (970) 669–0798 or (800) 459–6694

Other Attractions Worth Seeing in Denver and The Plains

DENVER

Denver Art Museum, (303) 640–4433
Elitch Gardens, (303) 595–4386
Ocean Journey, (888) 561–4450
University of Denver, (303) 871–2000

FORT COLLINS

Lincoln Center, (970) 221–6735

GREELEY

Fort Vasquez, (970) 785–2832

PLACES TO EAT
IN DENVER AND THE PLAINS

DENVER
Duffy's Shamrock Restaurant (Irish home-style; inexpensive to moderate); 1635 Court Place; (303) 534–4935

Imperial Chinese Restaurant; (expensive) 431 South Broadway; (303) 698–2800

The Normandy (French; deluxe); 1515 Madison; (303) 321–3311

Old Spaghetti Factory (Italian; good value; inexpensive); 1215 Eighteenth Street; (303) 295–1864

Papillon Café (French and Asian fusion; deluxe); 250 Josephine Street; (303) 333–7166

Wellshire Inn (steak, seafood; adjacent to a well-kept golf course; deluxe); 3333 South Colorado Boulevard; (303) 759–3333

Zaidy's Deli (kosher deli; inexpensive to moderate); 121 Adams Street; (303) 333–5336

FORT COLLINS
BeauJo's (American, pizza; moderate); 100 North College Avenue; (970) 498–8898

Coopersmith's Pub and Brewing Company (moderate); 5 Old Town Square; (970) 498–0483

Rio Grande Mexican Restaurant (moderate); 143 West Mountain; (970) 224–5428

GREELEY
Blackjack Pizza (inexpensive); 814 Sixteenth Street; (970) 356–2500

The Egg & I (American; inexpensive); 3830 West Tenth Street; (970) 353–7737

LOVELAND
Panchita's Mexican Restaurant (moderate); 251 Fourteenth Street Southeast; (970) 203–0750

Denver and The Plains General Information Resources

DENVER

Denver Metro Convention & Visitors Bureau,
1555 California Street, Suite 300, 80202;
(800) 233–6837; fax (303) 892–1636
E-mail: corr@dmcvb.org
Web site: www.denver.org

Fort Collins

Fort Collins Area Chamber of Commerce,
225 South Meldrum, 80521; (970) 482–3746;
fax (970) 482–3774
E-mail: general@fcchamber.org
Web site: www.fcchamber.org

Greeley

Greeley Convention & Visitors Bureau,
902 Seventh Avenue, 80631;
(970) 352–3567 or (800) 449–3866
E-mail: greeleycvb@ctos.com
Web site: www.greeleycvb.com

Loveland

Loveland Chamber of Commerce,
5400 Stone Creek Circle, Suite 200, 80538;
(970) 667–6311; fax (970) 667–5211
E-mail: info@loveland.org
Web site: www.loveland.org

Parsonage Restaurant (continental; historic; moderate to expensive); 405 East Fifth Street; (970) 962–9700

The Savoy (French; expensive); 535 Third Street, Berthoud; (970) 532–4095

The Summit (steak, seafood; moderate to expensive); 3208 West Eisenhower; (970) 669–6648

Index

Index

Index

Index

Index

About the Author

A Denver resident, Curtis Casewit has written more than forty books, eight of them travel guides. He writes travel columns regularly for newspapers nationwide and lectures at several writing workshops during the summer. He taught creative writing at the University of Colorado for thirty years.

About the Editor

Alli Rainey has lived in Colorado since December 1997, when she and her husband moved to Boulder. As an avid rock climber and all-around outdoor enthusiast, she discovered in Colorado a perfect fit for her passions. Alli writes a weekly column for a local newspaper on outdoor adventure sports in addition to freelancing for numerous other publications. In the past few years, her rock climbing travels have taken her not only all around Colorado, but also all over the United States as well as to the Cayman Islands and France.